S

Born and raised in Wigan, Kris Radlinski was determined to play rugby league for his home town club from his earliest years and made his debut in a team of all-stars in 1993 aged just 17. He went on to become the first player to score a hat-trick of tries and the youngest to win the Harry Sunderland Trophy in Wigan's 1995 Premiership Trophy victory over Leeds. Later that year he broke into the World Cup side aged 19 and soon became one of the first names on the international team sheet, amassing 20 Great Britain and 10 England appearances.

2002 saw Kris complete a historic double in Wigan's Challenge Cup Final victory over St Helens, becoming one of only a few players to win the Lance Todd Trophy as well as the Harry Sunderland award.

Persistent injury forced Kris to retire prematurely from the game but he returned in June 2006 to see out the season with Wigan, helping the team successfully fight off relegation.

Having finally hung up his boots, Kris had to adjust to being a retired athlete dealing with boredom and depression along the way. He's now embarking on a new career on the coaching staff back at Wigan Warriors.

In 2007, Kris received the MBE for his services to rugby league and embarked on a trip to Poland to research his ancestry. He still lives in Wigan with his wife, Rachel.

Simply Rad

KRIS RADLINSKI

VERTICAL EDITIONS

www.verticaleditions.com

First published in the United Kingdom in 2010 by Vertical Editions, Unit 4a, Snaygill Industrial Estate, Skipton, North Yorkshire BD23 2QR

www.verticaleditions.com

A CIP catalogue record for this book is available from the British Library

Excerpt from 'The Guy in the Glass' © 1934 Dale Wimbrow

ISBN 978-1-904091-46-2

Cover design and typeset by HBA, York

Printed and bound by JF Print Limited, Somerset

DEDICATION

This whole book, and in fact my whole life, is dedicated to my family. Without love and support from them, I would not have achieved half as much as I have done. I wrote this book as a thank you to them for making me the person that I am. I hope that by reading this book they will all feel a sense of accomplishment that we did it all together.

To my mum, dad and sister, Nicola: I want us all to celebrate a remarkable journey.

To my wife, Rachel: I love you dearly and hope this book helps build a picture of the parts that you missed but shows just how important you are to our future.

CONTENTS

ACKNOWLEDGMENTS

Even though I wrote this book myself, I could not have done it without Phil Wilkinson. He didn't complain once as I constantly bombarded him with texts and emails as I searched for clarification on certain points. He also helped with grammar and offered many ideas. I will never be able to repay the time and effort he has shown me.

I would also like to thank Andrew Heaton, David Groom and Phil Thomas for their support as I wrote this book.

Special thanks go to the *Wigan Observer* for permission to use their photographs and to RLphotos.com for use of the GB photo on the front cover.

I would also like to thank and pay tribute to Ryan Giggs for his kind words. The fact that he has just been named PFA footballer of the year a month before my book is published makes it more special. He is a champion sportsman but more importantly a champion bloke. Thanks Ryan.

FOREWORD
By Ryan Giggs OBE

As a keen fan of rugby league I followed Kris's career pretty closely and I have to admit he was always one of the players I looked forward to seeing in action. It's hard to have anything but total admiration for a local boy who came good with his hometown team, and there's no doubt Kris did it better than most.

I can still remember the day he scored a hat-trick as a 19-year-old when he was man of the match in the Premiership final back in 1995—no mean feat when you consider the stars they had in that Wigan side at the time. He had a hard act to follow, because Steve Hampson was one of the great full-backs, so it says everything about Kris's ability that the fans took him to their hearts as quickly as they did.

I got to know him pretty well as we bumped into each other over the years, and there's no argument about where the most impressive meeting place was—Buckingham Palace, in 2007. Kris was there to receive the MBE, while I was getting the OBE, and it was quite surreal, standing chatting in the grand hall. Our families were taken off into one room while Kris, me and a lot of military people getting awards were briefed over the protocol. Sadly Kris had already been forced to retire because of all the knocks and bangs he'd had over time, until eventually he decided he couldn't put his body through any more bashings. So we had a fairly good discussion about injuries, because I've had my share of them throughout my career. Fortunately for me, a different training regime, and doing things like yoga, has helped me to carry on. So having seen that side of sport, I have every sympathy with Kris for being forced to hang up his boots.

I suppose we're pretty similar in that we both still live in the north west, and have largely stuck with the same mates that we grew up with. The fans always love it when 'one of their own' comes into the team and stays there. And Kris certainly did that. I know his playing days are behind him now, and it's always sad to see someone having to retire. But he should be proud of the fact he left so many fantastic memories to so many people—me included.

Best of luck with the book mate. If it's as good on paper as it was in real life, it's going to be a good read!

INTRODUCTION

ONLY two people were ever supposed to read my life story.

When I was struggling to come to terms with the end of my playing career, I filled the tedious, empty days by writing my memoirs. It helped me come to terms with retirement, it helped me reflect on a career to be proud of and, to put it bluntly, it gave me something to do. It filled that gaping void in my days and weeks that appeared once my playing commitments finished. When I'd finished my memoirs, I printed off three copies, two of which I had leather-bound as gifts—one for my dad and one for my all-time hero, Ellery Hanley. They were both extremely touched by the gesture.

I've never met Ellery and, the truth is, I never want to for fear it may somehow dilute my magical childhood memories of him. But I sent him a copy because I wanted him to know the impact he had on a young Wigan kid who was never blessed with natural rugby league ability; just an ability to work hard. The third copy, I kept for myself, and for a while I pretty much forgot about it. But over the following weeks, and without any pestering or pressure, I allowed those close to me to read my copy—my wife, my mum and my sister. They liked it, and so I widened the circle to a few friends, one of whom was Phil Wilkinson, the rugby league correspondent of the Wigan Observer. When he returned the manuscript, he asked, 'Why don't you release it?' It was a question that was echoed by other mates. I was flattered my friends and family liked my story, but I wrote it for no other reason than it was therapeutic, and I dismissed any suggestions of making my story public.

Over the following few weeks, though, that question niggled in my mind, until it morphed into a new question, 'Why not release it?' When I failed to come up with any answers, I knew I should. The fact that I wrote my book with no intention of it being released will, I hope, prove that it has come from my heart. I decided from the outset that if I was going to tell my story, I was going to do it right.

Sure, I knew that by resurrecting past fall-outs and mistakes—and by discussing issues as wide-ranging as the eroding culture at Wigan through to salary cap breaches and even painful accusations of match-fixing—I risked upsetting a few people. I hope they realise that I didn't do so out of malice or mischief or a desire to sell a few extra copies. If I didn't include the bad parts of my life, how could I do justice to the good parts? Being Mr Nice Guy is great, but not at the expense of honesty, integrity and self-respect.

And so, through interview sessions, countless meetings and a steady stream of emails and text messages with Phil, chapters were added, points were clarified and expanded, and issues were addressed, so much so that the word count of this book is double that of the copies that sit on my dad's and Ellery's bookshelves.

But like those original documents, it all came from me. This is my story. It does not contain every try I scored and every game I played in—I've always found those books inevitably boring. Nor is it all cheerleaders and fast cars. By revealing the insecurities and setbacks a sportsman faces, I hope I've created a book that appeals to more people than just Wigan and rugby league fans.

From the unadulterated euphoria of making rugby league history early in my career, to battles with my twin demons of boredom and depression at the end of my career, this is all me. And in between, I remember the beers, the laughs, the friendships and the fall-outs. I also reveal just how close I was to joining St Helens; the real reason I rejected the offer to become the second-highest paid player in world rugby after Jonah Lomu; and how I caught the eye of Hollywood star Jennifer Love Hewitt. Okay, I admit, that final point is not strictly true—but I promise you, everything else you read over the next few chapters is. I hope you enjoy it.

1

RUGBY IN THE BLOOD

'In Lancashire, babies don't toddle, they sidestep. Rugby league provides our cultural adrenalin. It's a physical manifestation of our rules of life, comradeship, honest endeavour and a staunch, often ponderous allegiance to fair play.'

Colin Welland

THE PITCH where I **really** developed as a rugby league player is now a supermarket. It saddens me to think that, as you're reading this, shoppers are probably pushing their trolleys down the frozen food aisle on the same piece of ground I used to soar down the wing and score some amazing tries . . . usually providing my own, enthusiastic running commentary at the same time. No, I don't mean Central Park, Wigan's famous former home that made way for a Tesco store in 1999.

Before I played on that hallowed turf, before I'd pulled on a Wigan shirt, I was honing my skills on a field close to my home in Marus Bridge, two miles from Wigan town centre. That site, too, is now a supermarket. A Sainsbury's. And while Central Park holds a special place in my heart, I'll never forget where my rugby league education really began—on 'the field' where I spent so many hours of my childhood.

All I ever wanted was to be outdoors. Any toys I got at Christmas would rarely be played with, and while my school-mates were obsessing over *Paperboy* and *OutRun* on their Commodore 64s, I was looking for people to play with and against on the field. I'd spend hours out there until my mum called me in for bed. When I was too young to go alone, I'd drag my dad along with me. He'd walk in from work to find me changed and ready to go. Sometimes I'd play football, other times I'd be armed with my trusty eight-iron that my dad bought me. Most times, though, I played with my rugby ball, kicking, catching and pretty much doing my best to emulate my hero, Ellery Hanley.

I was born Kristian John Radlinski on 9 April 1976, the son of John and Susan, and brother of Nicola. I weighed a whopping 10lb 10oz, a chubby thing with big brown eyes. I had a normal, happy childhood in a nice, semi-detached house on Ashdale Road in Marus Bridge. My dad worked as a manager of an electrical store in Wigan, and my mum escorted disadvantaged children to school. Nicola was constantly helping mum out, and looked after me a lot, though I never believed her claims that I was a pest when I was a kid. Nicola and I weren't spoiled, but I don't remember longing for anything. Our mum and dad drilled good manners into us and every time I hear someone say, 'Isn't Kris Radlinski well mannered?' I don't take it as a personal compliment, but as an appraisal of the parenting I had.

I can't remember exactly when I caught the rugby league bug. There's no single, vivid, defining memory when I discovered and fell in love with the sport. I'm sure it was while watching Wigan and I think it was at Central Park, but I must have been young, because I can't remember a time when rugby league wasn't a part of my life. My Sunday afternoons were spent either on top of the dugouts at Central Park watching my heroes—Ellery, Dean Bell, Steve Hampson and Joe Lydon—or making visits to other grounds to watch them on the road with my mum, dad and sister. There were also, of course, the annual pilgrimages to Wembley—my first was in 1985 and I went to every one when they trampled over all-comers for eight years from 1988 to 1995.

It was a great time to grow up as a Wigan fan. Everyone wanted to play for Wigan. Like in the movie *Charlie and the Chocolate Factory*, kids would stand at the fence rails in the hope of catching a rare glimpse of Willy Wonka, that's how I remember visits to Central Park.

And—while you may see plenty of Wigan Athletic tops in the playground now—my lunchtimes at both primary and secondary school were spent in the playground, when games of touch rugby would unfold into full-on, physical tackling on tarmac. My dream was to play for Wigan. Everyone's was. We'd argue in the playground about who was Ellery and who was Joe and who was Shaun Edwards.

Later in my youth, I first heard the saying 'dreams give birth to reality', which really hit home with me. It was that passion for the game—and the dream that, yep, one day I could play for Wigan—which prompted me to join a local amateur side when I was about nine or 10.

Our team at Wigan St Judes was coached by my great friend Ken Owen. He would pick me up for training, twice a week, with his son Barry and then drop me off a few hours later covered in mud. I loved it . . . though I'm not sure my mum appreciated the dirty footprints across her clean floors! At the same time I started playing for my primary school team, which was also called St Judes. Mick Mullaney, who was well-known in rugby league circles, coached the team.

When I left primary school and moved to St Thomas More

High School, I began taking my rugby league more seriously. Under the guidance of Ken and Mick, I would play for school in the week, on Saturdays for the town team and then on Sundays for St Judes. Throw in training three nights a week and it was a pretty hectic schedule, but I couldn't get enough, and in between I'd still find time to squeeze in jaunts onto the field with my dad.

As I got older, and bigger, our father-son sessions became more physical. We would run at each other, and he would call me 'soft' so I would get angry and fight back. We would launch high bombs for each other to see who would be the first to crack and drop one. We would go out there when the sun was out and come back when it was dark, covered in mud with burst lips and noses. And we wouldn't walk back, instead we raced home through the streets. He always won . . . and he retired from our duels at a time when I was getting close to beating him! They were magical times, and I'm convinced that those encounters with my dad created a spirit inside me. My dad used to say to me, 'Play every game as though it's your last', and I did. Now, if ever a coach asks me to deliver a few words of advice to kids' teams, that's the message I try to get across.

Despite what some people think, Wigan is not always sunny and dry and so, for the days when it was too wet or too dark to play on the field, I'd spend my time hanging about in my shed at the bottom of the garden. This was no ordinary shed. My dad had carpeted the walls to keep it insulated, and it had an old bed in it and a black and white TV. Sometimes I'd spend nights in there with my mates, feasting on chocolate and crisps. Spilled Coke, lots of sweat and way too much Lynx deodorant perfumed the air. I also had an old multi-gym in there, which my uncle Carl from London had sent me.

My dad's mum, my other nan, died when I was a young lad

but I remember her fondly, and I used to love our trips down to London to visit her, my uncle Carl and auntie Jean. Nan used to adore me, and after she died, my dad would still occasionally make trips to the capital just to clean her grave. My granddad died before I was born, in Poland. Uncle Carl and auntie Jean still live in London, they send birthday cards and Christmas cards: auntie Jean was an actress—her stage name was Catherine Neilson—and appeared in some big films such as the 1987 film *White Mischief* with Charles Dance and Greta Scachi. She also appeared in popular TV shows like *Coronation Street* and *Bergerac*.

I was so grateful to my uncle Carl for his multi-gym. From an early age I would spend a couple of hours a day lifting weights and training hard whilst looking at the shrine I had created to the king, Ellery. I literally worshipped him. I had pictures cut out from programmes and magazines stuck all over the walls, and I would scrutinise every story that appeared about him in my dad's newspapers. I knew everything about him—I still do. I even gave my class speech on him . . . it was one of the most thorough and detailed pieces of school work I ever did!

I spent a lot of my youth with our next door neighbours, the Baines'—Colin, Kath and their two daughters, Jennifer and Sarah. They became like a second family, and as Jennifer and I were a similar age we would spend most days together— we were inseparable. Nicola, being older, kept an eye on us, reporting everything we did wrong to our respective parents! One of our favourite things to do every year was to search for Christmas presents in each other's parents' bedrooms. And we didn't just stop at finding them; we would get things out of boxes and play with them as if it was Christmas day, and then carefully repackage them! One year, though, we came unstuck when Kath arrived home to find us heavily involved with all the presents. Forget the festive spirit, she was furious, and she bounced me back across the fence to my mum, screaming and shouting. She laughs about it now! We would go on holidays together and spend Christmas together. Every New Year's Eve, the grown-ups would go to the local pub, The Ben Johnson, and all the kids would stay at home with Nicola babysitting until our parents returned just before midnight. One year, Jennifer received a karaoke machine for Christmas and so everybody took turns, giving it everything they had. My turn arrived and I belted out my best rendition of John Travolta doing the 'Grease Megamix'. I didn't realise at the time that my performance was being filmed, and a tape of it still lives on to this day—I'd emigrate if it ever appeared on YouTube! Sarah was the youngest out of us all, and I adored her. She was so laid back and relaxed, yet so loving and caring, and I became very protective of her—almost like a big brother. I was happy when she started going out with Sean O'Loughlin, the Wigan skipper, because he's a champion bloke and the pair are now happily married with their own family, and still good friends.

I was also very close to the Gregorys, Maureen, Joe, Paul and Damien, who lived on the same road. I would just wander across the road and hang out with them. Paul and Damien were about 10 years older than me but were the coolest guys. Damien signed for Warrington Rugby League Club, and so I used to run with him and he would give me all his old training gear. It was miles too big for me, but I wore it anyway! He once gave me a tackle shield that I had for years, and my dad and I would spend hours in the garden or on the field smashing each other. Damien's career ended prematurely because of injury, but I never threw the shield away and a few years ago—when his son John was beginning to get into rugby—I signed it and sent it back, with a message saying that it had brought me great luck.

Maureen, sadly, passed away and during my pre-game ritual of visiting my grandparents' grave at Gidlow Cemetery in Wigan, I would always nip across to check on Maureen too. My nan and pop, my mum's parents, lived about two minutes' walk away when I was growing up. My nan's dad is actually a local legend in Wigan folklore as he used to have sit-on-scales in the Little Arcade in town; paintings of him with his scales are still on sale. My pop was a brilliant man who I adored. He died after contracting gangrene in his leg, after a fall whilst holidaying in Thailand. He came back home and had his leg amputated, but his heart was too weak to recover. I'll never forget my dad meeting me off the school bus to break the news to me. It was the first time I had experienced the death of someone I loved, and it tore me apart. It hit us all hard, especially my nan. I would go and see her and she would be sat in her chair in the front room crying, listening to the *Phantom of the Opera* soundtrack—they had seen the musical shortly before he died. Just before my pop's accident, he had been planning to take all the family to Disney World in Florida, so nan granted his wish and took the whole family, including my auntie Connie, my mum's sister, and my cousins, Mark and Gareth. It meant the world to her.

My auntie Connie is so much fun and always up for a laugh. And whenever she came around to our house, even if it was 10 in the morning, and you asked would she like a drink, she'd always reply, 'A small brandy wouldn't hurt!' A few years ago I was drinking in a Wigan pub with some of my mates and my auntie Connie was in. I went to chat with her and asked if I could do something that would get a laugh out of the lads. At this point I should tell you that she wears a wig. So I asked her if I could get the lads' attention and then whip the wig off her head! She enthusiastically agreed, and when I did it, the lads were falling off their chairs laughing! She loved every minute. My cousins Mark and Gareth are brilliant fellas. Mark is a computer whizz who always sorts out any of my laptop problems, while I can't tell you the number of times Gaz has had to kick people out of my house after a party, while I'm fast asleep in bed. He is into this strange, American wrestling in which contestants dress up and dance around, but there's no actual fighting. His stage name is The Phoenix. He made the mistake of telling some of my Wigan team-mates about his passion and they wasted no time testing his ability, taking him down instantly and soon realising that he couldn't wrestle a 10-year-old kid. My other cousin, Alison, lives in London and is happily married to a great guy called Alan. In my testimonial she bought the Wigan shirt I wore when I won the Lance Todd Trophy in 2002 for more than a grand.

My nan died a few years ago, she slipped from us with her family around her. I think about them all the time and it's a real sadness of mine that my pop never got to see me play for Wigan as it would have meant more to him than anybody. My nan got to see me play and she loved it . . . even though she didn't have a clue what was going on! My mum was actually in hospital getting her leg plastered after breaking it in a fall when I got a phone call from my nan's neighbour. He told me she had taken a terrible fall and was very ill and I was to meet the ambulance at the hospital. I made my way quickly there, first to find mum and then to take her to my nan. When I did find my mum, she told me that I should not have bothered going to see her and that she was fine. I told her that I had not come for her, it was my nan. A nurse helped me load mum into a wheelchair and then we went to another ward to find my nan in a horrific state. All the family and my mum, still in agony from her fall, sat and held my nan's hand until she sadly left us. It was heartbreaking for us all but it tore my mum apart. My mum is my hero in life. She's such a loved lady who everybody adores.

My family played such an important role in my upbringing. My mum and dad weren't overly-protective or intrusive, and they certainly didn't pamper me, but their involvement in my rugby league was always appreciated. They followed me everywhere watching me play. Mum drove and cleaned, and made sure I kept warm, and dad would tell me to toughen up and get stuck in. Sometimes, if I'd had a bad game, dad wouldn't speak to me for a few hours! I'm sure my consistency throughout my career stems from that childhood determination to play well each week to impress my dad.

I had a lot of personal success at St Judes with my pal Barry Owen. We were very close. He was a good player too, and signed a professional contract with Widnes, but things never worked out for him because of a knee injury. I once scored six tries in a game but didn't get the man of the match award, because he set every one of them up for me. His brother, Lee, was also a good player but (and he'll kill me for saying this) he was too into his looks! Sadly, with numbers dwindling, Judes were unable to raise a team when I reached 14 so I had to move to their close, but bitter, rivals Wigan St Patricks. There were no hard feelings—Ken advised me to do this, saying it would help my career. He remained a huge help to me, taking Barry and I on extra training sessions—he even made a pulling sled at work, which we used on the field to strengthen our legs.

St Pats had a great tradition of producing top players. Shaun Edwards, Andy Platt, Mike Gregory and Joe Lydon were among their most recent graduates when I arrived, but I struggled to make my mark at first. That wasn't the club's fault. I reached the age of 14 and I was tall and very thin, but I hadn't filled out like others had. I didn't really look like a rugby player. I was scrawny, and my rugby suffered. I knew I was one of the better players until that point, but I began falling down the pecking order until I dropped out of the town team completely at under 15s level. I didn't make the squad the year later, either, and that was really upsetting because rugby was all I lived for. People would try to comfort me, telling me that I would 'fill out' over time, and that I had to let nature take its course, but I wasn't going to wait for time to solve my problems. When my mates went training for the town team on Thursday evenings, I went to the Robin Park indoor sprint track—alone—to work on my speed. Every week, for two years, I followed that same monotonous, lonely and, seemingly unrewarding, routine. But by doing the extra sessions, and by training with Ken Owen, Ray Unsworth and Brian Foley as well, I began to flourish as a player. Fitter, faster and sharper, I made my switch from loose forward to an out-and-out back.

Looking back on that time now, I have no doubt that a huge part of my success comes down to the extra work I did when I was overlooked for the Wigan town team when I was 15 and 16. That was my first major setback as a player, and I responded by training harder when it would have been so tempting to just accept the decision or even quit altogether. A decade later, I was eating at an Indian restaurant in Wigan—about a week or two after winning the Lance Todd Trophy—and one of the coaches who had not selected me walked in. Seeing him, and remembering his snub, my chicken tikka bhuna tasted a whole lot better.

While St Judes and St Pats played a huge role in my rugby development, I've got to mention my school, too. I loved my time at St Thomas More, which has since, sadly, been demolished. They had a leaving party before the school closed; I was gutted that I couldn't make it, though a few years earlier

I'd been invited to speak to the students who were leaving, and that was a very proud moment. I've never had a problem with public speaking, I get a buzz out of it, and I told them to have a dream and not to let setbacks put them off, citing my fall from the Wigan town team when I was a pupil myself and how I used it as a launch pad to bigger and better things. I also spoke about the importance of working hard, a quality I had even when I was studying at school—I was never the greatest pupil and my results weren't great, but I always tried hard. We had a very successful school team at St Thomas More and won quite a few trophies, under the supervision of a great teacher called Nigel Green. My last game for the school was the final of a school competition, and it was played at Knowsley Road, the home of Wigan's biggest rivals, St Helens. That day, we played a St Helens school, Cowley High (where BBC commentator Ray French used to teach).

They had a fearsome reputation; they'd been destroying other school teams all year, and several of their players had already signed professional contracts with top-flight clubs. True to form, they slaughtered us 48–0, yet despite the scoreline—and remember, I'm a fierce critic of my own performances—I had an absolute blinder. My dad had always said 'Play every game like it's your last', and it was my last . . . at least for my school. I worked myself into the ground, defending like a Trojan from the loose forward berth, and my own team actually applauded me off the field.

My performance hadn't gone unnoticed by some of the others who were watching, either. After that game, St Helens approached me. But that's another story in itself . . .

2

SIGNING ON THE DOTTED LINE

'Play every game as though it's your last.'

My dad

I AM, and always will be, inevitably linked with my hometown club Wigan. But not many people realise just how close I went to joining St Helens. They were the first professional club to show an interest in me, the first club I trained with and, when Wigan were reluctant to give me a full-time contract a year later, Saints wanted to take me on board. After playing at Knowsley Road for my school, St Thomas More, a St Helens club director approached my teacher, Gwen White, and asked about me. She was a lovely lady, who I adore to this day—the director actually thought she was my mum, but she corrected him and they exchanged phone numbers. She told me about their conversation, and I went home so excited—I'd finally got the break I'd longed for and, I felt, deserved. With no other options, it was a chance I couldn't turn down, so I agreed to join St Helens for pre-season training.

It feels almost surreal now to remember those few sessions I spent at Knowsley Road several days after I'd left school. I trained hard, kept my head down and tried to make a good impression. I was actually enjoying it, and I got some good feedback. All I wanted to do was play rugby league professionally and, while I'd never envisaged playing for St Helens, this was the break I had longed for. I was on top of the world. Then I got an unexpected knock at our front door which was to change the course of my life.

Two guys called Jim Hartley and Haydn Walker came around to my house. They explained they were from Wigan, and told me about the new academy system that they had created. In short, young professionals that the club had signed up would play alongside amateurs in the same team, under the Wigan club badge as the academy side. The professionals would get paid, the amateurs wouldn't, but the incentive for the amateurs was that they would also benefit from the same expert coaching and advice that the young professionals were getting. Jim was the manager, and Haydn the coach. Jim asked if I would join the academy set up at Wigan—as an amateur.

Saints, I knew, were very keen on me and were close to offering me a professional contract, but Jim told me that I would receive free boots and training gear—freebies always excite players—and he assured me that, if I proved my worth, the club would consider offering me professional terms. They made it sound very exciting, telling me I would get the chance to train in sessions with first team players—the same players I'd idolised.

My mind was made up. They didn't pressure me into making a decision, insisting I speak to my family first, and even though St Helens could, and probably would, have offered me a professional contract earlier, the chance to play for Wigan—however remote—was too good to turn down.

I had two years to prove to people that I had what it took.

After that, I would be too old and ineligible for the academy set up. I knew that I had just been given a massive opportunity and if I was going to fail, it wasn't going to be through lack of hard work. I've always been a big believer that the harder you work, the greater your reward. My mum told me she would help me out wherever she could, and told me that she had no doubt I'd succeed. I think she was just so glad that I hadn't joined St Helens instead! But Saints had been nothing but good to me, so I phoned Tom Ellard, a St Helens director, and told him I was going to join Wigan. He understood, and wished me luck in my career. I then called Wigan and agreed to join them and, on the same day I collected my GCSE results (an A in PE and eight Cs, for the record) I walked through the Central Park doors for the first time as a Wigan player, rather than a fan.

That day, I swapped school and the comfort blanket of my parents for gruelling training regimes and constant banter. For most people my age, the change from boy to man is a gradual transition, but for me, that day was the day I became an adult. My development as a player accelerated in the Wigan academy teams; those two years also gave me some close friends and many great memories. I gained respect because I just came in as an amateur and worked my ass off, kept my head down and went about my business. People knew how much playing professionally meant to me—I never hid the fact that I was desperate for a contract—and I think they were impressed by my work ethic. I was playing in the same team as lads who had come to the club with massive reputations as juniors, players who had received a fortune for signing on and who had believed every word of the local newspaper stories hailing them as the next Hanley, Edwards or Schofield. That, unfortunately, was their downfall. They received too much, far too soon, and sadly it happened to many talented young players. They thought they had made it as soon as they had signed on the dotted line, when the truth was the opposite—signing for Wigan was when the hard work began.

I had no contract, so there was no danger of complacency creeping into my lifestyle. Wigan were the glamour team at the time, and there were many others who just wanted to put their new club tracksuit on and swagger around town thinking they were the next big thing. I'm sure, now, many of those players look back on their promising but ultimately doomed careers with a tinge of regret, because many had real talent. I can sympathise with what they went through because many pitfalls come along with becoming a professional sportsman and, going from school to being involved in a club like Wigan, they can easily be seduced by a whole range of off-the-field distractions. It's as if they wanted to be rock stars, not rugby players, and they didn't realise that having the time of their lives at pubs and clubs would impact so heavily on their performances.

While there are many anecdotes in these pages of nights out and beers, believe me when I tell you that those events occurred fleetingly—once every month or two, at most. It also happens that some of my best memories are from those nights, hence their inclusion in these pages, but when I was a 16 and 17-year-old, when many of my peers were going out, I didn't really have a social life. I was determined to get somewhere with rugby league; I put everything else on hold, which is why I didn't spend my weekends standing on my tiptoes, trying to convince a burly bouncer that I was 18. I did extra training instead.

With Wigan prepared to take a chance on me, without rewarding me with a contract, I became an apprentice at the club with guys like Simon Haughton, Sean Long, Rob Smyth and David Whittle. We hung around Central Park all day, learning different aspects of the club—from helping John Martin in the Riversiders' club to leading school tours, you name it, we did it. We also went into schools to coach, and studied one day a week at college. We had some laughs, but we pushed each other too, and became competitive with weights and sprints training.

I was earning £40 a week, plus £30 a win with the academy side. In a good week, that would be £70 . . . not a fortune, and certainly less than the current minimum wage, but I could hardly have been happier. Every Monday, our crazy fitness coach Chris Butler would take us fell running up near Rivington Pike, on the outskirts of Wigan. We had to run over the bogs and up steep hill sides for about 90 minutes and then, on the way down, take our clothes off and dive into an icy cold pond. It was a great way to recover from the torturous run, but the drive back to Wigan was the horrible part, freezing our nuts off!

We also became close friends with Martin Offiah. He was a genuine superstar and we were 16 and 17-year-old apprentices, with no recognition and little money, yet he just acted like one of the lads with us. We would have mad sprints through town at lunchtime, trying to get to Tasty Bite to buy our jacket potatoes first. Three guesses who won those races most of the time! We would also do sprint training at the local athletics track, and we'd get there an hour early just so we could play hide and seek! Martin shared our sense of fun and, because he was from London and not one of the local guys, he hung around with us. Every so often he would bring in bags of old training gear and we would all take turns choosing an item. We've kept in contact since—he tells me I'm always the first person to text him every time he appears on a reality TV show, though only he could make ballroom dancing look so cool! Around that time, in 1992–93, he was awesome, and did things on the pitch no one else could. Although he was down -to-earth, he was always aware of his talents, and I always wanted to be a bit more like him in the way he carried himself so confidently. He was an extrovert and extremely secure, while I was the opposite. I remember walking through an arcade in Wigan when the schools were on half-term and I felt so uncomfortable, almost claustrophobic, by the stares, smiles and pointing fingers that came my way. Martin was happy when people were looking at him—why not, he was a superstar? But I was never relaxed or comfortable with it. Even now, if I am going out, I will always have a beer at home first to relax and I can never walk into a pub knowing my mates are not there and wait for them alone . . . I always ring first to make sure they are in there!

Our mentor at the time was Ray Unsworth, who had followed me from St Pats to Wigan. He looked after all the apprentices as well as coaching the academy side. He was a great character, who had so many jokes and stories, and a massive knowledge of the game, but he also had a serious side, too, and it was his job to shout at us if we stepped out of line. One of the groundsman's jobs at Central Park was to shoot the pigeons in the rafters, as they flew up there and left bird muck all over the seats in the grandstand. Every so often, after we'd nagged and begged, the groundsman would let the apprentices have a go with the air rifle. One day, half our group were shooting while the other half were showing a school around the ground. I was in the group taking the children around. I was explaining to the kids where the players came out of the tunnel and onto the pitch—and I was doing a pretty decent job of being a tour-guide, I must say—when dead pigeons started to fall right in front of these kids. The children started to scream and, in trying to control them, I couldn't help crack up laughing! Ray was not happy, and called us into the changing room to put us in our place. But he hadn't got a few seconds into his rant when he started choking on the banana he was eating! He went bright red, and had to leave the room to settle down. He returned a minute later, but there was no way he was going to tell us off—everyone, including him, was in stitches.

Whilst playing for the academy I was beginning to turn a few heads. People were asking who the kid with the red hair was, and why wasn't he a pro? A huge benefit of having luminous hair was that I stood out. I was now playing in the centre and gaining a reputation as a tough defender—I was on a mission to impress, and sometimes made up to 40 tackles a game, which was far too many for a centre. Other clubs were beginning to take note, including St Helens, but I kept being assured by Johnny Jackson, a Wigan scout who really supported me, that my hard work would pay off and, in June 1993, those forecasts came true. The gamble I had taken paid off when Wigan offered me a professional contract.

My family were immensely proud, and rightly so, because they had dedicated so much of their time to helping me. They had spent countless hours crossing the M62 to watch me play, given me lifts to training, not to mention handouts when I was broke . . . you name it. They had sacrificed so much of their time. My mum bought me a new, trendy green blazer and we all went to the boardroom at Central Park to sign my contract. The directors at the time were Jack Robinson, John Martin, Tom Rathbone and Jack Hilton, and as we sat down to sign the contract, they told me they had high hopes for me. 'I won't let you down,' I assured them, as confidently as I could. Twenty minutes later I walked out of that room £6,000 richer. If I'd been given a million I wouldn't have been happier. It was not about the money, it was about the professional contract, and the chance to become a first team player at Wigan. I knew I had taken a giant step towards realising the one thing I'd dreamed about my whole life. As for the money, I actually still have that same £6,000 in the same bank account. Well, that's not strictly true . . . for some reason, I went to Southport and blew £180 on a gold chain that I hardly ever wore—why, I don't know—and put the rest in an account, where it remains to this day.

With an increased work-load in training, and a new hunger to succeed, I had to drop out of college after one year. Besides, though I liked it at St John Rigby College in Orrell—their PE teacher John Ireland was very supportive—I never really fitted in. I trained every evening and weekend; the other students spent their free time drinking cheap cider.

I started the 1993–94 season in the alliance team, the reserves, which was a big step up from the academy league. Not only were the skill and fitness levels far greater, I was also playing against grown men and I still had a lot of growing to do myself. With no salary cap back then, squads were so big that those players not picked for the first team on weekends would drop down and play for the alliance side. Suddenly, I'd gone from playing with and against 16-year-olds to becoming team-mates with players like Joe Lydon and Martin Dermott, which was overwhelming at first. Joe was a hero of mine, but it wasn't long before I struck up a strong bond with him. We were completely different in our approach to games as he was so relaxed and natural—and very funny—and I was the complete opposite. Dermott, like Joe, was also a bit of a character but he too was a class act; he passed a ball from the ground better than anyone I have ever seen. We were coached by John Pendlebury, a genuine, fair and thoroughly decent man, but also one of the toughest people you could ever meet, and if we were a man short he wouldn't hesitate to take his teeth out and pull on a strip. He helped me out enormously.

I made my first team debut aged 17—details of which are outlined elsewhere in this book—and spent the rest of the season trying to make an impression with the reserves. All the while, we would each put part of our winning money into a kitty to pay for a trip to Salou at the end of the campaign. Those end-of-season breaks were a fixture of the alliance season, usually to such trashy resorts as Magaluf or Benidorm . . . not the best places for sightseeing!

I had lived a pretty sheltered life before signing for Wigan. I'd never drunk, and rarely done anything reckless in my life, so the Salou trip was a real eye-opener. My mum made me promise that I wouldn't hire a moped when I got there but, in the company of 20 lads, I couldn't turn around and say, 'I can't, my mum told me not to'. Truth was, with bravado and testosterone present in equal measure, I didn't even have the courage to admit I'd never been on a moped, so I just hopped on and tried to act like I knew what I was doing. I watched a couple of the lads start up, and copied them, easing the throttle by twisting my right-hand grip. But I moved off too fast and, instead of using the brakes to slow down, I tried to pull the bike back to me, which, of course, resulted in my hand turning further and the bike moving faster. And faster. And faster.

Not knowing what was going on, I flew across a dual carriageway and disappeared into an amusement arcade, my terrifying but short journey coming to an abrupt halt against an air hockey table! I stepped off, relieved to be still in one piece, and turned around to see 20 lads on their hands and knees in hysterics, and the owner of the hire-shop running across the street waving his hands angrily at me. I laugh at it now, and that story is brought up each time I see one of the lads from that holiday. It was on that trip that I learned the rugby player's holiday drinking rule: if you woke up with a hangover, the first thing you had to do was order another beer. I survived my first lads' holiday, and the friendships forged during that week survived too. One of my best mates was Anthony Hatton, a guy from St Helens and a big signing for Wigan from amateur side Blackbrook, who unfortunately never got his break.

He was one of the funniest men you could ever meet. After one season had finished, we had a drink in Wigan, but Anthony lived in St Helens so he didn't stay long. He had about seven pints, then phoned his girlfriend to ask her for a lift home. He went really giddy when he was drunk, and that summer evening—it wasn't dark yet—he thought he would surprise his girlfriend when she picked him up outside Central Park by being completely naked. He hid out of view until he saw Liz's car turn onto the car park, and then jumped out in front of the car shouting, 'Surprise!' His wide grin switched into a look of horror as he realised Liz's dad was driving. Apparently,

Anthony then sat in the passenger seat with just his clothes covering his privates, and pulled his seat belt on normally!

There was no harm in this guy, just good no-nonsense fun, and I loved him for it. The following year, I couldn't go on the end-of-season trip to Benidorm because of my commitments with the first team. Anthony couldn't go as he was a bit strapped for cash, which upset the lads because he was brilliant fun. I felt sorry for him and, as I'd started earning a bit of money, I told him I'd pay for him. Two weeks later, Ant pulled me to one side. 'Rado, thanks for paying for my trip,' he said. 'I really appreciate it—I owe you a pint.' Now I am not sure how much a pint was in 1994, but I am sure it was not worth £230! But if he ever offered me the money back I wouldn't take it. His friendship is enough for me.

Andrew Johnson was another guy I became good friends with. We didn't hit it off immediately, we just didn't connect, probably because I was the complete opposite to him in some ways. AJ lived the student life to the full and played rugby, while I just lived for my rugby, but we enjoyed each other's company and were soon close mates—and, a few years later, neighbours. He's hilarious when he lets his hair down, and also the weakest person I have ever met with a hangover. AJ was very popular around Super League having played for five different clubs—Wigan, London, Castleford, Huddersfield and Salford. In fact, he was so popular, he nearly won the Super League Players' Player of the Year once because all his mates from different clubs voted for him, but the RFL got suspicious!

From those early days, it's strange to look back on how our playing careers panned out. Out of all my friends who never quite made it to the top, I would have loved it if Craig

Murdock had. He was a big signing for Wigan, who came down from Whitehaven with a huge reputation and an endorsement from the great Wally Lewis. He embraced Wigan life, and lived rugby league—success with Wigan and Great Britain would have meant more to him than anyone. It wasn't to be, though he can still lay claim to having scored one of the greatest ever tries at Twickenham in the 1996 cross-code challenge against Bath, when he finished off a flowing move from behind our own in-goal, a try that even the rugby union crowd applauded.

Another player and mate who became a huge hit with the Wigan fans was Simon Haughton. Our careers mapped each other for a while. An absolute monster of a man with a kind heart, he scored some amazing tries in the early years of Super League but he never really liked the sport, just found he was good at it. We spent a lot of time off the field together as we enjoyed each other's company and loved to travel. One of our greatest trips took us to the west coast of America. It was one of my best experiences as we hired a convertible and drove down the Pacific coast highway from San Francisco to LA. It was a nine-hour journey on a boiling hot day, roof down, driving the rugged coastline and living the American dream. We were young and determined to enjoy the ride. He had a great attitude to life. He did what he wanted no matter how much banter he would receive off the lads. One afternoon we met in a local restaurant to watch a game on TV. Most of the team was there but Simon arrived late. Suddenly he strutted in with brown leather pants on and shirt unbuttoned below the chest, he looked like Mick Jagger. You can only imagine the abuse he got from the boys, the truth is, though, he actually pulled it off. Some people have a style about them that will support this sort of thing, obviously I didn't have that style. After the initial laughter calmed down, we all agreed that he looked pretty fantastic.

Yep, I certainly loved my early days at Wigan rugby league club. In those two years, I definitely served my apprenticeship—I virtually lived at Central Park, and being involved every day whetted my appetite to succeed. Being surrounded by such great players, I became greedy: not financially, but with my career goals. Having played one game for the first team, I didn't just want to represent the club again, I wanted to be involved in the history of the place. I wanted to be remembered in years to come. I wanted old men to talk about me as a 'bloody good un', as they did other top players. As I spent more time around the Central Park ground, I regularly came into contact with the first team squad. They would ask us apprentices to clean their boots and do little jobs for them, but they didn't act like prima donnas—they would always look after us. In 1994, when the squad was flying out to Australia to face Brisbane in the World Club Challenge, three of us were asked to hire a van and take all the players' luggage to the airport and check them in. This was so the players could get on and off the coach with little hassle. We didn't mind it, we loved being involved with them, and they were always grateful. Just before the team coach departed for the airport, Gary Connolly arrived late. He hadn't even packed—he opened his boot, got his suitcase out and started picking out clothes from his boot and packing them into his case. I watched him, part amazed by how casual he was, when he turned to me and threw me a shoebox with a brand new pair of Mizuno boots in. 'Thanks for taking my bag to the airport,' he said. I was made up, and I actually played in those boots for two years, even though they were a size and a half too small! But it's amazing how small gestures like that can have a profound effect on young players and throughout my career, I tried to do little things like that, knowing how much it would mean to those younger players. I would never have guessed that Gary and I would become best friends and neighbours.

Though I was playing for the alliance team, I was still eligible to play for the academy team, and I was desperate to make the Great Britain academy side for their tour of Australia. But I broke my wrist in a training ground accident and didn't play for four months, only returning with two games left of the season. The clock had beaten me, I didn't have enough time to impress the selectors, and I didn't get picked. I was upset about it but, just like when I'd missed out on town team selection two years earlier, I turned my disappointment to my advantage. That summer, while many of my Wigan mates were away on tour with the GB academy, I worked tirelessly lifting heavy weights. I really bulked up, putting on over a stone. I had been hungry enough to make that leap into the first time and, now, I had the physique for it too.

3

PHONE CALL . . . SURPRISE, SURPRISE!

'It's the team that matters. Where would The Beatles be without Ringo? If John got Yoko to play drums the history of music would be completely different.'

David Brent, *The Office*

IT WAS a typical Saturday evening for me when I was 17. I had my tea about six, and then sat down in my bedroom to watch my favourite TV programmes—*Gladiators* followed by *Blind Date*. Fantastic. As Wolf and his pals were bashing some poor guys around the head with giant cotton wool buds, the house phone rang (this was a time long before mobile phones). My mum answered and shouted upstairs that the call was for me. Upset that my TV ritual had been interrupted, I dragged myself to the top of the stairs to find my mum clasping her hand over the mouth-piece. 'It's John Dorahy,' she whispered.

Wigan's head coach wanted to speak to me? That was strange . . . he'd never called me before. Confused, I said, 'Hello' and he told me that he had liked what he had seen from my performances in the alliance team. John told me that he thought I was ready for the next step, which was great to hear. Everyone likes positive feedback, especially from their bosses, and I must admit I had been happy with my own form. Then he said the next step was playing at Castleford the following day.

I thanked him, hung up the phone, and forgot all about Cilla Black playing cupid. In an instant, my relaxed Saturday evening melted away and became the most nerve-wracking night of my life. It was like the night before taking a driving test . . . times 20. I was still nursing bruises from playing for the reserves the previous night, though the only feelings I was conscious of were the butterflies racing around my stomach. I hung up the phone, collapsed on my bed and stared at the ceiling, gathering my thoughts, and allowing the words John had just said to sink in.

I was scared to death. This was what I had wanted my whole life, but I was petrified. As the minutes ticked by, I convinced myself that I was ready for it. Besides, I assured myself, John wouldn't pick me if I wasn't up to it, would he? So I took a deep breath, stood up, went downstairs and into our lounge to tell my mum, dad and sister. 'We're going to Castleford tomorrow,' I said, 'I'm playing.'

They were thrilled and hugged me, showering me with congratulations. I was already feeling anxious, but when Nicola pointed out that it was live on Sky Sports . . . well, let's just say I struggled to get to sleep that night.

The next day, the morning of the game, I followed my usual routine, which was basically keeping my own company and saying little. I did that throughout my career; I hated people stressing about match tickets or bar passes on game-day—I had a match to think about. I ate something light, and listened to music. Okay, here's a confession—before I play a game, I listen to the same song—Diana Ross, 'When You Tell Me That You Love Me'. I like it; certain songs remind me of certain people and that song always reminds me of my family—but please believe me when I tell you I'm not a Diana Ross fan!

Oasis and The Verve are more to my liking, but I always put on that song in the hours before a match as I read, and re-read, our tip sheets.

Tip sheets are usually a couple of sides of A4 paper, and they give a run down on our opponents' strengths and weaknesses—which foot players step off, whether they have a weak shoulder, things like that—and also tell you how we are expected to play. Sometimes there was too much information to take in, so I tried to digest the information that affected me. As my career progressed I used these tip sheets more.

I always did my homework, at least when it came to rugby league, and before any game I could tell you which foot the kickers used and what style of kicking they favoured, which helped a lot as a full-back. Rugby league is a game of territory, and good positional play from your full-back—anticipating where the kick was going—could get you to where you needed to be on the field a lot quicker.

After gathering my thoughts about Castleford and my equipment, I took a hot shower to clear my mind. Before I got out, I quickly twisted the control to cold to really wake me up. From that day, I followed that little routine all through my career. I was not a robot on match day, but I hated things being changed, and many players are the same. They are creatures of habit, and that's probably why teams struggle when they go to France or London. On those overnight trips, I could never understand why coaches used the extra time to hand their players more information, when they'd have been better served trying to keep the routine as normal as possible. We used to joke at Wigan that the coaches threw a meeting just to tell us when the next meeting was! If there was any spare time, they'd fill it, when they'd have been better served just leaving the players alone.

I wished my family farewell, but there was one last stop

before I met the team at Central Park. I visited my nan and pop's grave every week, and I said a little prayer and wished that they could have been alive to see me make my debut. I arrived early at Central Park, and I'm pretty sure my Vauxhall Nova SR 1.4 was the worst car on the car park! I acted cool and calm, like I belonged. The last thing I wanted was any fuss. I boarded the coach, shuffled down the aisle, sat in the first available seat and kept my head down. 'What do you think you're doing?' came the voice seconds later. I looked up to see Andy Platt, the toughest, most rugged and intimidating prop you could ever wish to meet, looking down on me in disgust. 'Come on,' he said, 'let's be 'avin' you.' I wasn't sure what I'd done wrong, but I shot up and walked off the coach. I waited until I was sure all the other players were on board, and then went and sat next to the club masseur, Andrew Pinkerton. Whispering, not to be overheard, I confided in him what had just happened and he told me that certain players liked sitting in specific seats. He filled me in on some more protocol, too, such as when they made trips to Yorkshire they'd always break the trip up with a 10-minute walk, just to stretch the players' legs.

Castleford was, and is, a real rugby league town, and Wheldon Road is a real rugby league venue. They have old-fashioned wooden stands built close to the pitch, so the crowd feel like they are practically on top of you. You can smell the greasy burgers they eat; you can hear every word of abuse aimed your way. It is a tough place to make a debut.

The changing rooms are small and cold, with the toilets outside in the narrow corridor. I know because I made about six trips! Once changed, I sat quietly, collecting my thoughts. I afforded a glance around the room . . . it would have been an autograph hunter's paradise. The squad had been stripped of some of its stars by injuries, but there were still many big names in the side, including seasoned campaigners such as Platt and Dean Bell, one of my childhood heroes. I felt like a boy. A pale skinned, red headed young and innocent boy, getting ready to play the hardest game in the world at a tough venue, against a physical side.

Castleford are always difficult to play against and were at maximum strength that day. A complete Wigan squad would have had their hands full. In those days, before the salary cap, the club could pay you what they wanted—it would vary from game to game, depending on the side and the opposition. The players only found out about 20 minutes before kick-off what they were getting for their match bonus. A few were already speculating what it might be when Jack Robinson, our chairman, came in and whispered in Dean's ear. Jack left, prompting Dean to stand up and announce that we would be getting £600 if we won. I couldn't believe it—£600! I was 17, I don't think I'd ever seen that much money in my life. Without prompting, and with no fanfare, I ran out with the rest of the team for the warm-up and I could sense the mutters among the spectators, wondering who the red-headed kid was. At any other ground, I'd put that feeling down to paranoia but, as I said, at Castleford you can hear what the fans are saying.

Dean came over and told me to enjoy it, then he said, 'I don't know too much about you, but you must be half-decent to get this shot'. John, our coach, named me as a substitute that day—it was back in the day of two replacements, not four—and I hated warming up, as I had to run past the Castleford supporters who were always willing to tell our players to 'Bugger off back to Wig'in'. For some reason, a red haired teenager seemed an easy target. I don't really remember too much about the game, though I quickly realised I'd never see the £600 as we fell to a 46–0 defeat. We were being battered, St John Ellis scored a hat-trick, and I whispered a prayer that if I got on, I wouldn't be marking him!

In the 72nd minute I got the call to say I was on. I didn't care about the result—this was the moment I had waited my whole life for. After this, it didn't matter—I could say I had played for the most famous club of them all, and no one could ever take that from me. I was proud, not just for myself, but for my parents and my sister—I wondered what they would be feeling at that point, too. I puffed my chest one last time and stepped to the sideline. Of all the people to get substituted to make way for me, it was Gary Connolly. He shook my hand, uttered a quick, 'Good luck' and I was on. I'd like to tell you I had a super game. It'd be nicer still to be able to report that I scored, but I did neither of those things. I never touched the ball, I never made a tackle, and quite honestly I didn't care. I had done little, and lost, but I loved it, and I savoured every one of my modest eight minutes on the pitch, replaying them in my mind on the coach home to Wigan. I must have been the only Wiganer who returned from Castleford that day happy— we'd been hammered, after all! I was 17, rangy and 13 stone, but I felt seven-foot tall and bullet-proof. I even had fans asking for my autograph after the match, which was crazy . . . it'd not been long since I'd been asking Wigan players for their signature and there I was, signing them myself. I had an inner-glow—a happiness that is impossible to describe.

My mum and dad taped the game, so as soon as I got home, I watched it back on TV. As I came on the pitch, pale skinned with my bright red hair, the commentator Eddie Hemmings said, 'Forget the scoreboard, this lad will remember this for his entire life'. I know some fans say that Eddie exaggerates things sometimes, but I'm happy to testify that, on that occasion, he couldn't have uttered a truer word.

In the days that followed, Wigan welcomed back many first team stars from injury; I wasn't surprised to return to the alliance team, and I certainly wasn't deflated. By contrast, I was full of energy. John thanked me for playing—I felt like I should have thanked him, but I didn't—and he told me he wouldn't think twice about calling on me again. He was a fan of mine, and a few years down the line he actually tried to sign me when he was at the Australian club Perth Reds. He even faxed a contract over, but I was too young and I still had things left to achieve in England. I went to see Jack Robinson and he offered me a new two-year contract, so I called John and told him I was staying at Wigan.

John didn't leave Wigan on the best of terms. I think he had disagreements with the board and he was a lonely figure on the training ground, just walking around while Dean Bell and Shaun Edwards took training. He confused plays, which annoyed some of the senior players. I made my debut in October 1993, and though I didn't play again for the first team that season, I did enough in the alliance side to earn a contract the following February. By that point, John was basically seeing out his time, and by the end of his time 'in charge' I'm not sure how much he actually was 'in charge'. I'm not sure if he was still picking the teams. I'm pretty sure he had little to do with the success on the field. It was a strange and embarrassing situation, and I felt sorry for him as he worked hard. I'll always like him—he handed me my debut after all!

John was the man who had allowed me to realise my dream. I continued to train with the first team, as well as with the reserves, so I was training about eight hours a day. I played for the reserves, I was full of beans, and hoping to catch John's eye again, but before I knew it the season had ended. I had really earned a rest, I knew I deserved a good summer break, but after three weeks I was desperate to get back into training.

I had a first team to break into.

4

GRAND SLAM ERA

'The biggest thing is to have a mindset and a belief you can win every tournament you're going into.'

Tiger Woods

WHEN JOHN Dorahy left Wigan, there was a massive public debate around town as to who would be the next coach. Top of the fans' list was Graeme West. A former player who also worked in the lotto office and coached the reserve grade, Westy was a great man. He had honesty and integrity, and from playing under him in the reserves, I knew he was a fan of mine—another reason I was so pleased when he got the job in early summer of 1994.

The directors bowed to public pressure and appointed the big guy, his first head coaching position. He had a baptism of fire, his first task was taking the team to Brisbane to play the Broncos in the World Club Challenge before the summer break, which I watched on TV with the rest of Wigan. It was an epic match that Wigan won, not bad for Westy's first game! Brisbane had beaten Wigan at Central Park two years earlier, so even for a club like Wigan—burdened by the expectations of success in England—their triumph in Australia was against the odds. With the season finishing on a high with that 20–14 win, making Wigan World Club Champions, there was a great feeling around the town.

I'd still not played for Wigan since my debut the previous October, and I was as keen as the fans for the new season to roll around. When the off-season was over the summer, before the switch to Super League, fans would be so miserable and depressed around Wigan in June and July. They were like junkies craving their next fix, they sorely missed their rugby, and once the fixtures were released they enthusiastically counted the days to the opening game.

To whet their appetite, before the season began, Wigan hosted a summer sevens tournament, and teams from division one—the top-tier, then—and division two took part in at Central Park. It was also a useful warm-up for the players and they could put some training ground combinations to the test and blow away a few cobwebs that even the toughest training runs couldn't sweep away.

Westy selected a squad of both young and experienced players, with teenagers like Simon Haughton, Sean Long and me there with guys like Martin Offiah, Frano Botica, Andrew Farrell and Jason Robinson. Even though it was not really a big event, the young lads took it very seriously; we were in the shop window, and we had a chance to show our coach that we could handle this level. I'd worked over-time during the summer in training, and was fuelled by frustration and excitement. Wigan won the trophy and, to crown a great day, I took the crystal decanter home for Man of the Tournament—my first individual honour as a professional.

It was during the tournament that I first became aware of Gary Connolly's pranks. The players had to pass a 50p piece around on the pitch. There was only one coin, but the rule was that if somebody passed you the coin, you could not refuse it. Whoever was caught in possession at the final whistle had to buy a round of drinks for the team in the bar afterwards, and so players would accept it, put it down their sock and a couple of minutes later—at an appropriate break in play—pass it on to somebody else. It was bizarre—I'd never done anything like that, even at junior level. I was always one to focus on the game, on the next tackle, on the next play, and here I was at Central Park—a nervous 18-year-old desperate to impress—playing a silly coin game in front of thousands of oblivious fans.

I won the Player of the Tournament award, but I knew that wouldn't ease my passage into the first team. Westy's first-choice back-line at the time was: Henry Paul; Jason Robinson, Gary Connolly, Inga Tuigamala and Martin Offiah. His half-backs were Nigel Wright or Frano Botica and, of course, the mercurial Shaun Edwards. And they were all at their peak. I was not stupid, but nor was I impatient. I knew I had to bide my time, learn what I could and wait for my opportunity. Usually, as a fringe player pressing to get into the team, versatility can help but my ability to play either on the wing or centre seemed irrelevant—the choice of trying to disperse Connolly or Tuigamala at centre, or Robinson or Offiah on the wing was daunting, improbable and seemingly impossible.

Those players were absolute perfectionists, every one of them. And Westy did the best thing possible—he didn't try and over-coach them. Other coaches may have been tempted to let their ego interfere, but not Westy—he was as much a man-manager as a coach. He realised he had exceptionally talented players, and he didn't want to shackle them with set-pieces and instructions. Instead, he allowed them to express themselves on the pitch. Training was taken just as seriously as the games. The players would seek the perfect session, where a ball would not once be dropped, or a move not once executed incorrectly. I've been in that position when I was the one who dropped the ball, or mistimed a run, and it wasn't nice to be on the receiving end of one of Shaun Edwards' angry expressions. He didn't need to say anything, he'd just dip his head slightly and his piercing eyes would stare right at you—it would frighten anybody!

Shaun was a unique individual. He could be joking in the changing room one minute, then completely in his zone a minute later. He was a born winner, and was put on this earth to be involved in rugby. He also had, by some distance, the worse dress sense, and wouldn't think twice about turning up in a tracksuit, finished off with a smart pair of shoes. I distinctly remember him wearing tracksuit pants that had 'Soul 2 Soul' written down the leg, but he didn't care; he knew he had the respect of the whole changing room. His mental strength was unbelievable.

I'd watched him play all of my life and seen how influential he was on the pitch, but he was just the same on the training ground, in every session, every day. He had a burning will to win, such fight, and though his frame was relatively small he was one of the toughest men I ever saw. I think that environment really honed Andrew Farrell's qualities as a leader. He was already confident enough to boss players around, even though he'd only been in the team for 18 months or so, but he acted like a seasoned veteran. With his towering physique, opposition defences used to give him so much attention, and that took the pressure off the rest of the Wigan players. He also used to get abuse hurled at him, too. Why rival fans picked on him, I've no idea, though I imagine it was jealousy—bad players rarely get booed. Either way, Andrew was blinkered, like Shaun: his only focus was on winning. I was still 18 and, in one respect, I felt a little out of my depth, but in another I felt right at home because the players' attitudes were like mine. They all had that same stubbornness that I had, that same drive to improve and get better. Two or three years earlier, I'd felt like the only lad in the world who did my own training on top of the training I did with my school and my club. Now, I was with guys who'd clearly done the extras to get ahead.

It aggravated me so much when I used to hear remarks like, 'Frano Botica's a naturally talented goal-kicker' or 'Henry Paul's a real natural'. Frano practised relentlessly, taking as much time with the easiest of kicks as the hardest. Granted, he obviously had a knack for it, but he mastered his craft over hours and hours of practice. Henry was another. He is a natural entertainer, that's his character, but fans don't realise the hard work he put in during training. He has the body of a Greek god, and no one gets a six-pack like that naturally. That is all down to hard work on his part . . . I looked like a little schoolboy next to him!

It seemed like all the players did their own little extras, no one wanted to let the team down. Phil Clarke and Denis Betts spent a lot of time together, they were training partners, and great students of all sports. They would always be the first ones to bring new exercises into the gym. We were doing Olympic weight lifting—picking up a bar from the ground, snapping it up and lifting it above our heads—well before anyone else was. And, though now common practice, we were the first to take the rowing machines seriously as a workout. Denis and Phil were behind both of those ideas.

Phil was always a bit distant, he never really socialised with the team, which was probably due to the fact he was still studying at university. I tried to get to know him better, but I couldn't break down the barriers and I always felt that I had something to prove to him. Denis, on the other hand, was the complete opposite. He made me feel welcome from the start, and appreciated my hard work. I grew in confidence during those weeks in training, but I was still a little intimidated by the squad. I was always the quiet one, which is a sin in rugby league—when I was a senior player, that was the first piece of advice I gave to young players, be vocal. Without communication, the team falls apart. Inga Tuigamala, the former All Blacks star, took me under his wing and treated me like his little brother. We'd stay behind after training together to do one-on-one sessions, which helped bring me out of my shell.

Fitness-wise, I could hold my own against most of the team, but it was the gym that scared me the most. The weights that these guys were throwing around were frightening, with big guys like Faz bench-pressing 170kg (the equivalent of two 13 stone men being perched on a bar).

I made a surprise appearance on the first day of the 1994–95 season against Warrington, owing to injury, and as the season progressed, I edged myself into the side more regularly—either as 16th man (there were only two substitutes back then), a substitute, then playing if someone was injured. In all, I scored 18 tries in 23 games, a haul that included my first professional hat-trick in a Regal Trophy match against Rochdale. On top of that, I also played for the reserves so I would often have two games a week, and I was also doubling up on training sessions too—the club's masseur Andrew Pinkerton saw a great deal of me! I didn't mind though, I was young and if I was struggling, they wouldn't have picked me. The appearances and the victories also brought in money, and I received my first sponsored car, a Nissan Primera. Life was going pretty well. None of it went to my head, though. I was getting recognised more and more, I was taking home plaudits, but I knew that the minute I got in the comfort zone it would all evaporate. Besides, how could I get a big head when I was still living in a box room at my mum and dad's house?

We had a great team spirit and genuinely enjoyed each other's company. I think fans could see that in the way we celebrated our tries—Martin and Shaun worked out a few different ones, such as high-fives and nodding to each other. As part of a bonus for the players, Nissan offered to throw £50 into the players' kitty every time one of us celebrated a try in front of their advertising hoarding during a televised match. That didn't last long—it cost them a fortune! There was a real bond in the team.

It was so exciting to be involved in a team of all-stars, and to be accepted by them. They treated me like one of them, and if ever they went out they phoned me up and invited me along. This was in an era when there were four domestic trophies up for grabs. We got the Regal Trophy under our belt at the end of January (I didn't play), we were closing in on the league championship and we had two other trophies to win—the Challenge Cup, and the Premiership, which staged their finals four weeks apart. This was an era before the play-offs, so we knew the league would take care of itself—by the time we'd progressed to the semi-finals of the Challenge Cup, we'd only lost two of our 35 games that season.

Trips to Wembley had become an integral part of the calendar in Wigan. They'd made the last seven finals, and it just got bigger each year. By 1995, after defeating Oldham 48–20 in the semi (again I missed out) it seemed like a mass-migration down the M6 to watch the final against Leeds, who they'd beaten 12 months earlier.

Though I'd played quite a bit in the first team leading up to Christmas, I dropped out of the side in early spring, missing the Regal Trophy and all the knock-out stages of the Challenge Cup, so I wasn't surprised when Westy didn't name me in the line-up for the Wembley final. Others may have been disappointed, but I wasn't. I'd turned 19 just a few weeks earlier, and I was happy to go along for the experience. As a travelling reserve, I still got the traditional Cup Final suit and appeared on the team photo. I'd been in the team a few months, I was no longer pinching myself that I was living my dream but, on the coach down to London, I relapsed into being a Wigan fan again. I couldn't help it—I'd wanted this all my life, and there I was, right in the middle of it.

In London, the preparation was intense and meticulous. Jason Robinson injured his foot—I'm still not sure how—a few days before the final, and Westy pulled me to one side. 'If Jason doesn't recover in time, I'm going to start you on the wing, how do you feel about that?' he asked me.

'Yeah,' I said, clearing my throat. 'No problem. I'm up for it.'

I lied a little—no, correct that, I lied out-right. I was crapping myself. My stomach began churning, and the realisation that I could be about to start a Wembley Final sunk in as I trained in Jason's position all week, just in case he didn't make it. There are always more players than there are places in a team, but in rugby league, players don't rejoice at others' injuries—even if it helps them out. They just see injuries as being an inevitable by-product of our game. Truth is, I wanted Jason to play. I liked him, he was a real friend, and he was desperate to take part. Plus, I'm not sure I was ready for it at that point. I'd done well for Wigan in the appearances I'd made that year, but Wembley was always an emotional day for me as a fan—I couldn't imagine how I would have felt playing at that stage.

Westy left it to the very morning of the game. Jason replaced me in training on the wing, he ran through a few sessions, with all the staff gawping at him and his injured foot. I stood with Westy and Joe Lydon, who was effectively working as an assistant coach, and Jason walked over to give his verdict. 'Anxious' does not do justice to how I felt as he approached. 'It's painful,' Jason said. 'But I've got great movement.' Westy asked him if he could play with a pain-killing injection, and he nodded his head. No one doubted him. Jason is an honest man and if he was not fit, there is no way he would have played simply for selfish motives. He wouldn't have done that to the team.

Everyone carried on training—there was no big cheer, just a few quiet remarks—though Jason later pulled me to one side, thanked me for covering for him all week, and asked how I felt. 'Don't worry about me,' I told him. 'I'm happy for you, and I know one day my shot will come.'

Even then, I still couldn't switch off. If Jason broke down in the warm-up, I would be in, so I prepared like the other players. I was very nervous, even just walking down the Wembley tunnel behind the players—that alone had been a dream of mine. When I entered the stadium, the Wigan supporters gave me a huge cheer and were chanting my name, which was fantastic. They knew I'd been on stand-by all week and missed out at the last minute. Their appreciation calmed me down and, as soon as the game kicked-off, I finally relaxed. I could at last enjoy the biggest week of my life.

Wigan were brilliant that day, especially Jason, who scored two tries and won the Lance Todd trophy as man of the match in a 30–10 victory. Jason is such a humble person, and in the dressing room afterwards, he weaved through our giddy team-mates to get to me, and then thanked me again. I didn't know what to say, so I hugged him. I'd heard plenty of stories about Cup Final celebrations and, like all good fishing yarns, I thought they'd been exaggerated over the years. Turned out I was wrong.

The party was brilliant, with directors, players and coaches all enjoying the sounds of a glam rock band—everyone was so overjoyed. It'd been a crazy week for me. I didn't have that much to drink—I was emotionally drained, but very happy. The following morning, I went down to breakfast to see a few players loading up the team coach with more crates of beer than I could count. There were about 30 grown and thirsty men on the coach for a four-hour journey back to Wigan—I'll leave you to do the maths! It was a great trip back up the motorway, with everyone letting off steam, relaxing, singing, laughing, even dancing. Then a call came from the front of the coach to smarten ourselves up—we were approaching Wigan, and we had to switch to an open-top bus to take us the rest of the way to Central Park. It was so surreal. Just two years earlier, I'd been on the other side of the fence, cheering my heroes' names and here I was, on the open-top bus with the Challenge Cup and superstars of the game thrusting beers into my hands. I hid my drunkenness behind a pair of sunglasses.

We returned to normality days later, soon securing the league championship and putting ourselves on the brink of a grand slam—a clean-sweep of all of the trophies. That had never happened before, so even for a club like Wigan that thrived on expectations of glory, it turned the pressure up a notch as we set out to win the Premiership Trophy. That tournament involved the top eight teams in the league, and we made smooth passage in our first two games—I played in both—to reach the final at Old Trafford against Leeds. My Challenge Cup experiences really helped me develop. I was coping better with big occasions, and with pressure, and I felt comfortable in the team. I thought I'd done enough to secure a place on the bench, but in the build-up to the final, Inga was informed about the death of a family member and had to fly back to New Zealand. We were very sad for him, and when Westy named me at centre for the final, I took no satisfaction in taking Inga's place—as happy as I was to get my chance to play in my first major final, I wished it had been under different circumstances.

The rest of the team had won the Challenge Cup Final a few weeks earlier, but Westy realised it was a big day for me. He told me he had confidence in me, and to go out and enjoy myself. He always looked after me, and I wanted to re-pay his faith. The worse part of final day was, I soon discovered, the waiting around. Because the game was in Manchester, we stayed at home the night before, and so when I woke up I had a few hours to kill doing nothing. The time dragged and, like a kid on his first day of school, I was showered, dressed and ready to travel before anyone else in the squad. Once I was on the coach, I was fine. I enjoyed the excitement.

Rarely have I been in a dressing room and known I was going to win, but I did that day. I looked around at the players, they were all on form, and they were all hungry to complete the Grand Slam. I think we would have defeated any team in the world that day—even Australia. We knew each other so well that we bordered on telepathy and everything we tried came off. On top of that, our defence was so mean. The opening was ferocious—Leeds were motivated by revenge, following the Challenge Cup Final—but I calmed our nerves by scoring the opening try, after an offload by Martin Offiah. As I celebrated, I thought of my auntie Connie—she always placed a bet on me scoring the first try. The game was going exactly to plan and, 10 minutes later, I scored my second try when Shaun Edwards put me through a gap. The ball was being swung right-to-left across the field, and I just hit Shaun's pass at full speed on an angle, darting past my marker's inside shoulder. In defence, the inside shoulder is the hardest tackle to make because a player has to readjust his posture and direction.

As I celebrated I tried to block out the thought that I may become the first player to score a hat-trick in a Premiership Final. Luckily, other players began to cross for tries, which dragged my concentration back to the team's success. But at half-time, Joe Lydon pulled me to one side and told me that the game was more or less won—we were over 30 points up. He told me to run like I had never run before, and to look for the ball in order to break the record.

I was a team player, and always had been, but I understood what Joe meant. I would never do anything to harm the team but it would do me no harm to go sniffing for a third try. As it transpired, I didn't have to wait too long before I was over again as, early in the second half, Henry Paul made a little break down the left, chipped ahead and I scooped up the ball to dive over the whitewash for a moment I will never forget. I had scored a hat-trick in my first final—no man had done that before. Sometimes, during games, it's only afterwards that players are aware of records but not on that occasion—every single one of my team-mates ran from wherever they were standing and jumped on me! It felt impossible for me to get any happier, though I did minutes later, when Gary Connolly—who had then become my closest mate—scored a hat-trick too. It was perfect.

For the last 10 minutes of the game, Westy moved me to full-back for the first time since I was about 16. Then the announcement came over the tannoy that I had won the Harry Sunderland Trophy as man of the match. I couldn't believe it. Wigan had just completed the Grand Slam, the very first team ever to do so, and I'd made a bit of history in the process as well. Players had only been given two tickets for their families, which my mum and Nicola took. I'd bought my dad one separately. As my team-mates celebrated around me, I scanned the stand for my mum and found her, stood cheering with Nicola.

'Where's dad?' I mouthed, animated, so she could understand. She pointed to the Stretford End. I cantered over to look for him—he was easy to find. He was the only one not stood up. He was sat down, his head in his hands, crying. It warmed my heart that I'd made him so proud.

Denis Betts and Phil Clarke were celebrating their last games for Wigan; they were both heading down under. In the dressing room Phil congratulated me, and told me to build on it—I felt, after nearly a year of trying, that I finally had his approval. It was a nice touch from him, and it meant a great deal to me. I was in heaven, on cloud nine . . . pick your cliché. I'd never felt so happy and satisfied in all my life.

'Kris,' I heard a voice yell. 'Come on mate, random drugs test.' That brought me back to earth with a bump. I'd never had a test before. I was taken into a separate room, given a sample pot, and asked to pee. But I was so dehydrated from the game and, combined with the stage-fright—I'd never been told by a man that he was going to watch me pee—I couldn't go. The biggest night of my life, and I celebrated it with my dad and two strangers waiting for me to pee in a cup!

I walked through the tunnel, drugs testers in tow, and sat on one of the seats in the now vacant stadium. In the relative silence, I reflected on the game. It had been three hours since the full-time whistle, and I apologised to the two drugs testers who were with me, but I still wasn't ready to pee. I think they felt a bit guilty about having to stay with me, because they'd watched the game and knew I was missing the party, where I should have been the star guest. The team coach left without me, so the drugs testers offered to drive me back to Central Park and said they could take the sample there. I appreciated their charity, and as soon as we arrived in Wigan I was bursting to go—the litres of water I'd drunk were aching to get out of my body. I thanked the drugs testers again, and made my way into the after-game function just in time—food was being served. I took my seat with my family, and Joe Lydon walked by and tapped me on my shoulder. He handed me a napkin. 'Open it,' he instructed. Discreetly, I unfolded the napkin and read the message he had written: 'Only a handful of people have ever won the Harry Sunderland Trophy and the Lance Todd trophy. I am one of them, and you're half way there. You'll be the next one.'

5

INTERNATIONALLY SPEAKING

'It's like trying to pin a kangaroo down on a trampoline, impossible.'

Sid Waddell

WHEN I SAT down to write this chapter about my international career, I didn't know off the top of my head how many times I'd played for my country. The internet gospel that is Wikipedia says I played 20 times for Great Britain and 10 for England (though the website also says I'm engaged to 'Carrie Hamilton', a girl I've never heard of). What I definitely knew was that I figured in three tours down under, two World Cups, and one agonisingly-close Ashes series that will haunt me until I die.

Like my Wigan first team career, my international call-up came out of the blue. There was little fanfare about my call-up—the first I knew about it was when a letter came through the post, in the early summer of 1995 saying I'd been selected to play for England and to report to Castleford a few days later. I was made up, but I never really expected to play a big role in the World Cup. I'd played that season as a bit-part wing or centre—I hadn't cemented a spot in a back-line that had Jason Robinson, Inga Tuigamala, Gary Connolly and Martin Offiah, with Henry Paul at full-back. I only thought I would play a similar role for England, maybe play in a couple of the 'easier' fixtures if I was lucky, but I knew it was a great chance to be involved at that level. I ran at full-back during training and then, after about three days, Phil Larder pulled me to one side and said, 'I'm going to start you at full-back against the Aussies'. On the outside, I was Mr Cool. I nodded my head, and told him I was ready for them. Inside, I was packing it!

I think Shaun Edwards had something to do with it. Stuart Spruce was injured and so they were short of a full-back, and I'm told Giz (that's Shaun's nickname) had a word in Phil's ear. Shaun was an influential figure in the game, and well-respected. At Wigan, there were times when we'd been training for 10 minutes and Giz would say, 'That's it lads', and then tell Westy that we were ready. And the scary thing was he was right! Phil respected Shaun's opinion. I never thought I had a chance of playing because I hadn't played full-back before, and I was still only 19. I'd always been able to tackle and catch. We had a press conference at the hotel at Brighouse and Phil announced I was full-back, and that's when the enormity of it all hit me. I became the media's focal point. Gary Connolly could have played there but he'd lost two stone through pneumonia.

My room-mate was Faz, but he got sick and—not wanting to risk me catching a bug—I was moved to share with Karl Harrison. Rhino was the worst snorer in history, but it certainly helped having him there; we didn't talk about the game or anything like that, but the fact that he was so relaxed and calm gave me confidence before our opening match against Australia. I'd been to Wembley three years earlier as a fan to watch Great Britain lose to Australia in the World Cup Final, Steve Renouf scoring the clinching try. If someone had told me then that, in three years' time, I would be running out at the same venue to face the Aussies, I'd have told them they were mad. Walking out at Wembley, seeing Diana Ross come past in an open-top car, I knew this was the big time. And when the national anthem played, a hundred thoughts went through my mind. It's very emotional; when players say a shiver goes down their spine, they aren't lying. It's impossible not to let the gravity of the occasion get to you—I didn't feel nervous, more a sense of pride.

I realised the Aussies would target me and I wanted them to; I wanted to catch the first bomb and to make my first tackle, to put myself at ease. Typical, I completely mistimed the first kick that went up, leaping too early, and the Australians scored! As the Aussies celebrated, John Hopoate gave me a real mouthful, calling me every name under the sun. But after that, I had a pretty solid game and pulled off a couple of good tackles on Steve Menzies, who was outstanding during that series running off Brad Fittler's inside shoulder. Afterwards, Giz criticised Hopoate in the press conference but to me, it wasn't a big deal—that kind of abuse probably happened 100 times throughout my career and I just brushed it off. A few journalists came looking for me to ask about what Hopoate had said, but I hadn't got a clue—I was just made up that in my first international, we'd beaten Australia 20–16 at Wembley. Days later, I scored my first try for England at my home ground, Central Park, against Fiji. I was enjoying playing at full-back, but in truth, I didn't really know what I was doing. Full-back is one of those roles where you learn game-sense—the positioning, and reading of the game— through experience and trial and error, and that's what I was doing. We had a good game against Wales in the semis to set up a rematch against the Aussies in the final, again at Wembley. In the build-up to the match, I had my picture taken with one of my heroes—no, not Brett Kenny, but Carol Decker of the band T'Pau! She had performed the official

World Cup anthem.

We were determined to win the World Cup Final, and not just because we were on £15,000 a man if we did—that was a huge sum then, especially considering not all players were full-time. We felt confident, we'd played pretty well throughout the tournament and the Aussies were far from convincing in their semi-final, needing extra time to see off the Kiwis. I played in the final with laryngitis, I could barely speak, but I couldn't pull out because I'd lost my voice.

My memories of the game itself are sketchy; I've not watched it on video since, but I know we went really close to beating them—it took a scrappy score on their part to wedge an eight-point gap between us, and they clung on. I was gutted we'd lost. I swapped jerseys with Tim Brasher after the final whistle, and though we hadn't won we'd played well enough to warrant a drink afterwards; my lingering memory of our night was being at the bar drinking pints with the actor Mark Little, best known as *Neighbours'* Joe Mangle.

Playing full-back for England helped me squeeze into the Wigan side regularly, once Henry Paul moved to stand-off to replace Frano Botica. The team's other stand-off Nigel Wright, a genius on his day, was injured. Wigan's Challenge Cup run ended in early 1996, but one silver lining of that defeat by Salford was that I was able to play in the World Nines in Fiji—only players from teams knocked out of the Cup were considered. It was a great experience for me. I'd never been anywhere more exotic than Benidorm before then. Thousands of people lined the streets as we paraded through town during an opening ceremony, all wearing sarongs! It was great fun. I also learned that my performances the previous year for England hadn't gone unnoticed. As I walked through our hotel lobby, Mal Meninga was walking the other way. He'd been a bit of a hero of mine; I smiled at him politely, acknowledging him, and he looked at me and said, 'Hi Kris'. Well, that blew me away! I was 19 and Mal Meninga knew who I was—I was straight on the phone to tell my mum and dad. Thinking about it now, that was the last time I was in awe that someone recognised me; I was surprised, though, when I was in Ayia Napa one year and, across the bar, Rio Ferdinand, the England football defender began pointing my way. I looked over my shoulder, thinking he was trying to get the attention of someone behind me, but he again pointed at me, so I went over to say hi and he told me he always bet on me as first try scorer, which was nice to hear!

Fiji was in the middle of a monsoon, so the entire Nines competition was played over two days. We were held up in our hotel, frustrated and unable to do anything but train. Everyone, that was, but my Wigan team-mates Martin Hall and Gary Connolly, who were told when they landed that they couldn't play because they'd signed contracts with the Australian Rugby League—they spent the entire time in the bar having a whale of a time. We lost to Australia in the semis and, afterwards, all the squads had a post-tournament party. Because Henry Paul was in the New Zealand squad, the England and Kiwi players mixed well together. The Aussies didn't—they kept themselves to themselves. It was at that party that I had my only experience of being high from drugs . . . though it's not what you think! Fiji has a drink called Kava, which is made from the scrapings of a Kava plant's root and is a natural tranquilliser. The Kiwi boys were serving it in half a coconut shell and I must have drunk three of them. I was in trouble. I didn't get drunk, it was—I imagine—like taking too much of a strong anaesthetic. For some crazy reason, I started walking the four miles back to our hotel, down the dark roads. When I saw a car approaching I collapsed in front of it, and the driver took me back to my hotel. I was sharing a room with

Simon Haughton and Mick Cassidy and, for no reason, I flipped. I completely lost all control, I turned the beds over, I threw a chair from the balcony—the next day I woke up to find Simon and Mick laughing their heads off. It scared me that I'd done those things; I spent the next hour cleaning up my mess, completely embarrassed.

I returned to Fiji later that year on our tour of the South Seas Islands. I was proud to be picked, because only when you've toured with Great Britain are you a real British Lion. Apparently, because of that, I can get into any sporting event in the country for free, though I've never tried it out!

Before we landed in Fiji, we flew to Papua New Guinea first, which was like nothing I could have imagined. From the minute I had to go and get my own bag off the plane, I knew it was going to be a crazy experience. On the way to our hotel, I looked out the window at the locals sat outside their shacks, eating a local delicacy which looked like a piece of raw flesh—they would literally take a bite and blood would drip out of their mouths! It was called betelnut and was bright red in colour—needless to say I didn't try any. Rugby league is the national sport of Papua New Guinea, and international players are treated like Gods. When Adrian Lam flew in from Australia for the Test, locals walked for up to two days from the mountains to greet him at the airport. Lammy was already a superstar; he'd captained Queensland to a shock series win in the Australian State of Origin the year before, and he was followed with devotion in his homeland. There was even an Adrian Lam-themed fruit-machine in the airport at Port Morseby—the jackpot was three faces of Lammy!

The PNG Grand Final had taken place the day we landed and the referee had, apparently, endured a shocker. He was staying in our hotel and there were 2,000 locals outside trying to kill him! Because of safety concerns, we were under armed guard, unable to leave our hotel. We felt imprisoned; we played games of ticky-off-the-ground to try to conquer the boredom. The only time we left the hotel was to train on the pitch where we were to play the Kumuls, and it was so hot we had to train at 7am. I jogged out onto the pitch, thinking that the surface had a few stones on it, but when I looked down at the ground I discovered they were spent bullet cartridges! The police had fired them to disperse the riots after the Grand Final. On the morning of the Test, we changed into our kit in our own hotel rooms and then went by minibus to the ground. It wasn't a stadium, at least not one with any seating; it had one stand, with tall trees surrounding the pitch on the other three sides. Many of the locals climbed up the trees to get a better view, and if they fell, the crowd would cheer—even when the poor guys had fallen 40 feet! Their fans were so passionate; many lived in third world conditions, and didn't have television, and the prospect of their national side facing Great Britain really excited them. We were told that, as soon as the game finished, the crowd would invade the pitch so we had to dash straight to our minibus. I was particularly worried because I had red hair, and I was told that the locals had probably never seen anyone with ginger hair before—it was like when the Ewoks worshipped C3P0 in *Return of the Jedi*! Mick Cassidy, with his mop of hair as white as Tipp-Ex, was also petrified. Genetically, the PNG players are made for rugby league—their bodies are like granite, like the ageless Stanley Gene—and they threw themselves into tackles with reckless enthusiasm. In steamy conditions, and in front of a hostile crowd, we managed to cling on for a 32–30 win. The game was probably too close for comfort but, personally, I was thrilled, as I'd scored two tries on my GB debut. I didn't hang around afterwards to celebrate my double, though; as soon as the final whistle was blown we—as advised—dashed for the minibus after the briefest of handshakes with our opponents. On board, we weren't safe, as the locals mobbed our vehicle and began shaking it violently. No one admitted it at the time, but we were all terrified; we returned to the hotel and headed straight to the bar, dressed in our full kit and boots, and only then—with a calming drink settling our nerves—could we laugh about what had just happened.

Though I'd played for England and Great Britain Nines, it was still a special occasion to make my full Great Britain debut, and the prestige of pulling on the jersey hit home when Phil Larder presented me with a cap at the hotel. Rugby league players only get one, after their debut . . . my dad has mine in his office.

Having been made into a full-back by the international game, it was strange that—after a full season in that position for Wigan in 1996—I played all of that tour at centre. Daryl Powell was the other centre, I roomed with him and he really took me under his wing. I was only 20, and still living at home with my mum and dad at the time, and Daryl looked after me—he even washed my training kit to help me out. When players from different clubs come into an international side, sometimes you get little cliques, with players from the same club sticking together. Though Wigan and St Helens are big rivals, when we went into international camps we stuck together because we knew each other so well; better than the Yorkshire-based players. When you go on tour, barriers between players from different clubs are broken down more easily and I became good mates with Daryl, Alan Hunte and Paul Sculthorpe. Scully was a year younger than me, 19, and boy could he spend money—he told me he was still paying his visa bill off three years after that tour!

We flew out of PNG and I was relieved to find no monsoon greeted me when I returned to Fiji, it was like being on holiday, swapping our training shorts for Bermuda shorts as soon as training was over. On the field, we had a tough match against Fiji—they were very physical so we had to keep our discipline to win, which we did. All of us, that is, except Bobby Goulding, who fought throughout the match!

We finished our tour with three Tests against New Zealand. I'd never been there before, and I loved it. Unlike Australia, the locals are really welcoming—in Australia, they look down on Brits. They have a superiority complex. I know it's a generalisation—and keep in mind a lot of my closest friends are Australians—but many of them have an arrogance I don't like.

Our first Test against the Kiwis was a brilliant match. We lost narrowly, but in that game I pulled off what I regard as the best tackle of my career. Mathew Ridge, a full-back I always admired, was heading for the corner. I tracked across and caught him about a yard from the try-line. If I had carried out a normal tackle on him, he'd have scored, so I had to hit him high across his shoulder to force him into touch-in-goal— in the match review, team-mates told me it was one of the best tackles they'd ever seen, which made me feel great.

The closeness of that first Test—we lost 17–10—swelled our confidence before the second match. But as we waited for our flight to Palmerston North, coach Phil Larder told us that the RFL had decided to send nine players home as part of a cost-cutting exercise. It was like a hammer-blow—it deflated the whole squad. On the flight, there was a sense of unease, because the players didn't know who was going. Then when we got there, they pulled the nine aside and broke the news to them. I've never been one to blame defeats on referees or anything like that, but our losses in the second and third Tests were down to the RFL's decision—the squad was completely demoralised. We managed to put up a fight in the second Test, losing 18–15, but the mood was so flat that it surprised no one when we lost the final match so heavily (32–12). On top of that, homesickness was creeping in; I loved the touring experience, I was young, single and seeing new sights. But those with wives and children were becoming more miserable by the day. There was little to cheer about, with few events planned to lighten the mood. It got to a point where Faz complained to the management and said it was a farce, because we'd carried our official suits in our cases and not worn them. So they put on a function for us, which ended in a casino, and Scully and I went with Denis Betts to the roulette wheel. Scully and I were on our first tour, while Denis was a veteran of them, so we looked up to him.

We certainly took on board his gambling advice when he suggested we bet on our squad number. With his first bet, he put the minimum stake, $5, on his squad number, 11, and— bingo—the ball fell on the number 11. He couldn't contain his joy, though he tried to look cool as he turned to us with a grin and said, 'I told you so'—as if he knew it was going to happen. As he gloated, he didn't notice that the ball had been rolled again with his chips—all $180 worth—still on the table. Noticing his error, he turned to retrieve them, but the croupier waved her hand across the table with authority and insisted, 'No more changes'. Denis thought he'd blown it . . . until the ball landed on number 11 again! He couldn't believe it, we couldn't believe it. He'd won an absolute fortune off an initial $5 bet. Talk about luck. Having seen Denis score tries and win trophies plenty of times, those celebrations were nothing compared to his reaction to this bit of luck—he punched the air and screamed. To this day, I still bet on the number one whenever I'm near a roulette wheel, though I've never had the same luck Denis enjoyed in Auckland.

I finished my career with 20 Tests for Great Britain, including one as captain. I was proud to play in every single Test match, though the problem I found—and I know it's the same for other players—was that the internationals were at the wrong time of year. After a long, bruising season, I always carried various knocks and niggles and I was tired. I was always enthusiastic, always passionate; but it was often hard to find the energy, and while I looked forward to playing internationals, part of me felt like it was a case of wanting to survive.

I only beat Australia three times in my career, though we went close so many times it was painful. Some people think when you play the Aussies you need to come up with superhero plays—I disagree. A lot of their success comes from doing the little things right. They are clinical, ruthless and hungry. Physically, there is little between the players, the real battle is a psychological one. I've been there a few times when we have managed to win one of the first two matches and then the media storm begins, the history gets brought up and the pressure mounts, and we buckle.

Australia's game split in the late 1990s, meaning there were two competitions. We were beaten by the ARL team in the 1995 World Cup Final and, two years later, a team aligned with the Australian Super League competition came over for a three match series where we managed to beat them at Old Trafford, 20–12. This is one of my favourite Test memories. Our coach, Andy Goodway, gave a speech that inspired us. He drew a line in imaginary sand in the changing rooms—I later discovered it originates from the Battle of Alamo in 1936 when William Barrett Travis did the same with his sword, urging those willing to stay and defend the fort to cross it. I guess Andy wanted the same level of commitment from his team and he got it. What's more, Old Trafford had always been one of my favourite venues.

My other victory over the Aussies was in 2001, in the

opening Test win at Huddersfield. I was always content with how I performed on the international stage, though I never felt I really excelled—I never quite reproduced my Wigan form in a GB shirt, though it was not through lack of trying. In 2001, when we beat the Aussies 20–12 at Huddersfield, that was, in my eyes, my best performance for my country. Defensively I put on some big hits at crucial times, which made the win even sweeter. The only sore point of that match was having my nose broken as I drove the ball in from a scrum. This was courtesy of the elbow of Trent Barrett and I was quick to remind him about the incident over a few beers when he joined Wigan years later!

It's a well-known fact, and was the source of occasional amusement among my team-mates, that I never had a fight during my career. I always managed to keep my cool. But I did go close to trading blows once . . . against Quentin Pongia. I don't remember how or why it started, but I do remember getting up from a tackle, he shoved me and, instinctively, I shoved him back; Q looked at me with a menacing smile, as if to say, 'You don't want to do this'. And he was right! Wisely, I retreated.

The turn of the century wasn't a great time for the Great Britain rugby league team. Pongia was captain of the Kiwis when they came over and beat us in 1998. We lost both our Tests on a Tri-Series tour down under the following year and then came up short in the 2000 World Cup. I mentioned earlier the stresses and strains that accompany touring; that part-explains why I had my only ever argument with Gary Connolly when we were in Auckland in 1999. I was 23 and still had goals to achieve; I trained hard, I was serious and focussed. Gary, by contrast, had been playing for a decade and had pretty much done everything in the game, and took things in his stride.

We roomed together, but operated in different time zones. I adjusted my body clock to the local time, sleeping all night, while Gary would sleep during the day after training. Our room was constantly in darkness and it used to bug me that I had to creep around in the day time while he snored louder than a combine harvester. One night, when he had been out with Andrew Farrell and Denis Betts, I lost the plot. I packed all his bags and threw them into the corridor and told him he was out of order. Faz was in hysterics as Gary came into the corridor to see all his clothes all over the place. I wouldn't let him back in, so he gathered his belongings and went to reception to book a new hotel room. The next day, I did what I probably should have done in the first place and told him why I was so mad. He agreed he had been out of order and I let him back in.

I started my international career going close to beating the Aussies, and that's how it ended. And while the results may not suggest it, I truly believe we made progress when David Waite came in as coach in 2001. David was complex and his knowledge of the game was incredible. He was also incredibly thorough, producing DVDs of opponents—and each player's own performance—which are far more common-place now, but were revolutionary for us at the time. His appointment caused a bit of a storm because Britain had never had an Aussie coach before, but I didn't care about that. All I cared about was getting better. Those who didn't want him coaching the British side were given plenty of ammunition when we were beaten 64–10 in Sydney by the Aussies in 2002. That was a record defeat. But believe me when I say that it was not his fault.

That fixture should never have been agreed. We played our club match on the Thursday night, went straight from the JJB Stadium to Manchester Airport and flew out early the following morning to Sydney. We were mid-air when our bodies needed recovery, we were stiff and sore, and by the time we touched down we had only a few days to prepare for a match against the Aussies. Getting over the jet-lag of that flight is hard enough at the best of times. To do it within five days, and fit in training sessions and team meetings too, sapped our energy. We trained when we wanted to go to bed, we were eating dinner when we wanted breakfast and on top of that, we had official functions to attend in the evenings when all we wanted to do was sleep. On the outside, I put on a brave face and tried to remain upbeat, but anyone who was with that squad could easily have predicted we were going to get smashed.

We just weren't ready. The game was an absolute nightmare, and nearly every time the Aussies got the ball, they scored. About 20 minutes in, the Australian hooker Danny Buderus made a break down the middle of the field. He stepped to my right and, as the last line of defence, I darted at him—my arm outstretched—to bring him down. As soon as I did, a burning sensation shot across my chest. The top and side of my body felt like they were on fire, like nothing I had ever felt before. I stumbled to my feet, grimacing at the unbearable pain and unable to lift my arm—it was practically flapping to my side, I simply couldn't raise it. I tried to carry on—I didn't want people thinking I was deserting a sinking ship. But after yet another try, big Willie Mason ran straight through our front line from the kick-off and there was me between him and our try-line. As he closed in I thought, 'Bloody hell, this is going to hurt'. It was a kamikaze tackle, I flung my body at him, and my forecast was spot on. The word 'agony' does not come close to describing the pain I was in. I had to go off and the doctor quickly diagnosed that I'd torn my pectoral muscle. I was devastated as I sat on the touchline, and not because of the pain, but from watching my team-mates get completely embarrassed on the world stage, a position they should never have been put in.

Later that year, while I was still feeling like I owed David Waite something for my early Sydney exit, I had to drop out of the international squad because I needed wrist surgery— Wigan were putting a bit of pressure on me to get it done quickly. I felt like I'd let David down, so I wrote him a letter explaining what had happened and he replied to say that he never once doubted my commitment. The following year, we played a warm-up against a New Zealand A side and, with Faz rested and Scully injured, he pulled me to one side and said, 'I've still got that letter you sent me, I was so pleased to receive it, and I'd like to give you the honour of captaining your country because I know how much it would mean to you'.

One question I often got asked was how I got on with Paul Wellens, who rivalled me for the Test number 1 jersey. I dare say Faz and Scully got asked how they got on and the same with Keiron Cunningham and Terry Newton, who contested the hooker spot. The truth is we got on great—we were—and are still mates. A rugby league game is played by 34 passionate and aggressive men, and if tempers flared between Wigan and Saints—and many remember Faz and Scully trading blows once—then it was forgotten a split second after the final whistle went. The truth is I wanted those players who gave their all for the cause on my side. Guys like Scully and Morley were such ferocious players for their clubs, who wouldn't want them in the same Test team?

When we played internationals in England, we'd often be based at the Worsley Marriott outside Manchester. I never really looked out for the squads in the press so, when we reported for duty, I'd always look out to see who'd been called-up. There were a handful of players who gave me confidence in internationals— blokes like Scully, Faz, Jamie Peacock and Morley. Whoever was called-up, everyone got on. There are few egos in rugby league, even fewer superstars, and when the England football players stopped at the same hotel as us it made me realise the difference between the two sports. When we finished training, we'd hang around together, but the football boys had a huge entourage and even more interest from guests—many are celebrities, after all—that they would often disband and go to their rooms. A few rugby league fans may be surprised by how many footballers follow our game—when they play away games on Saturdays, they'll often watch the Friday night Super League match in their hotels. Once, at the Marriott, I got into the lift and David Beckham was in. He said, 'Hi Kris, how do you think you'll go tomorrow night?' which was nice to hear. A few would come over for a chat but they had so much security around them—especially Beckham—that they couldn't really hang around with us, which was a shame, because I sensed that they envied our relative anonymity.

Australia always had an abundance of talent, but the constant thorn in our side during all the series I played in was Darren Lockyer. And though we lost the 2003 Ashes series 3–0, I truly believe that had Lockyer not played, we would have won. That was the closest I ever went to ending Australia's dominance. All three Tests were end-to-end, nail-biting affairs. I was concussed in the first match—I had to have a brain scan afterwards to check I was okay. I was given the green light, though I wondered if the medics had made a mistake when someone told me Adrian Morley had been sent off in the first few seconds. I couldn't believe it!

When you lose the opening match of a three-Test series, the pressure really mounts in the week leading up to the second match. I used to deny it at the time—and other players did, too—but I used to challenge myself to beat my opposite number; to make it personal. The fact that Lockyer had done me in the opening match—he scored the game-winning try with five minutes to go, making it 22–18—made me more determined ahead of the second Test. I had a great game in Hull and it was one of the few times I felt I won my 'duel' with Lockyer. We led 20–12 at half-time but it was in vain, as the Aussies—with Brett Kimmorley outstanding—snatched the game in the dying minutes. I was devastated to lose that match, as it ended our hopes of winning the Ashes. I'd grown up seeing my heroes not able to win an Ashes series, and I thought we were going to do it. I was convinced of it. Of all the defeats I have ever suffered, that loss in Hull was the most painful. I genuinely believed we could, and should, have not only won, but won easily. I scored in the third Test but we still lost that match at Huddersfield—Lockyer and Kimmorley carved out a try right at the end to make it 18–12—meaning the series was lost 3–0, with six points or less separating the sides in all three matches. The Aussie players were complementary, because they knew they'd been in a fierce international series, and it really ignited the flame of international rugby league. I'd lost other series, 2–1, but—as bizarre as this sounds—we were much closer in the 3–0 series in 2003, than any of the others. It was heartbreaking.

Lockyer and I got on well in the few times we met at functions; we weren't mates, but there was a mutual respect between us, and during that series he made some nice comments about me, which were great to read. After the final Test, we swapped jerseys, which was scant consolation at the time. But of everything I own, his framed, green and gold top remains one of my most prized possessions. And it stays a constant reminder of an international career that I am extremely proud of.

6

SUPER LEAGUE TIME

'I've missed more than 9,000 shots in my career. I've lost almost 300 games. 26 times I've been trusted to take the game-winning shot and missed. I've failed over and over again in my life . . . and that is why I succeed.'

Michael Jordan

WINNING the Grand Slam in 1994–95 was great. It was great for the players, the club and the fans. Others, though, were becoming concerned at the grapple-hold Wigan had on British, and world, rugby league. We were dominating the sport to such an extent it was a surprise the monopolies commission didn't get involved. Instead, Rupert Murdoch did. And when he revealed plans to invest heavily into the sport, it was seen as the perfect chance to strengthen the league, expand the game, and give other clubs more of a chance of beating Wigan. I loved our success at the time, but looking back now, we were killing the sport. Our success had raised the profile of Wigan above that of the sport itself.

In 1994–95, my first full season, I was a teenager who was a full-time rugby league player. Other clubs, though, only had a pocketful of full-time professionals—the other players had day-jobs in addition to playing the sport, and it was difficult for them to get close to us consistently. It was certainly not a level playing field. In the days of winter rugby, it would be dark when many players finished work, and then they'd go and train on a field in the dark. That's another reason we rarely had an easy game, because every time we faced a side, we'd be up against players who were putting themselves in the shop window. Wigan were the only club with a full-time, professional squad, and opposition players knew that if they could impress our directors, they might get signed up themselves. I played in some fierce matches then, against fired-up players, and that's why Wigan lost occasionally—but over the course of the season, and in big Cup matches, our quality would, more often than not, prevail. You could have been forgiven for thinking that, at Wigan, we would be cautious of the creation of a Super League—after all, part of the plan included, inevitably, ending the domination that we enjoyed so much—but we were all excited at the prospect. The thought of playing in summer, on hard grounds, and with a new audience, sounded fantastic to us. The move to Super League probably took months at the top level, but for the players, it all happened quickly.

Not long after I'd joined the first team squad, I turned up to training one morning and was summoned to the boardroom unexpectedly. I was filled in on a few more details about the new Super League, and told that my existing contract with Wigan would be replaced by a new one that aligned me, like my club, to Super League. The purpose of the meeting was to tell me about what would change but, as far as I was concerned, nothing would change. My terms and work conditions would stay the same . . . I didn't see the big deal. I was just looking forward to playing in summer. They also told me that, in Australia, some clubs were breaking away to form a Super League while others were staying with the existing Australia Rugby League—a fact that didn't concern me. All I was bothered about was getting into the Wigan team. The move to a Super League wouldn't affect that, so I was happy. I was ready to leave the meeting, grateful that I'd been given a few more details, when they told me that they were going to give me a Super League bonus of £20,000. Yep, £20,000. For doing nothing! I'd only played a handful of first team games, I was salaried to about £8,000 a year, and I'd just been given a lump sum payment of £20,000, a sum of money I'd never seen before. I later found out that a crop of the league's young players were being offered the bonuses to stave off any approaches from the ARL, though I couldn't see why the Australian competition would want a teenager from Wigan with only a handful of games under his belt. Either way, I wasn't going to question their logic—if they wanted to give me £20,000, who was I to argue? I snatched their hands off. Not everyone in the sport was happy about the handouts, especially Garry Schofield, who publicly stated that I and the other recipients had not done enough in the game to deserve them. I wasn't upset that Schoey had been so outspoken; not one bit. He wasn't having a go at me, and I'm sure he didn't blame me for accepting the money; he was criticising the system that was giving a lad from Wigan who'd played only a few games £20,000, while he got nothing. For the most-capped Great Britain player ever, I can see why that was a bitter pill to swallow, but the payments were not rewards for services already given—they were bonuses to secure our playing services for the years to come. Like the footballers who dropped on it when the Premier League launched, or the cricketers offered huge prize incentives to play in the Stanford Series, I was just fortunate to be in the right place at the right time.

Once the details of Super League were hammered out—and before it was launched amid scenes of razzamatazz usually reserved for a Presidential race—there were just a few months to squeeze another full season in: the centenary season. This took place over the winter 1995–96 and it was crazy. We would often have to play two or three games a week, to make sure the campaign was finished for the start of a professional, summer era. We won the league easily. Phil Clarke and Denis Betts had gone, but Scott Quinnell—a giant of a man, and a terrific bloke—was finding his feet in league after switching from Welsh rugby union, and our back-line was star-studded. That league title felt a little hollow. Not only did it not feel like a full season— as it was squeezed into a few months—but also everyone was looking forward to Super League. The centenary season became a formality to complete before we could start a new era, and the comprehensive manner in which we won the league only served to heighten the excitement among non-Wigan fans about Super League. The best thing about that season was that we got to keep the Championship trophy—that felt good, because we'd secured a piece of rugby league history forever, and no one could take that from us. Throughout the centenary season, I kept hearing warnings that the new Super League would end the era of Wigan trampling over all-comers. We knew it would get tougher, and we knew that with every club running a professional, full-time squad, we would be up against it. But I never expected our Challenge Cup run would come to such an abrupt end before the new Super League had even begun, against Division One side Salford.

In early 1996, on the eve of the new Super League season, Wigan's Challenge Cup run ended. The glorious, unbeaten eight-year run had turned Wigan players into household names. It had made Wigan famous outside of the M62 corridor. I'd been to Wembley as a fan and a travelling reserve but—just like Australia's dominance of the international game—we all knew it would end one day. When I broke into the team 18 months earlier, we were enjoying victories in the league, but when it came to the Challenge Cup, it stopped being fun. I didn't play in any of the Challenge Cup matches, but I sensed it in the players. They wouldn't celebrate victories; they would breathe a massive sigh of relief, because the inevitability—the end of

Wigan's Cup run—had been deferred for another day. Shaun Edwards used to speak about the 'fear of failure', and he was right—that's what drove Wigan in those Cup matches. Nobody wanted to be in the team when it ended. Unfortunately, I was. As much as every Wigan player feared losing, opponents were excited by the prospect of being the team that ended Wigan's famous winning streak—every player wanted to add that to their CV. I know the real glory of sport lies in its unpredictability but, when you're the overwhelming favourite who ends up on the losing side, it's a horrible feeling.

Of all the away games, the one I detested most was going to Salford. It was a bitterly cold day and, at The Willows, that chill seemed worse inside the changing room. The visiting room is cramped, cold and has a sloping ceiling which means that—in parts—you can't stand up straight. This was not the ideal preparation to defend one of the greatest runs in British sporting history. That game was my first experience of playing in the Challenge Cup, and I was looking forward to being part of such a special tournament. A year earlier I'd missed out after a late fitness test taken by Jason Robinson and now, a few months later, it was my time. Unfortunately, we had one of those games where everything that could go wrong, did go wrong. Usually, when that happened, we'd still have enough defensive grit and individual class to overcome most opponents, but it was one of those games where our opponents executed everything perfectly. Salford played out of their skin that day. The great irony is that one of my heroes, Steve Hampson, played for Salford that day and had a blinder, even though he was coming to the end of his career. He loved Wigan, but the club did the dirty on him by releasing him a few weeks away from a lucrative testimonial and it was no secret that he was angry about it. It was obvious how much satisfaction he took from ending Wigan's run. They deserved their 26–16 win, but that was little comfort.

Afterwards, I wasn't upset as much as numb. I just couldn't comprehend what had happened. 'Wigan', 'winning' and the 'Challenge Cup' went together hand-in-hand—I'd been at primary school the last time they'd lost in the competition. Eventually, the severity of the loss sunk in and, that night, I felt terrible. I'd made Challenge Cup history, as I'd always wanted to, but in a way I'd never even contemplated. It was an early lesson to me that, even at a club like Wigan, where success seemed at times like a birthright, nobody handed you anything on a plate—it had to be earned. The Wigan fans were furious. Their annual jaunt down to London was over, and I understood their frustrations, but part of me wondered whether they really thought it could go on forever. No one felt the loss more than the players and, while it was my first Challenge Cup match, I was deeply hurt. But once the initial mourning had taken place, I thought our fans would have reflected on the eight-year run and celebrated it. Instead, they—and the newspapers—staged a drawn-out inquest into how it happened. What angered them the most was that we had been given some time off at the end of the truncated centenary season to go away and relax. I went to New York with my team-mate and friend, Simon Haughton, to do some shopping and sightseeing, but about seven team members chose to spend their break on the lash in Tenerife. Who knows if it affected the result—I actually don't think it did, as their drinking session took place about three weeks before the game. And, when they got back, possibly realising they'd over-stepped the mark, they trained flat out leading up to the Salford match. But the Wigan fans wanted to channel their anger and direct their blame and, unfortunately for those who went to the Canaries, they copped the brunt of it.

Two days after being knocked out of the Cup, I got a phone call saying that I had been picked to represent England in the world Nines in Fiji. The majority of the England side actually came from Wigan, they never expected any of us to be eligible as the selectors—like everybody else—thought we would still be in the Challenge Cup. Even in Fiji, the fall-out from the Super League war in Australia was not far away, and one night all the players who had received Super League bonuses, including me, had to get on a mini-bus to another hotel and sit in a conference room to watch the results of a court case on TV. The result was to decide whether the Super League in Australia could go ahead—in England, all the teams had signed up to the new concept. I didn't pay too much attention to the complexities of it all. This was not only because it didn't really affect me, but also because I couldn't believe I'd been whisked away to a conference room and I was sat with the likes of Laurie Daley, Wendell Sailor, Andrew Ettingshausen, Ricky Stuart and their coach, Mal Meninga (all of whom were heroes of mine).

The start of the Super League competition definitely brought a feel-good factor with it. Everyone associated with the sport, every player, was excited. Everyone loved rugby league, and we all bought into the vision to establish our sport among the big sports of Britain. I was happy to do the extra publicity, which ranged from being included in nude calendars to dressing in dinner suits for Sky Sports promotional films. It was good fun and we got a few extra quid for it too. At Wigan, we already had a professional squad but, with the injection of more money, our days became longer. It was as if the coaches wanted to justify the cash that was coming in, so instead of letting Giz dictate when training was over—usually within an hour—we would train in the mornings, then have rehab sessions, then lunch together and sometimes attend functions or make appearances in the afternoon. It started feeling like a job, and it wasn't as laid back— no longer could we say, 'I'll have to leave early, I've got a dentist appointment', and things like that. It was taken seriously.

The switch to summer rugby was brilliant. It suited the

steppers and guys with pace, and the harder pitches made it easier for individuals to showcase their skills. In the past, in muddier conditions, a lot of the tries were scored from cascading set-pieces but once Super League began, we saw more tries created by individual skill. We didn't win the league that year. All season it was nip and tuck between St Helens and Wigan, and Saints won in the end. They lost two of their league games all season. We lost two and drew one, but we had a better for-and-against, which meant that—had we not drawn to London at Central Park, had their Australian loose forward Terry Matterson not kicked a late sideline conversion to draw the Broncos level—we'd have won the league. Our Challenge Cup run had ended and now our arch-rivals were the league champions—it was heartbreaking. Even though it had all come down to a brilliantly-executed conversion, and we'd lost just three games in all competitions all year, it felt like we'd been derailed. We had one last chance to make amends when we played Saints in the Premiership final, and—after a nerve-shredding semi against Bradford, which we won 42–36—we weren't going to slip up. We were fuelled by revenge. Saints, who had won the Challenge Cup that year, were driven by the prospect of winning a treble. I wasn't sure what feeling was worse; us losing, or Saints winning, but I had a sneaky feeling we were going to win when I cast eyes on Henry Paul's boots. They were white. No one, but no one, ever wore any colour other than black, but that was typical HP. That year he'd already set trends among his army of young followers by wearing nasal strips, Thorpedo shorts and even gloves, and I can't say I was surprised when he turned up in white boots. HP is a gent, very modest and unassuming, but when it came to rugby league he was a showman. He was immensely talented and had a freakish ability to dance through defences—playing on harder ground had taken his game to another level—and, more than anything, he was a confidence player. If he'd have worn white boots and played badly, he would have been crucified, so the fact that he had turned up in the stylish footwear was a good sign—a sign that he felt we were going to win. As it happened, we did win, quite easily (44–14), with Faz playing immense rugby and Danny Ellison scoring a hat-trick—only the third player in the history of the competition to do so, after myself and Gary Connolly.

One of my closest pals in the team was a guy called Steve Barrow, son of the St Helens great, Frankie Barrow, and he played in that game against his hometown club. After the match, we did a lap of honour at Old Trafford, waving and celebrating with the fans. Henry, great showman that he was, unlaced his white boots and threw them into the Wigan fans. Stevie-boy watched this, saw the fans scramble to grab the boots—for whoever caught them, they'd have been prized possessions—and took his own boots off and lobbed them into the crowd. A few seconds later, someone threw them back! I'm still very good friends with Steve and, you won't be surprised to hear, that story has been told a few times. He still denies the boots were thrown back but we have witnesses to prove otherwise.

In February 1997, before the start of the second Super League season, our coach Graeme West was fired. Everyone loved Westy, he's one of the most genuine blokes you could meet, though the writing had been on the wall from the day we got knocked out of the Challenge Cup in 1996. That season also saw us adopt our new moniker for the first time—the Warriors. Was I a fan? I honestly wasn't bothered. I could see the logic of doing it. Super League was trying to emulate the Australian competition, giving a team a nickname seemed the inevitable next step, though I can't say I was a fan of the shirt that accompanied the new name—the traditional cherry and white hoops were ditched for an awful, arty Warrior design. It was a transitional period for the club . . . and not just regarding its name.

Wigan were no longer the super-power of the game—St Helens had won the Challenge Cup and the title. On the playing front, we lost Martin Offiah to London and, not long after, Shaun Edwards left too. Every fan realised that Giz had been a brilliant player and captain, but they couldn't have realised just how big an influence he was on the side. He left a huge void in the team—as big as any I saw in all my years at Wigan. Giz effectively led coaching sessions, and that's certainly not an insult of Westy's methods. On the contrary, Westy did the best thing possible. He realised that Giz was the half-back and the heartbeat of our side and, when it came to deciding who did what on the pitch, he let Giz run the show. That changed when Westy was fired and Eric Hughes came in. Giz only played one game and, as well as him and Martin, a few others left. Inga Tuigamala, who'd mentored me when I came into the team, returned to rugby union with Newcastle because their code had gone professional, and Longy was exchanged—with £100,000—for Widnes prop Lee Hansen. I'd played with Longy from being kids, I knew more than anyone just what a talent he was, and I knew as soon as they let him go, he would come back and haunt Wigan. In the club's defence, Longy had a boundless amount of energy and was a bit wild, so I can see why they did it but, even so, I knew it would prove to be a huge mistake. I actually didn't mind Eric, we got along okay, but not everyone was impressed with his old-school style. To be honest, a guy from St Helens coming to coach Wigan was always going to raise a few eyebrows. Eric was the only coach I've ever known who would take off his suit on game day to help the team masseur, and it's a very strange feeling getting a massage from your coach while he is talking to you as he is doing it. Sometimes he'd get excited about the game and rub harder, causing huge friction burns! With players like Offiah, Inga and Edwards leaving, and the arrival of guys like Paul Koloi, Stuart Lester and Doc Murray—decent lads, but hardly Wigan players—it wasn't really a shock that we didn't have the best of seasons in 1997. Saints won the Cup again and Bradford quickly embraced professionalism, but we did better than any of the other English teams in the World Club Challenge.

That concept involved all the Super League clubs—from England (and Paris) and Australasia—and it got widely panned by the critics for its one-sided scores, but I loved it. It was great to play against the best players in the world in the comfort of your own individual club, and not within the international set up, and it also gave non-international players the opportunity to play on the big stage, which excited them. We got pooled with Brisbane Broncos, Canterbury Bulldogs and the Canberra Raiders, three of the giants of Australia.

We travelled down under first to play them which meant a month on the Gold Coast, 10 minutes from Surfers Paradise. We were based in a small town called Coolangatta, which was right on the beach and an idyllic setting for us, but it was hard to keep our mind on the job in hand. We'd train in the mornings and then spend the afternoons relaxing on the beach, which was not exactly our usual routine back in Wigan. If ever we tired of the beach, we'd return to our hotel. With all of us on one floor, we carried chairs into the corridor to turn our corridor into a communal living area. One afternoon, we were sitting around chatting when the elevator bell rang, the door slid across—and Rolf Harris was stood there! Not only that, but he had his wobble board too. We couldn't believe it, it felt like a *Beadle's About* moment. We invited him out of the lift and asked him to sing us some songs and he was great. He stayed with us for about 30 minutes singing all his classics, 'Tie me kangaroo down sport' and 'Jake the peg' . . . it was awesome. The afternoon finished with us all singing a chorus of 'We love Rolf, because he is big and daft'.

It was during that trip to Australia that I really noticed the full power of the name Wigan Rugby League. The people in that little town treated us so well, like mini-celebrities. Everywhere we went, people bought us drinks or offered us things. Some of the guys judged fashion shows, presented prizes and one player, Martin Hall, had his own slot on morning radio! We were given a daily allowance by the club, and lined up like schoolboys at the kit man's room and he would hand out our pocket money. The funny thing was, we never needed pocket money because we never spent anything; we lived like kings.

We got off to a cracking start in the competition by flying down to Sydney and beating Canterbury Bulldogs. It was a great game to be involved in, both teams played well but a couple of big plays by Nigel Wright and a great try by Andy Johnson brought us home 22–18. We were already having a blast in Australia but by winning, it meant the spotlight was trained on us and our fame grew, which meant more invites, more free nights out and more attractive offers to appear at bars and restaurants. We worked hard in training. Though it was a different format, Wigan had won their last World Club competition three years earlier and we were eager to repeat that success. But when we were allowed to go out, we enjoyed ourselves to the max.

We paid the price for that when we visited Brisbane to face the Broncos. They absolutely battered us that night. The Broncos had all their stars playing—Renouf, Langer, Lockyer— and they were very powerful as they swept to a 34–0 win. The incident that people will never forget was the brawl between Terry O' Connor and Gordon Tallis. Big Gordy hit Terry about eight times before he could get a shot in. Andy Johnson went running in to help, but changed his mind when he got there and saw Wendell Sailor waiting for him! The morning after, in the team meeting, we watched the entire video of the game and Eric savaged us for our performance. When we reached the fight, and despite the fact we were being dressed down, we couldn't hold the laughter in. Fair play to Eric, he gave us about five minutes to reflect on the incident and take the mick out of Terry, before continuing with the autopsy of the game. I was disappointed with the game in Brisbane. It was a massive test for us, playing Brisbane in Brisbane was as big as it got, and after our first win in Sydney we wanted to give them a game. A lot had changed in the three years since Wigan had beaten them in the World Club Challenge, but everyone was watching and I wanted us to send out the message that Wigan were the team to beat.

When we were away from home, blokes coped in different ways. I was young and single and loved every minute of it, but I did feel sorry for guys who missed their kids. The only way we could keep the group happy was to make the most of each other's company, and try to have as much fun as we could. We only trained for a maximum of two hours a day, so we spent a lot of time slobbing around the hotel, and we became restless. We craved entertainment. Eric set a curfew and, after the Broncos game, the club sent home Neil Cowie for breaking it. It became one of the biggest scandals of my career at Wigan. It's true, Neil did break the curfew, by about an hour. But the entire team did—it wasn't just one man—and there was absolutely no way he should have been sent home. Neil was victimised, and I had a feeling the directors made the final decision. The scenario was blown out of all proportions, and the club just made an example of Neil. Before he left, about six of us went to a bar near our hotel and had a couple of goodbye drinks with Neil, but it annoyed me that the rest of the squad didn't come along. The whole team was outraged, but only six backed up their anger and joined him for an hour. Neil never forgot that.

Our final encounter was against Canberra. We left the wonderful Gold Coast, and the locals who had made our stay so enjoyable, and flew into Australia's capital the day before the match. Canberra is the home of all the government buildings, but it has little else, which is why we left it as late as possible before going there. Again, we lost the game quite convincingly, but I had a decent game in defeat and scored couple of good tries. No matter if we won or lost, the first thing I did was analyse my performance. My effort was always good, but sometimes there were games when things didn't go my way and I'd look at those things to consider how I could resolve them. I always found time at the end of a game for a brief reflection and, though we were well-beaten by the Raiders, losing 56–22, I knew I'd played well. When I watched a tape of the game, the Aussie commentator remarked that I could hold my head high, which made me happy because Canberra were the team to beat when I was growing up. I enjoyed my time in Australia, despite the results and the controversy, but I was excited about going home. I couldn't wait to play those three clubs again, at our Central Park home, and what's more, I couldn't wait to see my mum.

On the return leg, we again beat Canterbury (31–24) and at least put up some resistance against the Broncos, who pulled away in the last few minutes to win 30–4. Because the other English sides had fared so poorly we made it into the semi-finals where we just lost to the Hunter Mariners 22–18 at Central Park. The season did not finish trophy-less, however, as we again beat Saints in the Premiership final, 33–20, but that did little to mask a disappointing year. In total, out of our 33 games, we'd lost 14 and finished fourth. For a club like Wigan, even accounting for the key departures and the improvements of the other sides, that was unacceptable. The fans thought the same, and showed as much with their feet; for the first time in a long time, our average crowd dipped below the 10,000 mark. The previous year we hadn't won the league or Challenge Cup—a shocker by our impeccable standards—but we'd still only lost three games all year in all competitions. To lose 14 matches was unheard of for

Wigan and, when there was a shake-up of the board and Mike Nolan took over as chairman, no one was surprised that they wiped the slate clean and fired Eric. In a little more than three years in the first team squad, I was getting my fourth coach . . . I couldn't believe who it turned out to be.

7

CUP SHOCK, GRAND FINISH

'Sports do not build character. They reveal it.'
Haywood Hale Broun

THE THIRD season of Super League, in 1998, proved to be a truly historical one for Wigan—in more ways than one. The man, the myth, the legend that was John Monie returned to the club he had served with such distinction years earlier. No one questioned his pedigree. Jason and Faz had both played under him, and they told me he would be the right man to get Wigan back on top after two seasons without Challenge Cup or league success. John certainly had an aura about him, not just because of his past success, but through the way he carried himself. He was a laid back but serious Australian, and I soon realised he was a man of few words. I never feared any opponent in my career, no matter how big, but to an extent I feared John. He had that presence about him. He was smart and didn't suffer fools; he could cut you down with three words. His standards were exemplary, and he would scrutinise performances as he searched for perfection. Before John arrived, we'd rock into team meetings, roughly on time, but John ensured we were all there for the start and that we all brought our own pen and papers. With just a sprinkling of signings—no-frills but honest

Australians Danny Moore, Mark Bell and the hugely-pivotal Robbie McCormack, plus the returning Denis Betts—he brought in a few set moves, but his influence was noticed more in our attitude. He was ruthless—and he made us like that—and he brought in the perfect conditioner to help him achieve that in Marty Hulme.

We made a blistering start, cruising through our early Challenge Cup games—we even beat St Helens 22–10, which was sweet as they'd won the Cup for the past two years—and easing past London 38–8 in the semi. On that day, nobody would have beaten us. As a player, you get a sense of how your team will do in the week leading up to the game, and I could tell the guys were in their zone. I was proved right, and I scored two tries on the way to taking Wigan back to what I regarded as their second home. On top of that, we had no problems in the league, either, even beating Saints again. By the time we'd secured a place back at Wembley, we'd won all our eight games, and in the process scored 312 points and conceded just 56. We were on fire. McCormack had settled well in the side—he was at the end of his career, but as fit as anyone—and players like Faz, Henry, Jason and Gary were playing awesome rugby.

They say every kid dreams of playing at Wembley, but that's wrong. It should be every kid dreams of winning at Wembley—and I learned that fact the painful way. Since missing out on the 1995 Challenge Cup Final, I'd had to wait three years to get my chance of winning my first Challenge Cup. I was nervous before the match, because—in my mind—I was an hour-and-a-half from achieving my dream. I'd won a league title, three Premierships and played for my country by that point, but it was always about the Challenge Cup for me. When I think about my childhood, my mind is flooded by so many memories of making trips to Wembley, of seeing the players walk out, of bumping into friends on the motorway services on the way home . . . it meant everything to me. It's not hard to see why the bookmakers made us such overwhelming favourites to beat Sheffield in the final. Sheffield had finished in the bottom half of the table in the previous two years and had surprised everyone by reaching the final, though no one gave them a chance. I think I read that they were 12–1 to win which, for a two-horse race, were extraordinary odds. In truth, I don't think we gave Sheffield a chance either . . . and that proved to be our undoing. Looking at the team sheets, there was only ever going to be one winner. I never deliberately thought the game was won, but when you're told by so many people, so many times, that you are going to win a game, it's hard not to start believing them.

I think that, unintentionally, we'd begun to believe all the hype. People were predicting a record score, we were running white hot and feeling bullet-proof, but we made the cardinal, sporting sin of taking the result for granted, and we forgot the fact that the opposing side would have 17 blokes who all had the same dream I had. The Sheffield players ran their blood to water and grabbed their moment in time. In coach John Kear, they had a passionate leader. It's still hard for me to think back to that result, but I have to be diplomatic and say that they conducted themselves well, performed as a team and—yes—deserved the Challenge Cup that day. Even if the result did break my heart. I had a life-long dream to win the Challenge Cup, I had an opportunity to achieve it and our team fell short against an unheralded side—I can't begin to express how upset and angry I was. Upset that I'd lost; angry about the way we played. In big games like that, freezing is not an option, but that's exactly what we did and as soon as they got an early try from Nick Pinkney, they never looked back. We trailed 11–2 at half-time and even an angry half-time team-talk from Faz didn't raise our game. Afterwards, the dressing room was as cold and miserable as a morgue. There was an incredible sense of disbelief. Defeats are easier to take when you've given your all and been out-played, but when you lose like we did against Sheffield, it's the stuff of nightmares—recurring, sweat-inducing nightmares.

In the inquest that followed, the conspiracy theories were incredible. Two days after the defeat, I drew the short-straw and had to visit the Wigan supporters' club to field fans' questions. I was apologetic, and still a little shell-shocked, but I understood their frustration. They had a right to question the way we played, but one point was laboured repeatedly—rumours that all the players had bet on the match and backed Sheffield to win. As a Wigan lad, born and bred, who had always dreamed of winning a Challenge Cup and parading it in front of the club's fans, that suggestion really annoyed me. I was insulted that my integrity was doubted, and as I sat on the stage, I became wound up just thinking that the people in front of me—the very ones who cheered me most weeks—thought that I and my team-mates could stoop so low. Was it so inconceivable to think that Sheffield just had their one perfect game? Could they not believe that we'd just not played well? I wanted to be on that stage with a winners' medal, telling them how long I'd dreamed of winning at Wembley, and there I was after the worst day of my whole career, forced to deny that I'd bet on Sheffield to win. I was only 22 at the time, and that was one of the most painful experiences of my life. I could tolerate people making remarks about how I'd played in various games, but I could not tolerate them tormenting me by questioning my character.

A week later, by chance, we played Sheffield in Super League and won easily 36–6, but it did not heal the wounds of that final defeat. That, I've come to realise, will never heal. For the rest of the year, we only lost two more games—both Super League matches against Leeds. They had really picked up under coach Graham Murray and Iestyn Harris, a former opponent of mine from my junior days who had that killer step back then, was on fire. They lost two more games than us all season, which meant we topped the table four points clear of them. In any other season until then, that would have made us champions but that year the Super League had introduced the Grand Final concept, in which the champion wouldn't be decided by the 'first past the post' method, but through a play-offs competition involving the top-five teams. I'd seen the system work in Australia and I was excited about having a Grand Final in England. I wasn't bothered that we'd finished top and there was a possibility we wouldn't be crowned champions. Although I was sad to see the Premiership scrapped to make way for it, I accepted it pretty early on, even if traditionalists struggled.

Leeds visited Central Park, with the winner guaranteed a spot in the final, while the loser would play the team who had emerged from positions three to five. We won the match 17–4 and it was an epic; worthy of the Grand Final itself. The game was a pretty heated affair, and when Mick Cassidy elbowed Adrian Morley in the jaw, it really lit the touch paper. From a drop-out, Mozza had picked the ball up around the half way line and built up a head of steam, running straight and as hard as he could in Mick's direction. Mick could tackle as good as the best, he had a terrific engine, but for some reason he launched himself at Moz, leading with his elbow, and breaking his jaw instantly. Mick was shown the red card, and the game just erupted, but we hung onto win. Typical of rugby league, there was no bad blood afterwards. Mick realised he'd had a brain explosion, and Moz was never the type to hold a grudge. It's often said that these fall-outs get left on the pitch; I'll testify that is one cliché that is true about rugby league. Leeds beat St Helens quite convincingly a week later, setting up the rematch with us that they craved so much in the big game—the first ever Super League Grand Final at Old Trafford.

Super League wanted the last game of the season to be the

Me as child (my nose was straight back then) but that velvet jumper, come on mum!

Christmas day—do you think I wanted to play for Wigan when I grew up?

Signing professional terms with John Martin and Jack Hilton

Winning the Harry Sunderland Trophy (nose was still straight then)

Me, Craig Murdock and my first sponsored car

Me and a koala bear when visiting a zoo in Fiji during the World Nines in 1997

Training for Great Britain at the great Central Park

Hull v Wigan

Wigan v Bradford Challenge Cup semi-final, taken by Wigan fan Kath Nield

Me presenting Keith Mills with the last ball ever kicked in a game at Central Park. Keith has had a 40-year association with the club

Doing a lap of honour with Andrew Farrell at Old Trafford in 1997 after GB defeated Australia

Lost weekend in Florida Keys with Brian and AJ

Me putting a shot on the master Darren Lockyear—people ask if I tackled him off the ball but I did force it out of him I promise

Press conference after turning down a move to rugby union the first time. Maurice announced I had signed a new five year deal at Wigan

Me and our little family dog Kodie

most important, and I agreed with their logic. Like the SuperBowl in American Football, it gave the season a pinnacle, and that opening final in October 1998 attracted fans from all over rugby league. There were plenty of Wigan and Leeds shirts in the crowd, but replica tops from other clubs, too—Super League, National League and amateur—which was great to see. Both sides were packed with talent but the heavy downpour dictated that it was never going to be a free-flowing try-fest. It was a real arm wrestle, with both teams giving nothing away. In games like that, the team that makes the least errors and shows the best discipline usually comes out on top, and that rang true that night. Leeds' defence was resolute, and I knew early on it would need a moment of genius to pierce it. Step forward Jason Robinson. Shortly before half-time, he picked up the ball on the right before jinking his way through the line and turned on the after-burners to score our only try. Only Jason could have scored a try like that. People associate Jason with speed and acceleration, but his pure, unadulterated power was awesome. Faz kicked three goals on the night and Leeds replied with a solitary try from Richie Blackmore in the second half to make the final score 10–4. Our performance was gutsy, but all that mattered was the result. Faz collected the trophy, and we were awarded Super League rings for the very first time. John Monie had worked his magic again—he'd promised to deliver success and, despite losing to Sheffield in the Challenge Cup Final, a few months later, we were crowned Super League Champions 1998.

8

LEAVING
CENTRAL PARK

'Where we love is home, home that our feet may leave but not our hearts.'

Oliver Wendell Holmes

I RECEIVED an award at the start of 1999, at our pre-season training camp. I beat off competition from other healthy, 20-something men to come out on top for my agility, footwork, fitness and strength . . . though not in the way you're probably imagining. Let me explain. No matter how many times players say warm-weather training is tough, there are still a lot of people who think warm-weather training breaks are just a reason for a jolly boys outing. I can't count the number of interviews I've given over the years when I've said the training has been tough, and the reporter's raised an eyebrow as if to say, 'Yeah, whatever'. I'm retired now, I've no pretence to keep up and so let me tell you that they are definitely punishing. They're certainly not holiday camps. The Club La Santa, in Lanzarote, is a renowned training facility, with a rugby field, 400m track, Olympic-sized swimming pool and a large gym area all on site. Coaches take full advantage of the dry weather and the extra hours of daylight, cramming up to three sessions in a day. We'd often be up by eight in the gym, and then onto the field, take a break for lunch and then straight back out onto the field. Even then, we weren't done, as we would meet again for evening meal followed by a classroom session, either to review aspects of the previous season or to talk about goals for the upcoming year. Believe me, any spare time we had was not spent in the bars or catching rays— we would just head back to our rooms and collapse, and try to catch a nap before we were summoned again. We referred to our rooms as prison cells; they had very few windows and, with such a stringent routine, we felt like prisoners. Marty Hulme loved it—he saw it as a chance to push us as hard as we could go, stripping fat from those who needed it and testing all of our mental resolve too.

At the end of the week, as a reward for training so hard, we were allowed a beer. But we were so exhausted, no one could face one and so we ignored the bars, and headed to a coffee shop, where we all ordered hot cocoa! We must have looked a sight. As we sat in this little coffee bar, debating what had been the toughest part of the training week, two girls came in from the onsite night club and said they needed a volunteer to take part in a Man O Man competition. Those contests involve a group of guys, who would take part in a series of initiations and trials and—at the end of each round—one would be eliminated.

Our night off was going nowhere and we were all pretty fed up.

'When's it on?' I asked.

'In 20 minutes,' one of the girls replied. 'And we need one more contestant to complete the line-up.'

'Rads'll do it,' someone said, as I was gently pushed closer to the girls. I was always up for a laugh, but I was stone cold sober, so I laughed off the suggestion.

Then Jason Robinson joined in the chat and attempted to convince me to do it. Jason had not been in a nightclub for years, ever since his conversion to Christianity. He was still the same guy—great company and a really good laugh—but he was a changed man in that he didn't drink, and he didn't go out. I knew he'd never go along to a nightclub to watch a Man O Man competition, so I said, 'Jason, if you come in and watch, I'll do it'.

'Deal,' he smiled, triggering ear-splitting cheers from the lads as the girls locked their arms under mine, and whisked me off before I could lodge a complaint. I sought comfort from the fact that it was only a little after seven, and there would hardly be anyone there, but when I stepped out onto the dance floor, the place was packed! I couldn't believe what was happening. All my Wigan team-mates were on one side of the floor, cheering—and surprised, too, that I'd agreed to do it—and on the other side were the Castleford Tigers players, who were also at the training camp. They were in hysterics and, credit to them, they all cheered for me . . . which only made me more nervous. I felt a tap on my shoulder, and Simon Haughton stood behind me with a shot glass. 'I think you could do with this,' he said. He was right—I necked it in one. I'm not sure whether the Dutch courage helped or not, but I thought, 'What the heck . . . I've come this far, I may as well have a dig.' There were seven volunteers—if I could be called a volunteer—from various European countries.

In the first round, we had to do as many press-ups in a minute as possible. Easy—I'd just finished a week-long training camp and was in good shape. I think I knocked out about 80, to progress to the next round. After completing a round, we would all stand in a line and a girl would walk down the line; if you'd survived, she would kiss your cheek, and if you were out she'd push you in the chest.

The next round got a little trickier. The song from the *Full Monty* movie—Tom Jones' 'You Can Leave Your Hat On'—blurted out of the speakers; they didn't have to tell us what our task was, but they did anyway . . . we had to strip. I shook my head, but 'in for a penny' and all that, I gave it my best shot.

Some of the details are a little scratchy, but I vividly remember bending another contestant over and whipping his ass with my belt, to the encouragement of my team-mates. I was actually beginning to enjoy myself.

Next came the singing round and, while I'm no Frank Sinatra, I can hold a tune—mastering a couple of lines from a Backstreet Boys song wasn't exactly challenging—and again I sailed through. When the contestants' line-up got down to three of us, I realised that I had a chance of winning.

Next came the dancing round. We had to dance to a 1950s rock 'n' roll song with one of the girls. I don't claim to be to be the world's best dancer, but nobody could knock my enthusiasm; I rocked around the clock as best as I could and again the nightclub cheered. The girl walked down the line-up, leaned forward and kissed me on my cheek—I was into the bloody final, against a guy from Sweden.

The deciding round was a romantic waltz, with a different girl. I'd never waltzed before, but I just tilted my head back and went for it, gliding across the dance floor. It was a wonder I didn't trample on her toes, because I didn't know what I was doing and as the cheers and laughs from the Wigan and Cas' boys probably helped sway the decision—I was crowned the 1999 Man O Man Club La Santa champion! People congratulated me—Jason was smiling, I think he was glad he'd made a cameo return to the nightclub scene! The following morning, as I boarded the coach to take the squad to the airport, John Monie patted me on my shoulder and said, 'I heard you brought the house down Rads. Good boy.'

The battling qualities and strong work ethic that had helped us win the Grand Final in 1998 faded rapidly in 1999. Some of the new signings didn't appear to have the same drive I had. Australian Greg Florimo, who was signed to replace Henry Paul, arrived with a massive reputation and while I liked him as a bloke, he never lived up to his billing. Mark Reber and Brett Goldspink weren't big name signings, and though they were great guys, they just didn't seem to have the same energy or enthusiasm as the existing players in the team. At the same time, a few of the Wigan-born lads emerged from the alliance side; some thought they'd become stars before they actually had. A player I really did like, though, was Mark Smith, a hooker who gave his all for the club. Our mixed fortunes on the pitch prematurely ended John's honeymoon with Wigan half way through the season. The players had heard rumours of him disagreeing with the board; I think Wigan wanted to bring a younger coach in to freshen the place up, with John overseeing everything in a director of rugby role. John, though, was a very 'hands-on' coach—he preferred a tracksuit to a suit—and was never going to take a management role. He left the club on sour terms, but it didn't overshadow the influence he'd had on the place, and no one forgot just how much success he'd brought to the town. John's assistant coach Andy Goodway, a tough forward in his day, was handed the daunting challenge of finishing Wigan's Central Park chapter and carrying us into a new dawn at the JJB Stadium.

While our inconsistent form continued under Goodway, we were impregnable at home, which was important to us because it was our final season at Central Park and we wanted to do the old ground proud. I knew that would count for nothing, though, if we didn't win our final home match—against St Helens. It was only fitting that we would play our fiercest rivals in our final match before the wrecking balls rolled into Central Park. They were enjoying a better season than us under Ellery Hanley's coaching, which added to the pressure of the occasion—there was no way that the Wigan fans would have ever forgiven us if we had lost the last ever game at Central Park to Saints.

That game was one of the real highlights of my career. Obviously I was sad to see the old stadium go, but to have taken part in such a memorable event was sensational. No other rugby league venue in the world compared to Central Park. At the time, Wigan was like many other Northern towns. There was nothing to distinguish it from them, apart from Central Park; and then they went and knocked it down. It was such a special place, and no matter how big or small the crowd, it created an amazing atmosphere that was unmatched. Visiting teams used to fear playing there; it had an aura about the place, and when their coach pulled up outside they knew they'd be in for a tough day. I think the fact that I'd spent such a big part of my youth supporting Wigan at Central Park swelled my love of the place. Old Trafford had the nickname Theatre of Dreams, but Central Park was my theatre of dreams, and it's sad that young Wigan lads now can't experience the magic of the place. Tickets for our match against Saints were like gold dust; every Wiganer and rugby league fan wanted to be there. I was inundated with requests for tickets—I can't tell you how many people I had to let down.

Nothing could have gone any smoother on the day. The weather was perfect, the sombre crowd loud, the atmosphere electric. It had the feel of a celebration yet there was an underlying sadness around the place. That game meant everything to me and I don't know how I would have lived with myself had we failed to win—Saints would have the ultimate bragging rights to last an eternity. I was nervous but excited. Everyone's eyes were on us, and the enormity of the day hit home when I went out onto the pitch to warm-up. As we did our pre-game drills, the real legends of the history of our famous club were introduced to the crowd. All my heroes were there, and the hairs on the back of my neck stood up as they were all introduced. Ellery, Henderson Gill, Shaun Edwards, Andy

Gregory, Steve Hampson . . . it was amazing. The loudest cheer of all came for the great Billy Boston. I got to know Billy quite well and he was a gentle giant, I liked him a lot. I remember bumping into him one day when I was with my dad, he said, 'Hello Kris, how are you doing?' My dad was star-struck, he could not believe that Billy knew me!

Fittingly, one of our players we all knew would go on to join that elite group of legends opened the scoring for us. Jason Robinson weaved through the defence to score a screamer of a try. Nobody was going to stop him, he was fuelled by pure passion. Jason helped create the next try, a long-range effort finished off by Denis Betts from half way. I was right next to Denis, screaming to him to give me the ball because there was no way I was going to get caught. But he backed himself and managed to get there—which was a good job, because I was ready to shout at him for not passing! We went on to win the game 28–20, though the score flattered Saints, because we were always in control. Tommy Martyn touched down late to salvage some credibility for Saints but the credit for the last Wigan try scorer at Central Park went to Paul Johnson.

I've played so many times in epic derbies which have been instantly described as memorable . . . and then been forgotten about weeks later. But on that occasion, no Wigan fan present that day would forget it, and they counted down the last 10 seconds to the final whistle. In the last play of the game, Paul Sculthorpe chipped over and I dived forward to catch the ball. I got tackled, and the sharp sound from the whistle signalled the end of the game.

I had the ball in my hands when the whistle went, and there was no way I was giving it up. In the middle of the congratulations and hugs on the pitch, I found one of our kit men, Keith Mills, and asked him to take the ball into the changing rooms for me. The team then paraded for a long, slow, lap of honour to thank our wonderful fans. Not one of them left. I dare say not one of them had a dry eye. Some just sat on the floor and reflected on their own personal memories of the place. The venue where so many greats had cast their legacies, through blood and broken bones, was being closed. Reluctantly, after soaking up the applause, we headed towards the tunnel to depart the pitch for the final time.

The club's sponsors and hospitality lounge was at the side of the tunnel, and Gary Connolly cantered ahead of us all, and stood by the door to the bar. He directed us into the lounge, still dressed in our full kit and boots, and walked to the bar. 'Seventeen pints of lager please,' he said, coolly, like it was the most natural thing ever. It was an unbelievable sight for the sponsors. When everyone held a beer, a toast was issued, 'To Central Park', and echoed by us all, as we saluted the great stadium with a sip of beer. When we entered the changing rooms a few minutes later, Keith brought me the ball he had kept safe. I looked at him and said, 'Keith, I want you to have it'. He didn't know what to say, but I thought he deserved it. He'd had a 40-year involvement with Wigan Rugby League Football Club, often with little or no recognition, and I knew that the ball would mean the world to him. He later put in a glass box and I signed a letter of authenticity to say that it was, indeed, the very last ball used at Central Park. And so 96 years and 364 days after the first ball was kicked at the stadium, against Batley, the last ball had been caught by me and hand-delivered to a man who deserved to keep it. I didn't need it; every Wigan player that day had their own little piece of Central Park history to treasure.

I was against the move to the JJB Stadium from the start. I loved Central Park, and I still don't think we will ever know the real reason as to why it was sold to Tesco. I'm not sure that the whole truth was told. Fans often think that players know every secret about the club, but often we found out news the same way as they did, by word of mouth, or through newspapers. The move to the JJB Stadium was a controversial one, but one we all had to buy into. The ground itself was awesome, and I would grow to love it, but it had got something missing. Central Park had character, charm, and more importantly as far as a Wigan player was concerned, it was feared by opponents. Rival teams absolutely hated visiting Central Park, but the JJB Stadium seemed welcoming. I have played at grounds where the toilets were broken and the heating turned up to the max, deliberate ploys from the home side to unsettle us. Once, St Helens painted the walls of the away team changing room a dull pink colour as studies found it made players feel tired.

At the JJB Stadium, the visitors have exactly the same facilities as the home team, little wonder our opponents often looked forward to the fixture. Our very first home game didn't go to plan; we lost 14–10 to a Stuart Raper-inspired Castleford side. The crowd that day, 13,374 for a sudden-death play-off match, confirmed my suspicions that some die-hard fans would need time to get over the death of Central Park. We underestimated Castleford that day, and the Wigan owner, Dave Whelan, was not happy that we lost our first game at his new stadium. He came into the changing rooms afterwards with his head down and gave us all a bollocking that we probably deserved. Again, our coach—Andy Goodway—paid the price for a season without a trophy. By his own admission, Andy is a moody guy, and he failed to get the best out of a few guys because they never knew how to take him. I just got my head down and got on with my job; in all my time at the club, I never once complained about anything, and the only times I visited the chairman's office were when my contracts were due for renewing. I didn't want Andy to leave. He didn't know how to treat certain players, but he knew the game extremely well. In the off-season, Dave brought

Maurice Lindsay back to the club as chairman—I'd met him a few times, but only in passing—and he immediately made two great signings, Willie Peters and Brett Dallas. With Steve Renouf and Terry Newton already signed up, the disappointment of a quick and unexpected exit from the play-offs soon turned into excitement about the following campaign.

Willie, who had played for Gateshead that year, moved to Wigan earlier than most of the other players. He stayed in a house next to mine, and we hit it off straight away. He was a young, innocent guy who loved playing rugby. He was constantly hyperactive and looking for something to do. Every afternoon, he came to my house and asked what we were going to do. One afternoon, I was taking a nap—as I tended to do after training—and Willie let himself into my place. He had a look for me, and found me fast asleep in bed. Seeing how comfortable I looked, he decided that he would join me, got into bed and fell asleep right next to me. I knew none of this, until I woke up—expecting to be alone—and found a man asleep next to me! I jumped out of bed and yelled, 'What the hell are you doing?'

He was a lovable little character, and as soon as I'd shouted I felt guilty about it. He just looked at me with an innocent, almost-puzzled expression and said, 'Sleeping'. I laughed, apologised for my reaction . . . and then ordered him to get out of my bed.

9

INTO THE MILLENNIUM

'For me, it is nothing. New millennium or new century or New Year. For me it's just another day and night. The sun, the moon, the stars remain the same.'

Dalai Lama

WIGAN WENT into a new millennium with a new stadium, a new coach, and a new (well, returning) chairman. Not since the dawn of the Super League era had there been such a feel-good factor in the club. Everyone was smiling; there was plenty to smile about. On top of all that was the arrival of probably the biggest name the club had signed since I'd broken into the first team. A few superstars had joined us, but none had the profile that Steve Renouf had. I'd travelled to Wembley in 1994 as a fan and watched him score the only try in the World Cup Final for Australia, and I'd been a fan of his long before then. Steve and I were completely different players but we had one thing in common—distinctive heads! People always used to notice me for my red hair as I stood out. People noticed Steve because he wore his head-guard.

Though I held him in such high regard, there was no way I could have been overawed by his presence when he arrived because within a minute of him walking into training on his first day I realised that he was the most laid back, easy-going and relaxed guy I'd ever met. It was as if he wasn't aware of his own fame. He was nicknamed the Pearl but we called him 'swivel hips', because he entered a room like he was doing a cha-cha-cha. He had a reputation among fans for being a dashing centre and a reputation among players for being a somewhat lazy trainer; he definitely lived up to both billings. But before I get accused of criticising one of my heroes, and a guy I love dearly, let me explain. I usually detest lazy trainers, but with Steve it was easy to forgive him because he was smart enough to do what he needed to do. He spent time on recovery, he ate well to cope with his diabetes . . . but he was no gym monkey. In truth, he was probably one of the most unfit men ever to play for Wigan.

Training is always very competitive—coaches encourage it as it drives players on—but Steve never got involved in any of that. He knew that bench-pressing 120kg eight times wasn't going to make him a better player. He knew how quick he was; when we did timed runs, he'd regularly get lapped, but he knew in a game, when he needed to, he could explode. He was smart. He was often described as a natural, yet while I haven't exactly given his training style a glowing endorsement, it wasn't just down to luck that he often found himself in so much space. At Brisbane, he made the out-ball into an art-form. Kevin Walters fired out passes faster than they needed to be, and Steve had both the acceleration and the anticipation to peel away from his marker at just the right time, pluck the ball from the air and go. He hadn't been at the club long before he had a word with Andrew Farrell, a master of firing out missile passes, and he employed the tactic expertly for Wigan. It was simplicity and yet genius at the same time.

If his arrival didn't lift the spirits enough, we also had a new coach in 'Happy' Frank Endacott. I'd never met Frank before, but he acted like an old friend to me, and all the other players.

When he arrived, he walked in and hugged everyone, and was full of energy and life; he was like your favourite uncle at Christmas. Frank prided himself on never forgetting anyone's name, and I've never known anyone make so many friends so quickly. The first thing he did when he came in was organise a bonding weekend in Edinburgh. He banned balls and boots; the team had gone through quite a lot of changes and he wanted us to get to know each other. He said the best place for that to happen was in the pub—and he wasn't going to get any disagreements from the players! Our first night out was superb, a harmless, fun night out. The following morning, we reported downstairs in our hotel, only for Frank to issue us with instructions: we had one hour to raid the charity shops for the most outrageous outfits we could find. Our squad dispersed to roam the Scottish capital's streets for charity shops, and we all got back on time. There were some horrific sights, not least Denis Betts and Andrew Farrell, who were dressed as old women complete with purses and nylons. It was a laugh a minute, until Brian Carney spiked David Hodgson's beer with a urinal tablet. Hodgy didn't notice the yellow tablet at the bottom of his pint, nor did he notice a change in taste, he just carried on drinking it. We laugh about it now, but Brian could have poisoned poor Hodgy.

The trip definitely served its purpose. We had a new hooker (Terry Newton), half-back (Willie Peters) and two marquee recruits from Australia (Steve Renouf and Brett Dallas), and it was important that we became a strong unit quickly. Frank's plan worked a treat—straight away we played some awesome rugby league. We hammered Whitehaven 98–4 in our opening match, a Challenge Cup tie, and all season we showed we had tries in us. I scored 20, Pearl and Jason each got 23 and Brett got 21—that's nearly 100 between just four back-line players. We were dumped out of the Challenge Cup at Hull, but in the league we only lost three matches all year, two of those to our arch-rivals St Helens. In the final match of the regular season, we travelled to Saints with us on 47 points and them on 46 points. It was effectively a Grand Final to decide who would finish top of the league, going into the play-offs, and we hammered them on their own ground 42–4. The bragging rights didn't last too long, however, as in the opening week of the play-offs they came to the JJB Stadium and were white-hot, beating us 54–16. We regrouped, and overcame Bradford in the next round to book a place at Old Trafford—our second Grand Final in three years.

Frank had been brilliant all year. He'd brought the fun-factor back to Wigan, sure, but he'd also instilled some grit into our side, too: we had the best defence in the league, conceding fewer points (405 in 28 matches) than any other team. But in the Grand Final, I think he made a big error. Gary Connolly was injured and couldn't play so, rather than putting a young David Hodgson at centre opposite Paul Newlove or Sean Hoppe, he reshuffled the back-line. He moved me to centre, put Hodgy on the wing and Jason at full-back. It was Jason's final game in league before he joined Sale, and he hadn't played full-back for a long time. I think playing Jason at full-back diluted what made him brilliant. A full-back is constantly moving and involved, but Jason performed better when he came in and gave one maximum, all-guns blazing play, and then moved back out to his wing to recover for his next barnstorming play. The St Helens team kept him involved and therefore sapped a lot of his energy. St Helens beat us 29–16.

It was a tough loss to take, because we'd dominated the league and finished top of the table, but did I bemoan the fact that the recently-introduced play-off system robbed us? No, I didn't. Although a team who finished behind us in the league table beat us, I didn't feel bitter. Once the Grand Final was introduced, it effectively made the league table a competition to decide the starting grid, not the champion. I understood and accepted that. I was more disappointed for the players who were leaving. Jason deserved a dream send-off—few players had given more to the club than him over the years.

On a personal note, I was sad to see my mate Tony Mestrov leave. The Australian prop loved rugby league, though not training, and he tended to eat the unhealthiest thing on the menu—he was the opposite to me, but we became really close. He thought he was a lot better than he was, and had an infectious personality. The first time he came with me to my mum's house, he followed me in, said, 'Hi Mrs Rad', and went straight to the fridge to see what there was to eat. And she loved him for that . . . she always loved people who felt comfortable in her house. Tony and our physio, Rob Harris, shared a house for a while and my mum invited them around for Christmas dinner so they wouldn't feel left out, even buying them each a sack of presents too. Mestrov had a big heart—at last orders, he would order 20 Bacardi Breezers to share with anyone who wanted one—but he would regret it the following day, when I'd wake him up and insist we go for a run to sweat it all out. He said on more than one occasion that I nearly killed him. I think he was right.

Willie Peters also left after just one season with us. He was 21, getting some good reports and his agent in Australia drummed up interest from NRL clubs. It was hard for Willie to turn down; he'd once been tipped as 'the next Peter Sterling', and a tag like that is a big burden, but after a successful season with us he felt ready to challenge himself in his homeland. It never really worked out for him, and I always wonder whether it may have been a different story if he stayed at Wigan for a year or two longer to hone his craft. One big problem Willie had was that he pored over every word written about him. Each Monday morning, he would rush to the shop to buy the two trade papers at the time, *Rugby League Express* and the *Rugby Leaguer*, to see what they said about him. That wasn't too bad at Wigan, because he generally played well and the reports reflected that, but the Sydney press are brutal—they can murder an under-performing player, and often do—and while he was finding his feet in the NRL, I can only imagine he tortured himself by reading reports about himself.

Willie's departure meant Wigan needed a new half-back, a quality one . . . and they got one in Adrian Lam. The deal wasn't done over night. There was speculation in the newspapers for a few weeks over whether he would leave the Sydney Roosters to join us. Fans in shops would frequently stop me to ask whether we were going to sign him. Like I knew—they all thought I had insider knowledge! I just replied, 'I hope so'. I'd played against him earlier in my career—while on tour in 1996—but he blossomed later in his career. Brett Dallas had played alongside him for Queensland, and he told me what an outstanding player he was. In a double coup, he wasn't the only quality half-back Wigan signed, with Australian Matty Johns also signing. If there was one signing who was vastly under-rated by the fans, it was Matty.

He loved playing rugby league so much. He talked constantly, had great footwork and a great ability to dissect defences with his brain—rather than through his brawn or speed. He left Wigan after just a year, with three tries to his name, because a member of his wife's family was ill. Though anyone who used that statistic to beat him with should really look at the bigger picture—I finished top try scorer with 30 tries, Renouf got 20 and Andy Farrell—who had a lot of the pressure taken off him by Matty's arrival—got 17. Matty has to take a lot of the credit for those tries. He also helped accelerate the rate of Brian Carney's development after he'd joined to replace Jason—sizeable boots indeed. Brian was still very raw then, he'd only been playing the game three or four years, and Matty took him under his wing. It helped that they were both mad and had the same sense of humour. I remember one time, we went yachting for a team-bonding exercise at Scotsman Flash in Wigan and Matty and Brian turned up pretending they were American tourists! They both had such sharp wit and impeccable comic timing that they pulled it off.

Playing in the same team as Matty, Lammy and Terry Newton was the happiest time of my career. We all got on, we all worked hard and hung out together, but on the field it was awesome; those players were carving out openings all over the field, and I was there to finish off many of the moves. Terry loved playing in that triangle, and that season I truly believed he was the best hooker in the world—a big plaudit, considering how well Keiron Cunningham, at St Helens, and Australia's Danny Buderus were playing. After a Challenge Cup loss to Saints in our opening game, a defeat I put down to the fact we had new players to bed into the side and they were buzzing from a World Club Challenge win over Brisbane, we found our feet pretty quickly. We went on a five-game run without defeat against some decent teams like Warrington, Leeds and St Helens. Bradford were too good for us at their place, but a narrow loss at London—New Zealander Richie Barnett, a full-back I always admired and a bloke I got on well with, was awesome that day—was sandwiched by two big wins, over Huddersfield and Wakefield. Everything seemed fine. Nine Super League games, two losses . . . granted, it was one more than the previous year but we felt okay. Incredibly—and to think of this loss is still painful—we lost at Salford, 31–30, with Matty just pushing a late drop goal wide to deny us at least a point. The following day, on Monday morning, we were all hanging around the players' room waiting for training to begin when Frank walked in and told us he had been fired. He started crying and it was horrible watching such a proud man break down like that.

It was honestly one of the worst days in my career, because everyone loved him. I imagine, though, that his popularity ultimately led to a little complacency creeping in—which was no doubt at the root of our loss to Salford. I liked Frank too much, we all did, and in becoming our friend, I think he stopped being a figure of authority. In 15 months or so with him, I'd never once seen him bollock anyone; his style of management was far more 'arm around your shoulder', but I wondered if he'd have been better served dishing out a few tongue-lashings on a couple of occasions. Who knows? It may have saved his job. Then again, given the fickle nature of the Wigan coaching job, maybe it wouldn't have. One thing I knew was that he was going to get a good send off, and I arranged a drink at Mawdesley Eating House, a few miles outside of Wigan, which every player attended. Frank had been a real mentor for me, a bloke I could really confide in, though over our fifth or sixth pint it was his turn for the confession. 'You know, Rads,' he said, putting his arm around my shoulder. 'I always knew Gary Connolly was an enigma, and when I came to Wigan I promised myself, "before I leave I'm going to work out what makes Gary Connolly tick".' I looked at him with a smile on my face. I knew what he meant. Gary, my best mate in the whole world, has a quirkiness that makes him truly unique. 'And you know what,' Frank continued, before bellowing with a hearty laugh, 'I still can't work the nutter out!'

We didn't realise how good it was with Frank until he'd gone. Stuart Raper was a different character altogether—I liked him, though others found his style too abrupt. Either way, no one was complaining with our results—of the following 18 Super League games, we won 16, and our mid-field combinations between Lammy, Matty, Terry and me grew stronger. I wasn't the only outside back benefiting—Pearl was on fire, while the performances of Denis Betts, Mick Cassidy and Dave Furner in the back row meant—sadly—that my good mate Simon Haughton was squeezed out of the frame. Simon and I had both progressed into the first team together, cemented our places in the side at a similar age and both went on to play for our country. I was sad that his career with Wigan turned sour; sad, because not only was he a close mate, but also because I knew what he was capable of on his day. He scored some of the best tries I've ever seen from a second-row forward. He was such a big man and also incredibly fast, and in the early days of Super League he was unbelievable. His biggest problem, and I think he'd admit this, was that he didn't love rugby league—he simply found himself to be very good at it. He scored tries for fun when he was a youngster, which alerted Wigan, and when they signed him up so young it seemed like the logical career path for him. He trained hard, but he didn't have a strong affection for rugby league and I can't remember him ever watching any games as a spectator. He now lives in Brisbane with his wife and children. At the time, Maurice Lindsay and Dave Whelan were trying hard to get Orrell promoted to the rugby union Premiership and Simon signed for them. I was excited about the possibility of having a top-flight union side in town. I always liked Orrell—there was a cracking atmosphere in their clubhouse on game-day—and when they went professional, we'd share the same gym under the JJB Stadium's East Stand and I always got on with their players. Their coach, Ross Reynolds, was a good bloke and really knew his rugby league, and it was sad to see the way Orrell demised over the following years when Dave and Maurice withdrew their financial support.

During our imperious run through the 2001 summer, I scored tries with familiar frequency and loved playing for Wigan. It was a blast. But not everything went my way. I felt a little queasy before we played Bradford at home. I put that feeling down to big-game nerves—after all, this was one of the biggest fixtures of our year, and the 15,000 crowd was making a racket. In the first two minutes of the game, I fielded a down field kick and returned it to the wall of Bradford defenders. Just before a collision in rugby league, a player tenses his muscles to receive the impact, but as I did this, my stomach groaned and I unwittingly followed through into my Speedos! I'd never done that before. I played the ball and cantered back to my position at the back of the team, wondering what to do. I couldn't go off, we were live on Sky Sports, so I had little option but to continue my game. The next time a water-carrier came onto the pitch, I told him that I'd need to change my shorts at the next break in play, leaving the reason why deliberately vague. I think he knew, the smell was horrifying and I was retching, so I dreaded what the other players would think.

Two minutes later, Terry Newton scampered from dummy-half and carved through the defence, I raced to support him and he offloaded the ball to me, and I crossed for a great try. My team-mates rushed to me and jumped on me to celebrate, and I had to fend them off as I ran off the pitch straight down the tunnel and into our changing room where the kit man, George Unsworth, was waiting for me with a towel, some new trunks and playing shorts. It took about 30 seconds for me to whip my shorts off, clean myself and put on the new clothes—all the while apologising profusely to George—and run back on the field. It was definitely a sickness bug—I spent most of the half-time break being sick in the toilets—but I told Stuey Raper I'd be fine. I played the rest of the second half and scored two more tries to complete my hat-trick. The Sky Sports commentators, who didn't know about my little 'accident', named me man of the match and presented me with my prize, a Tissot watch. I'd played okay, the whole team had (we won 44–30), but I knew a more fitting recipient of the prize. Still feeling sick as a dog, I walked into the changing rooms and said to George, 'Here you go mate, it's the least you deserve for having to wipe my arse'. I later watched the game back on video to see if anyone would have picked up on my unexpected exit. They hadn't, but a few minutes earlier, when I took the ball in for the first time, there are definite signs of an 'incident' occurring. Stevo and Eddie missed it, though it didn't escape the attentions of my team-mates, who ribbed me mercilessly for the next few days about it!

We finished 2001 strongly, hammering Saints twice and booking ourselves another place at Old Trafford. It was our third appearance in four Grand Finals, and we were desperate to make amends for the previous year's loss. Bradford and Wigan were well-matched that season; we finished the Super League campaign with 45 points each (they won the minor premiership because of a better for-and-against) and of the four meetings that year, we'd each won two. Everyone expected an epic. Unfortunately, the game was an absolute nightmare from start to finish for us. We were two well-matched sides but, on the night, we were outclassed, out-enthused and completely outperformed by an inspired Bradford effort. In sport, that happens sometimes. You can prepare meticulously, but for whatever reason, it may not go your way. We were never in it and got entirely humiliated in front of a full house at Old Trafford. The game started terribly for us, as my old mate Henry Paul—making his final appearance for Bradford—made a break. Brian Carney and I dragged him down, but as we did, my blades boots raked across Brian's shin and left a seven-inch gash that blood pumped out from. He was carried off the field, and I knew then he'd not return: his injury was too severe. I was disappointed for him because his dad had flown over from Hungary for the game.

From Bradford's first try, they gathered momentum and when they got going, they were a juggernaut, impossible to stop. They won the match 37–6, which I was completely embarrassed about. I couldn't bring myself to look at the Wigan fans on the customary defeated lap of honour, I just kept my head down until I could get back into the changing room. Maurice Lindsay was furious. He'd always felt our defeats—he prided himself as being a player's chairman—but that night, he shocked us all. I'd never seen him so mad. He was livid and, before he left, he basically told us that we could forget about getting a bonus.

At the start of the season, our captain Andrew Farrell arranged our bonuses with Maurice—which was the usual protocol. Maurice then compiled a list to say that, if we won the Grand Final, we'd get a certain amount, a little less for finishing second, and so on, all the way down to sixth position, the final play-off berth. They bonuses were calculated pro rata, so—for example—a player who had featured in 20 games would get twice as much as a player who'd played in 10 matches.

Maurice hated talking about losing pay. He told us that no matter what happened in the final, he would look after us. We never got his promise in writing because we didn't think we'd need to—we trusted him. We'd lost the Grand Final the previous year and still got our second-placed bonus. After the Bradford defeat, I was so disappointed with our performance that I didn't really think about what he said. Money was the last thing on my mind. But in the days that followed, I—and the other players— realised the injustice of what he'd done. We were all annoyed about it. Okay, we'd embarrassed ourselves in the Grand Final, which we were ashamed of. But we'd still finished level on points with Bradford at the top of the table and reached the Grand Final . . . it was a pretty successful season.

Some of the lads were furious. I was in a difficult position— I wasn't that bothered about the money because I was well paid, but I was on their side. There were players in our team on modest salaries and, depending on how many games they'd played, the bonus could have been about £7,000 or £8,000. They may have already earmarked that money—money that was owing to them—to pay some of their mortgage, or take the family on holiday. It wasn't fair that Maurice didn't pay the players, especially when Wigan would still have received the money from Super League for reaching the Grand Final. The players were deeply upset about their performance, but they were still entitled to what they'd been promised. Some lads needed that money.

Andrew went to see Maurice to argue the players' case, hoping he may change his mind after having a few days to calm down, but it made no difference. Maurice stuck to his guns, and that was that; we'd worked our balls off the whole season, finished joint top and reached a Grand Final, and got no bonus for it. There was nothing at all we could do about it. Despite how angry I was, it wasn't Maurice's worst decision of the year. Pearl was desperate to stay for one more season, he'd scored more than 40 tries since joining Wigan and all the lads knew what a class act he was, but Maurice decided to let him go. It was a terrible decision, and one I couldn't believe. Before he left, Pearl gave me his final head-guard, a memento that I have treasured; in that respect, I got my end-of-season bonus, even if no one else did.

10

ONLY ONE CODE
FOR ME

*'I am 49, I have had a brain haemorrhage and a triple bypass
and I can still go out and play a reasonable game of rugby
union. But I wouldn't last thirty seconds in rugby league.'*
Graham Lowe

I FIRST HEARD the rumours that union wanted me in 2001.
I was having a good season, and people from union had sat up
and taken notice. Jason Robinson had joined Sale and they were
on the look out for other league players to switch as well. I didn't
know whether there was anything in the rumours or the
occasional newspaper report, until—completely out of the
blue—I got a call from Sir Clive Woodward, asking if I would be
interested in meeting him to discuss the possibility of playing
union. It's not every day that you receive a phone call from the
England coach. At the back of my mind, I wondered whether it
was a wind-up, but after hearing his voice I was satisfied that it
was him. I was a fan of Clive's and I liked his approach to sport
and how methodical he was in his preparation, so I thought, why
not meet him?

Clive flew up to Manchester to meet me and we had a coffee
and a chat in the airport. He laid his cards firmly on the table,
saying he saw me playing full-back for his England side and that

he was going to do his level best to get me there. He had made his intentions known to the Rugby Football Union and they fully backed his decision. Not wanting to write anything off there and then—and needing some time to digest this information—I told him I was interested and that's all he wanted to hear at that stage. We spoke about rugby league and his great affection for the game and the athletes that played it, he never once said a bad word about the game; it was clear he was a fan from his great knowledge of our sport. We must have chatted for an hour and, just before leaving, I pointed out that should I decide to leave, I was still under contract with Wigan. He told me not to worry about it, and that they would buy me out.

As you can imagine, on my drive back to Wigan my head was everywhere—I'd gone there for a chat and left with a chance to play for England! Not knowing what to do, I headed to my mum and dad's house to fill them in and the responses I got from them couldn't have been any different: mum was the emotional one and dad was the business one. I understood both sides, and I realised that I had to give it some serious thought.

A few days passed before Clive contacted me again, and he explained that my salary would be split up, half paid by the RFU and the other half paid by the club I would play for. He said that he had a number of interested clubs wanting to take me on. At no point during my first meeting with Clive, at the airport, was money mentioned. All he wanted was to hear that I was interested, but the next time he called he said it was time to discuss figures. He told me how much I could earn, and the money offered was astronomical. He said I would be one of the top earners in world rugby, with probably only Jonah Lomu earning more than me.

I was amazed. If I accepted, I could literally buy whatever I wanted, everything I had dreamed of as a kid. All of a sudden 'keeping my options open' became something far more serious.

One thing I wanted to do all along was to be up front and honest with Maurice Lindsay, Wigan's chairman, who had returned to the club the previous year. I didn't want him hearing about the offer second hand, so I arranged a meeting and filled him in on the situation. I have always got on well with Maurice. I know he has his critics, but you can only judge people on how they are with you and I can honestly say that we have not crossed words in over a decade. Nobody felt a Wigan defeat more than Maurice and, while he made mistakes, he only ever had Wigan's best interest at heart.

So I told Maurice everything that had gone on, and when I told him the figures that were being thrown around he was blown away. He told me straight away that there was no way they could ever compete with it. I knew that already as there was not that much money in our game—especially with the salary cap rules—and he said he needed time to evaluate everything.

My head was still all over the place and, to make matters worse, the press found out about it and so the spotlight was on me. Despite what some may say, players read the newspapers like everybody else and my team-mates constantly asked me if there was any truth in the rumours. I was always open and honest with my team-mates; they needed to know as they would also be questioned about it. They joked about the situation, especially Tony Smith, who used to sing, 'Who wants to be a millionaire?' One thing you need in rugby league is a thick skin—you wouldn't survive the dressing room banter without it.

A few days later, Maurice returned with an offer of a new five-year contract. It was a good deal, and under any other circumstances I would have snatched his hand off. But it was a mile away from the money that the RFU were willing to pay. Let me make it clear that I never wanted to leave Wigan or rugby league. I had never once dreamed of playing union professionally; I never once played it growing up. In fact, the only game of union I'd ever played was for Wigan in the cross-code challenge against Bath!

I was living my dream playing for Wigan, but this offer came along and made me sit back and think about my career. Professional sport is a short career; anyone would be a fool not to consider other offers, especially such lucrative ones. At this point, the Rugby Football League got involved. They did not want to lose their valuable assets so they invented a system called Club GB to pay a sum to international players in danger of changing codes. The only two players ever to receive these payments were me and Keiron Cunningham, who was being chased by the Welsh RU. The Club GB money boosted my salary a bit, but the RFU were still offering me a chance to more than double my money. My agent, Andrew Clarke, had reached a stalemate with Wigan and said it was time for me to fight my own corner.

I don't think my performances were affected by the drawn out saga, but everybody was aware that my mind was elsewhere at times. No matter how hard I tried, it was hard to block out this distraction especially when so much was at stake. Our coach at the time, Stuart Raper, realised it needed sorting out and gave me a morning off training to make a decision one way or the other.

I'd spoken to my friends and family a lot. My mum and dad said the decision was all mine, but my dad asked me not to sign anything without speaking to him first. I arranged a meeting with Maurice, and when I met him in the boardroom at the JJB Stadium, I had a figure in my head that I thought, 'If they offer it to me I'll stay'. Even though it was nowhere near the RFU offer, I just wanted an end to the situation. I'd got to the point where I was sick of reading about myself in the press; I can only imagine what the Wigan fans were saying. Wherever I went around town people asked me what was going on and they didn't hesitate to voice their opinion.

The meeting didn't start straight away; Maurice said we had to wait for someone, then a couple of minutes later, the club's owner Dave Whelan walked in. The players never really came into much contact with Dave. Every now and then he would come into the changing room to have a walk around after a game, but it was never on a personal level. He walked in, made a few comments, then walked off before you could respond. On a few occasions we got told off for leaving the lights on in the changing rooms! Dave would even call the coach, whoever was in charge at the time, from his Barbados home to make his thoughts known. I suppose checking up on those little things are what made him successful in business—but I know if I was in Barbados, all I would be thinking about was how many ice cubes I would want in my piña colada!

To say I was nervous when he walked in and shook my hand was an understatement—I was going head-to-head with one of the most successful businessmen in the country! He asked Maurice to get him up to speed with the situation, and even he was amazed at the money I was being offered. He then asked Maurice who the highest earner at Wigan was. Maurice told him it was Andrew Farrell.

Dave paused, looked at me and said, 'If we give you the same money as the club captain, will you stay?'

I replied, 'If you give me that for five years I'll stay.'

He agreed, but before I agreed I kept my promise, and nipped outside to phone my dad to tell him what had happened. He simply said, 'Good on you, kid'.

I had just agreed a big contract that, if used wisely, would secure my future. I strolled back into the boardroom and shook hands with Dave and Maurice. The sense of relief was like something I'd never felt before. Maurice was delighted, but it was just another business meeting to Dave, he simply said,

'Right, that's sorted, back to work', and then left!

As soon as I had made my decision, I called Clive and he understood. He was a true professional, easy to get along with and didn't pressure me once. He knew it was a difficult decision that only I could make.

Maurice arranged the press conference straight away, and that's where he excelled. He was brilliant with words, and spoke with passion about how union had been defeated. A day later, the local Wigan papers went crazy; I think the headline on the *Wigan Evening Post* was, 'The player money couldn't buy', and they called me their favourite son.

Money is important as it gives you security and that's what we all wish for. But it was different for me because I was on a good wage anyway, so the money didn't really appeal too much. To give up what I had for money would have been foolish. I was wearing one of the most famous jerseys in world rugby, the number one for Wigan. When I was at school, sure I dreamed of being rich, but what I dreamed of most was being Wigan's number one. You can't put a price on that, and looking back now it's bizarre to think I considered giving it up. But having said that, I could understand why it appealed to other players. The money, the higher profile and the prospect of proving yourself all over again are huge incentives.

Over the following years, out of all the other players that left league for union, I was really gutted when Andrew Farrell left in 2005. We're a similar age, we'd been together at Wigan for many years and he was our leader. He left a massive void in our squad that was never really filled. But he had done everything in rugby league and had nothing more to prove. Rugby union was a challenge to him and I admired him for having the mental strength to try a new sport that he had no real experience of. I wasn't completely surprised he left—he'd told me he was thinking of going weeks before news leaked out that union were interested in him.

At about the same time that Andrew left, I got my second approach from union. I had a meeting in Wigan with Andy Robinson, the then-England Coach and his assistant, Joe Lydon. I had a good long chat with them and they felt that it was the time for me to make the transition. I must admit, they painted a nice picture of playing union.

One thing I was concerned about was how the other England players would feel if a league lad came in and got fast-tracked into the international set up, but they said that if it benefited the team, they wouldn't mind as it was all about winning to them. I asked what club they would want me to play for and they said that a few were very interested. I left that meeting and really started to consider switching codes.

A few years earlier when I'd been approached, I was in my early 20s and I still had a lot to achieve. This time, I was coming to the end of my career, I'd enjoyed many great moments with Wigan, and I thought union may open other avenues. The more I thought about it, the more attractive it became.

The first meeting I had was with Phil Davies from the Leeds Tykes, at a service station restaurant on the M62. We chatted for a good couple of hours and, again, I was surprised that he had great knowledge of rugby league. He said he would love to work with me and that he had already spoken to his players about it—I didn't want anyone thinking that, if I did join, I was stepping on their toes.

My second meeting took me down to London to meet London Irish coach Brian Smith. Brian had a rugby league background, and so he could relate to all my queries, questions and concerns. He was more interested about what I would bring to his game. I loved his approach and how he made me feel that I had something to offer. He showed me all around the Madejski Stadium, the Reading football ground where the Irish play. He then took me to their training ground in West London to meet Mike Catt. Mike was a terrific guy. I'd met him during the cross-code challenge in 1996, and had a beer with him when I went to watch Jason Robinson and Henry Paul play for Bath earlier that year. He said he was really excited at the prospect of playing alongside me and told me that the players had a great time away from the game. I really felt I could have joined that set up. They seemed professional and everything they told me was positive. It was a long drive back to Wigan for Andrew Clarke, my advisor, and me. I'd been in this position before and I knew there would be a few sleepless nights, but after talking to my family I again turned down both offers. It was not for the same reasons as before. I've always been extremely close to my family and, at that time, things at home weren't great—they needed me and I had to be in Wigan. And I can honestly say I've not regretted my decision once. I explained things to Maurice, he gave me a year's extension and that was the end of it.

Well, that was the end of that particular offer from union, but the press failed to report one more approach.

After I'd retired, in 2007, I went to visit my buddy Brian Carney in Cork. Whilst there I had another approach. After Brian's team, Munster, played I went on a night out with them. I'm always amazed by how many people love rugby league and know who I am, and it was a terrific night. After a few hours of drinking the black stuff with Brian, he introduced me to his team-mates, and I really got on well with Ronan O'Gara the British Lions fly-half. He loved talking rugby and asked me to play for Munster. For some strange reason, I told him that I was interested. I continued to drink Guinness and forgot all about our chat. Two days later, I took a call from the chief executive of Munster saying they were interested in signing me. I had a flashback to the night out, and at that moment I learned an important life lesson, never talk business on Guinness!

Looking back now, I don't think union would have suited me. I'm a player who likes to drift all over the field, I love to support, I love to tackle. I don't have anything bad to say about the other code; I like it and I respect the people who play it. I found the Graham Lowe quote at the opening of this chapter hilarious, and that's why it's included; I don't share his view about the 15-a-side code. Their game has many fine athletes in it. I don't think badly about people who have made the switch because it's their choice, whatever the reason.

Two years after I first turned down the RFU, England won the Rugby World Cup with my old friend Jason Robinson scoring their only try. That win made them national stars and, given we were beaten 3–0 in an Ashes series at the same time, people asked me whether I regretted my decision. The honest answer was no.

I never dreamed that one day I would grow up and win the Rugby World Cup; Jonny Wilkinson probably did, that's why it meant so much to him. I really admire Jonny, as a rugby player and as a person. Jason's told me he's a great guy. He trains harder than most of his colleagues and while he's a high-profile star, he doesn't go around seeking the limelight. I always wonder which rugby union players would make good league players and I think Jonny would. His defence is so strong, and he's got tremendous mental strength. When he had a bad run of injuries a few years ago, I asked Jason for Jonny's email address and I sent him a message telling him to remain positive, and that he would come back stronger and to use his rest wisely.

I got two email replies, one from his mum and the other from his dad, both saying they couldn't believe that I had gone to such lengths to contact Jonny, and that it meant the world to him. I knew he was a big rugby league fan, and a Wigan fan, and sometimes you can gain strength from messages like that.

I did the same with Matt Dawson when he had to retire. I

became a fan of his when he represented the British Lions in South Africa in 1997. He did some amazing things on that tour and I really enjoyed watching him. I emailed him to tell him how highly I regard him, and he replied to say he would treasure my email as he was a rugby league fan and that he considered me one of the great league players. That was great to hear because that's all I ever wanted to be—a great rugby league player. Not a rugby union player.

Rugby league has certainly taken me to some wonderful places all over the world, but I never thought that it would cross the great divide into rugby union territory!

In 1996, Wigan were twice involved with union when we played in the Middlesex Sevens and then in a fully-fledged game against Bath. No rugby league team had ever played at the Middlesex Sevens before, so there was a huge buzz in our squad as we had some massive names who used to play union. Our squad that day was unbelievable, and I don't think anybody could have beaten us. Our squad included Martin Offiah, Inga Tuigamala, Andrew Farrell, Scott Quinnell, Jason Robinson, Shaun Edwards, Gary Connolly, Henry Paul, Sean Long, Craig Murdock and me. It was a fast, mobile team with our bigger players, Faz, Scott and Inga, all able to move quickly. Frankly, it was a dream-team of talent, and what's more we weren't just a collection of stars—we were a real team who really enjoyed each other's company. We got on as well on the field as we did off it, we were so relaxed, and in between games we would just lie around in the changing rooms chatting and chilling out.

Our coaches, Graeme West, and Joe Lydon told us to go out and have fun. You can't really train for a seven-a-side tournament, you just have to be very fit and enthusiastic and have a fair degree of skill. Union had only just gone professional, while we were all full-time athletes, and we breezed through the early rounds to reach the final against Wasps.

We noticed during the day that many fans went to their mobile picnics in the car park when their team was not playing, but every time we played the stadium was full, and that was certainly the case for the final.

Wasps were captained by Lawrence Dallaglio and, as we stood side-by-side in the tunnel at Twickenham, he shouted to his team-mates, 'Let's send these northern bastards back to where they came from'.

We looked at each other and began to laugh! We were relaxed and wanted to get out there and play. In sevens, possession is everything, and we had no ball for about eight minutes during which time Wasps raced into a 24-point lead. But when we got the ball, we staged an amazing comeback to win the match in the very last minute.

It was a great competition to win, as we'd proved ourselves to a whole new audience, and the team had a celebrity-feel about it because there was so much interest in us. It really lifted our confidence before we played Bath in a cross-code challenge where we were to play one game each under the other code's rules.

The lads were excited to take part in such a unique event—we were on a guaranteed pay-day, and a big one at that, but we also knew that, after the win at the Middlesex Sevens, there would be a massive spotlight on the two games. Wigan's Challenge Cup run had ended, but we'd dominated the sport for a decade and Bath were doing similar things in the union code. I can see why the powers-that-be thought it was a logical idea to see who the best 'rugby' team was but, to me, I thought the cross-code challenge was stupid. Rugby league and rugby union are two completely different games, and there was never going to be one definitive winner.

We played the league game at Manchester City's Maine Road

first, and for the union boys, the hardest aspect was the pace of the game. The constant moving and short bursts of speed really took it out of them. They could all tackle, but the relentless speed eventually took its toll and we won the game easily with Martin Offiah scoring six tries.

I knew the union game was going to be a huge test for me, as I had never played that game before. But we had blokes like Gary Connolly, Martin Offiah, Henry Paul, Joe Lydon, Inga Tuigamala and—in the pack—Scott Quinnell and Shem Tatupu in our side, who had all played union. They all thought that we could run them close, so the training and preparation was full-on—their confidence fuelled our desire to do well.

In the weeks leading up to the game I had to learn all the rules because, honestly, I didn't know any. We went up to Orrell Rugby Union Football Club, on the outskirts of Wigan, and had sessions against them to gain more experience. Orrell were a pretty strong side back then and all their lads were brilliant . . . with one exception. Austin Healey showed a complete lack of respect by going for drop goals in trial games. The players were supposed to be teaching us about rucking and mauling and the intricacies of union. The Wigan boys' opinion of him was not too great after that.

As for union itself, I enjoyed playing it, which backed up many stories that I had heard about it being a better game to play than to watch. One training night up at Orrell, around 2,000 people came to watch us play a full-on practice game. Joe Lydon warned us that it was not easy in the rucks, and the first one I found myself stuck in the middle of, I realised he was right! It's a tough game, and definitely easier for backs than the forwards.

The game at Twickenham was a fabulous day out. The car parks were full of people having picnics or barbeques, their boots opening up to a feast of food and champagne early in the morning. It was a social event and there was a lot of interest in the game—it made me realise just how famous Wigan Rugby League Football Club was outside traditional rugby league territory.

Rugby union is a technical game and we certainly found that out in the first half—Bath murdered us in the rucks. We tried to play them at their game, which was against all our pre-match plans. We got sucked in—the Bath lads had been playing union all their lives and we were naïve to think that we could match them. They raced to a 20-point lead very quickly and the half-time break couldn't have come at a better time. Our coach, Graeme West, who had laced up the boots in the opening half, and Joe didn't hold back. They wanted to know why we hadn't followed their instructions.

I was amazed how seriously we took the game. There was a lot of pride at stake, and in the second half we went out and played what we knew best—rugby league. Every time we got the ball, we kept it alive, supported each other and just had fun. We didn't have a particular pattern but we played to our strengths and it allowed guys like Jason, Inga, Gary, Henry and Martin to showcase their talents. It definitely worked, we drew the second half and Craig Murdock scored a blinding try that will go down in Twickenham history. The game gave me a real taster as to what union was like.

I respected union players—they were all good blokes. But union is a more forward-oriented game than league and backs can go for long periods without being involved. That would not have suited my game.

11

RADLINSKI FINAL

'The greatest thing of all is to do something that others thought you couldn't.'

Text message from Ellery Hanley, morning of Challenge Cup Final

THE FIRST Challenge Cup Final I watched was the 1985 epic between Wigan and Hull at Wembley. As a nine-year-old fanatic, I marvelled at the tries—and celebrations—of wingers John Ferguson and Henderson Gill but, in the days, months and years that followed, that match became referred to by everyone as 'The Brett Kenny Final'. I still can't believe that, 17 years later, I would effectively have a final named after me, too. I was proud, if a little bit embarrassed, that the press and many fans started calling the 2002 showcase 'The Kris Radlinski Final' for the role I played in the 21–12 win over St Helens. Yet, while the build-up to that match was dominated by discussions about whether I would recover from a foot infection in time, only a few knew just how close I went to missing out on one of the biggest milestones of my career.

It all started with an innocent trip to the Trafford Centre, a week before the final, with my then-girlfriend. The Challenge Cup Final was a big occasion for my family and friends, and I'd promised my girlfriend a new outfit for the weekend in Edinburgh—Wembley was being rebuilt, so the game took place at Murrayfield.

Shopping with a woman for clothes is not easy at the best of times, and after a couple of hours being dragged from one store to the next, from one changing room to another, I was fed up. To make it worse, I began to get an itch on my right foot that wouldn't go away. It was becoming more irritable. I put it to the back of my mind—the last thing I wanted to do was prolong the shopping trip—but the itch, gradually, got worse. We walked into another shop and, as my partner tried on more outfits, I sat down. My trainer seemed to be getting tighter, I untied the shoelaces, but that didn't ease the discomfort and so—after a cursory glance around to check no one was watching me—I took off my trainer and sock. My foot was massive and, worse still, it was a burning red colour. I knew that something was very wrong. I abandoned our shopping trip, I had to get home. On the way back to the car, I started to go light headed. I weighed up my options—phone the doctor or the physio? Dr Zaman would probably send me to hospital as a precaution, so I called Alan Tomlinson, our physio, and asked if he could meet me at my house in half an hour. 'Something's not right,' I told him. I began driving home, hoping I'd feel better. Instead, my condition deteriorated; I began feeling sick, I was burning up and I was dripping with sweat.

By the time I arrived at home, Alan was already there, and checked me out immediately. He was completely baffled—he noticed a red line tracking up my leg and phoned the doc. Dr Ansar Zaman was Wigan's club doctor and had been my GP all my life. He referred to me as his boy. Within 10 minutes, he'd driven from his home in nearby Parbold to check me out. He couldn't be sure what had caused it, but knew it was some kind of blood poisoning. 'We've got to get you to the hospital,' he said. Within two hours, I'd gone from frowning outside changing rooms, thinking I'd rather be anywhere else, to being on a hospital bed with an IV drip in my arm, wondering what the hell was going on. My entire leg had swollen and turned bright red. The doctors assessed me but they couldn't agree what it was—maybe an insect bite, maybe a bad reaction. I wasn't bothered about what it was, the only thing I was worrying about was whether I'd be able to play in the Cup Final against St Helens in a week's time.

The Challenge Cup was massive for me. I made nine trips to Wembley with my family to watch Wigan—I had vivid childhood memories of going to school the day before the match wearing cherry and white coloured clothing, and driving past shops with their windows covered in good-will messages and streamers. Yet, since the day I'd covered for Jason Robinson in the 1995 final but not played, I'd never won the Cup. It was the one piece of silverware that had eluded me and I was desperate to break that jinx. Now, it looked like I was going to miss out. The doctors and advisors tried to comfort me, but I could tell they were all seriously concerned. They had no idea what was wrong with me—they just hoped the drip and pain killers would do their job.

I got hundreds of get well cards from my family, friends and Wigan's fans. When I was alone in the day time, I ripped the cards up—I had nothing else to write on—and used them to jot down everything I knew about St Helens; their players, their kicking game, their style of play, everything. I just wanted to make sure I was as prepared as I could be even though there was a real risk I wouldn't play. Doing something productive eased the frustration and helped the minutes pass. Those minutes rolled into hours and days, and still nothing changed. The swelling was still not going down and when I got up to walk to the toilet, I could not put any pressure through my foot. I had to shuffle to the bathroom with a slop limp. Our coach, Stuart Raper, told me that he would give me all the time I needed—even up to the morning of the game—to recover, which settled me down a bit. But, alone in a hospital bed, with my foot showing no sign of improvement, many things ran through my mind. If I'd been injured, I could have tolerated the misfortune, but this was a foot infection that no one knew anything about. I was heartbroken.

I thought my Cup Final was over. I kept my foot elevated, and after a few hours it looked better, but appearances can be deceptive. As soon as I stood up, all the blood drained down my leg and my foot blew up like a balloon again. It looked like a clown's foot.

With three or four days to go, I got a phone call from our chairman Maurice Lindsay. He was such a positive man, and he perked me up. 'I'm going to put a bet on you winning the Lance Todd Trophy,' he said.

'Maurice,' I replied, 'no offence but I think you're mad.' I told him that I didn't think I'd make the team but he wouldn't hear it.

'Keep the faith,' he kept reiterating.

Quite a few of the lads came to see me, and a visit from Adrian Lam and Brian Carney really helped. They spent a couple of hours with me, chatting and joking, and making me feel a million times better. Lammy was engaging company, and spoke with such passion and enthusiasm. He told me that my injury was part of the script, that we were going to win the cup and I would play a vital part. He said that's why he loved sport so much, for the unexpected scenarios it threw up and the opportunities to overcome the odds, and that he was excited about playing with me at the weekend. For the first time all week, a tiny bit of optimism crept into my mind. Lammy had ignited a flicker of hope.

They said their goodbyes, hugged me and assured me again that everything would be fine. I didn't tell them that my condition had not improved—they'd made me forget about it for a couple of hours. Not long after they'd gone, there was a tap on my door, and a nurse walked in. 'What have we here then?' she asked. Confused, I told her I was fine and ready for bed. She shrugged off my reply with a wave of the hand and compassionately told me I had no reason to be embarrassed, she'd sort everything out. 'Your friends have just told me that you've had an accident and that you're too embarrassed to say anything,' she said. They'd got me—I laughed, and then pulled back the covers to prove to her that I'd not had an accident. Finally convinced, she said, 'You have some strange friends'. I already knew that.

I went to sleep thinking about what Lammy had said, and forced my mind to try to think positively. I had no energy, I had not eaten properly all week, so I asked my mum to bring me some supplements, energy drinks and protein milk shakes and I gulped down as many as I could manage.

In a Cup Final week, the team would travel on the Thursday before the big game on the Saturday. Usually, the team would train on the Thursday morning in Wigan before being waved off by the thousands of adoring fans. It was part of the Cup Final build-up, a really exciting time, and I didn't want to miss out. On Thursday morning, while my team-mates were training in Wigan, the doctors at the hospital agreed to release me—not that my condition had improved, but because they had complete faith in Dr Zaman.

I called my mum and asked if she could pick me up and run me home for my playing equipment. Just walking to the car was a huge effort. I opened the door, collapsed into the passenger seat and told her how awful I felt. She asked if I would be fit for the game . . . I told her I didn't think so.

Dave Whelan, the club's owner, actually offered to fly me up to Scotland in his helicopter but I decided against it. I just wanted to be a part of my team, and being around the lads would help me recover. It also returned my thoughts to the game. I needed to play in this game. All the way up to Edinburgh, I sat quietly on the coach, and thought about my favourite Challenge Cup moments: Ellery Hanley's try against Saints in 1989, when he weaved his way through the Saints defence; Shaun Edwards' heroic display against Warrington the year later, when he played with a depressed cheekbone, and Mike Gregory's unbelievable cover tackle on him; Martin Offiah's unbelievable try against Leeds in 1994, when he ran the length of the pitch. That's probably my favourite try of all time. As a full-back, I always watched how other players dealt with situations and Alan Tait, the Leeds full-back, did everything right that day. He waited as long as he could before moving in, he showed Martin the touchline and, had I been in his shoes, I'd have done everything exactly the same. I think Martin would have made me look stupid that day too!

These were magic moments, which not only left a mark on my memory, but became engrained in Challenge Cup folklore. These were the moments that were talked about in pubs and at office water-coolers. Thinking about them only fuelled my desire to play. In Edinburgh, Alan Tomlinson and Dr Zaman constantly observed me, making sure I was having no more funny turns. On Friday morning, the day before the game, while the other players were training, Alan spent two hours massaging the swelling away. It was painful, but it looked like he had done the job. My spirits lifted as quickly as they plummeted when I stood up, and the infected blood drained back down. If I didn't make the starting line-up, Gary Connolly would be playing full-back, and though he started his career in that position, he hated playing there. All week, he'd been calling to ask if I would be playing. When the lads returned from training, I told Gary that I didn't think I was going to make it. My foot was not improving.

That afternoon—24 hours before kick-off—we made the traditional trip to the stadium to have a look at the surroundings. I'd not had my trainers on for a week and, when I tried them on, my right shoe wouldn't fit because my foot was still so swollen. I had to wear carpet slippers as we walked around the stadium, which certainly got the photographers' attention!

That night, I had an early evening meal and then went to my room to lie down and think about the game. There was no way I could relax, I had too many thoughts running through my mind. I knew it was going to be a long night so I called the doctor and asked him for a sleeping pill. He reminded me that I needed to keep my foot elevated, so I looked around my hotel room for something suitable. In the wardrobe I found a fold-up suitcase table. Perfect. I took my position in bed, raised my foot on the table and popped the sleeping pill. Nine hours later I woke in exactly the same position . . . I'd slept like a log. Immediately, I looked up at my foot—it looked perfect. There was no swelling and it was back to its original size and colour. My heart was racing at the prospect of being able to play. I controlled myself, took a few deep breathes and stood out of bed—I had one more test. Slowly, I walked to the bathroom to brush my teeth, which would give it the two minutes it needed to see if there was any reaction. Half way through brushing, the all-too familiar burning sensation returned. I looked down and my worst nightmare had been realised—my foot had ballooned again.

Downbeat, dejected, demoralised, I limped downstairs quickly to fill people in on my situation. I was still a part of the team, and the team came first. Gary needed to know what position he was playing, Stuart Raper needed to decide who was going to come into the side, and I wanted to give them as much notice as possible. It was still pretty early in the morning and only a few players were up, but the doc and Alan were at breakfast with them. I headed in their direction, they lifted their heads to enquire how I was, and I showed them my foot. 'I've no chance,' I sighed. It appeared like just the response Dr Zaman wanted to hear. A veteran surgeon, he loved the drama of professional sport and he could certainly perform under pressure. As he treated players, he would often tell stories about wonders he'd worked in the past, getting players back onto the pitch when they had no chance. He calmly finished his breakfast and then asked Alan to follow us to the treatment room. A few of the lads who were up for breakfast heard this exchange, and thought that there was no way they were going to miss it. Andrew Farrell was the most blood-thirsty of them all, he loved watching anything like that. He even ran to his room to get his video camera!

Dr Zaman didn't mind, it was a perfect chance for him to perform. He even gave a pre-operation interview as I lay on the treatment table, a woolly hat pulled over my eyes. Alan again worked hard to massage all the swelling into place, as doc gathered his apparatus together. Terry Newton was giddy, excitedly dancing from one foot to the next. Julian O'Neill watched casually, while Craig Smith was squeamish, so he stood in the corner and listened. Andrew took his position over the top with his camera, and we were ready. First, doc injected pain killers all around my foot. Then he got a scalpel and carefully but unceremoniously sliced open the top of my foot. I never felt or saw a thing; I just heard the lads giggling like schoolboys as the blood and infection oozed out. Alan continued to press as much fluid out as he could. Eventually satisfied that they'd got all they could, doc packed it with gauze—he said he couldn't stitch it up as there was a chance that it could refill with fluid.

He calmly cleaned his equipment and put it away, and told me to go and see Stuart. The first thing I noticed when I stood up was that my foot did not enlarge. Fluid wept out, but there was no pain. I felt a bit sick, though that was probably nerves. I found Stuart and explained what had just happened—as head coach, it would be his call whether I played or not. He suggested that we go to the hotel gym and try some running on the treadmill. Alan came along with us to check the situation. I started jogging and I felt pretty good. Alan then increased the pace gradually until I was sprinting flat out. Stuart then hit the stop button on the machine, and told me to get off. I was a bit out of breath, but I was encouraged. 'Mate, d'you feel okay?' he asked.

I drew a breath and thought hard about what he'd asked. Then I nodded my head and said, 'I'm ready to play'.

He grinned. 'Well let's do this then.'

Stuart trusted me. If I didn't think I could play, there was no way I would have lied and said that I could play, because if I broke down in a game it could be the difference between winning and losing. I was always honest with my coaches.

It was two hours before the coach would leave, so I went back to my room and made a couple of phone calls to let my family know, and then I showered and put on my Cup Final suit. I felt good. I felt excited. And I'd forgotten all about my foot problem until it came to putting my shoes on, and my right shoe wouldn't fit. I called for some scissors and cut all the leather away, before squeezing my foot into it.

Then it dawned on me. If I can't fit my foot into a shoe, how would I get it into my playing boot? Luckily, our kit man George Unsworth had thought ahead and realised it could be a problem, and had a pair of size 10 boots shipped up to

Scotland the day before just in case. Good job he did—I played in one size nine and one size 10!

The trip to the Cup Final is always a special one. Supporters from every team mingle together in the streets, many drunk but the atmosphere never hostile—there was not a policeman in sight. I had all kinds of thoughts running through my mind on the way to the game, but the main one was not to let Stuart down. He had showed a massive amount of faith in me—I'd have understood if he'd not picked me, and I did not want to fail him. We got to the ground and kept our usual pre-game routine. In the dressing rooms, I tried to focus, but I was becoming increasingly nervous. I went for a pee and stood next to Andrew Farrell. He'd played in 1995 when I missed out, and he was the captain in 1998 when we'd lost to Sheffield and, like me, he was a Wigan lad—he wanted it as much as me. 'I can't believe how nervous I am,' I confided.

He simplified it all perfectly, telling me to take away the occasion, take away the fans. 'It's just another rugby field, a piece of grass,' he said. 'That's why you play the game, because you love it. You've played hundreds of games, this is no different—play for the moment, not for the big picture.' He added that I had a room full of team-mates next door but, more importantly, a room full of friends who would help me through.

It was pure wisdom—the pressure I'd been feeling was from what I'd put on myself. I calmed down and, at last, began to enjoy the occasion. It's amazing what little details I remember, but stood in the tunnel, waiting to walk onto the pitch, the hymn—and rugby league's unofficial anthem— 'Abide With Me' came on, and I had a flashback to singing it as a child while I waited for my heroes to come out onto the pitch. I shivered at the memory, goose bumps covered my arms. I was dragged back to the here and now when I noticed the girl-band Atomic Kitten, who had performed in the pre-match show, walk past us—I couldn't believe how tiny they were.

I'd love to detail the match, but to do that I'd have to read a newspaper report or watch the video of the game, and still it wouldn't trigger any recollections. The match was mostly a blur to me. Early on, I chased a grubber kick into the in-goal area and I dived to reach it but missed, and I head-butted the floor. I hit the point where you get temporary memory loss—that happened a few times during my career—and so my memories are hazy at best. I only remember little points from the game. Brett Dallas scored a try early on. St Helens were big favourites to win—mad, really, when you look at the team we had that day, but our form had been scratchy until then despite the presence of players such as BD, Gary, Andrew, Lammy, Craig Smith, Tez Newton and Dave Furner.

Saints were in the game for a while, and Jamie Ainscough came up with an interception when momentum seemed to have swung in their favour. It was a massive play that probably sealed the win for us. I made a few crucial tackles, but they were done on auto-pilot. The only other thing I remember was when the announcement of the Lance Todd Trophy winner came over the loud-speaker. 'And the winner is . . . Kris Radlinski.' Straight away, I thought back to the hand-scrawled message on a napkin that Joe Lydon had given me years earlier after I'd won the Harry Sunderland Trophy. I had now entered an exclusive club by winning the two most coveted man of the match awards in rugby league. The game still had eight minutes to go but we refused to be beaten. When the final whistle went, my tank was empty—I had nothing left to give.

I'd imagined the scene a million times in my mind, and each time I was jumping on my team-mates, but when my dream finally came true I was too drained. I was feeling a little sick, I was light-headed and happy, but my over-riding emotion was relief that it was over. I looked for Stuart and walked over to him—I wanted to thank him before I spoke to anyone else. I told him I'll be eternally grateful to him.

On the way up to receive the Cup I walked past mum and dad. By this point, I couldn't control my emotions. Mum was so emotional, I hugged her, and I thought she was never going to let go. I think she was happier that I'd got through the game than the result. My dad just shook my hand firmly and gave me the look that every son strives for. No words were spoken, and none were needed—I knew he was the proudest man in the stadium. When I got to the top of the steps, I saw Maurice and I made my way over to him. I hugged him and he thanked me for winning him his bet—I'd forgotten about his chat earlier in the week! Winning the trophy was a truly fantastic experience, but what made it so special was the group of guys I did it with. Those men meant the world to me, and we all shared something that will never be forgotten. In years to come, we'll bump into each other and—with just one look—we'll be thinking about the same thing: that special weekend in Scotland.

Craig Smith approached me on the field and said that what he witnessed earlier in the morning was one of the toughest things he had ever seen from a rugby player, and that he was proud to know me. To hear that from one of the toughest men in the game was awesome. Rugby players aren't known for their sentiments, but in the minutes after a Cup final, any barriers of bravado come down. Guys had to say what they were feeling, and it was great. As soon as we got back into the changing room, I pulled my boot off, and it was one of the best feelings ever. I then had to get my foot stitched up, which gave me the reflection time I needed, so I lay back and put a towel over my head as if to signal, 'Do Not Disturb'. I thought of my family and the week they must have had. I didn't think about the pain of the stitches being sewn through my flesh. Sportsmen try their best and give their all and, if they work hard enough and sacrifice enough, it can take you to places you can't describe. A couple of journalists and a photographer were invited into the changing room, and I asked the photographer, Nick Fairhurst, to take one of me with Alan Tomlinson, Dr Zaman and the Challenge Cup trophy. If it wasn't for the hard work of those two men—and the faith of Stuart Raper—my place in Cup Final history would not have been achieved.

There was only one thing left to do—party. I had a brief drink with my family in the bar and had a chat with some of the St Helens players. I am very close to a few of them, and it was important to be humble in success. I had been on the losing side and it is a bad place. Rugby league players throughout the world know how to win graciously.

I got on the team coach, turned on my phone and it buzzed non-stop for a few minutes with incoming text messages from friends. Then I called my nan, who was in tears, and I told her that I loved her and that I was going to get wasted! Dr Zaman came to me and, ever the professional, he advised me not to drink any alcohol due to all the painkillers I'd taken. 'Doc,' I replied. 'I love you, but there is not a chance that I am not drinking tonight.'

He shrugged his shoulders, defeated. 'Fair enough,' he said, before adding that he would keep checking on me. One thing our team did very well was party.

I sat with David Furner and Craig Smith and drank about 10 bourbons as we watched the team wreak havoc. For some strange reason, Mick Cassidy had brought his hair clippers with him to Edinburgh and said it was a great idea to shave everyone's head. So, one at a time, we marched to Mick's makeshift salon for our buzz-cuts. I was one of the first in, and it was quite funny to sit by the bar watching the players disappear—with their full heads of hair—and returning a couple of minutes later bald. Everyone saw the funny side. Everyone, that was, apart from Kath Connolly (Gary's wife), who was really upset—she thought Gary looked like a thug with his new cut!

We had a live band on, and Andrew Farrell took his favourite place at the front with the microphone. It was a brave man who tried to take it off him. All year, Stuart Raper had told us that he could play the drums but none of us believed him, so he took this opportunity to prove it to us and, I have to admit, he rocked the place.

I was asked to give a speech, and so I stepped onto the stage and again paid tribute to Stuart—it was important to me that he knew how I felt about the decision he made. I tried to spend a little time with everybody. I sat down and had a beer with Jamie Ainscough, who was looking subdued. He just said to me he couldn't believe it, and that it was the best day of his career, which was a surprising admission from an Australian who had played State of Origin football.

I'd wanted to win the Challenge Cup all of my life, but it was great to hear other people's perspectives. The party eventually ended at about 5.30am. Dr Zaman had nothing to fear, as I was not drunk, just tired. I went to bed, though I'd only had about three hours sleep when there was a knock at the door. I got up, wondering who the evil person was who'd woken me at 8.30am, opened the door and saw Brian Carney. He said we had to collect £10 off every player and staff to load up the party bus for the trip back to Wigan. We then went to the hotel bar and cleaned them out of every single alcoholic drink they had! We loaded a bell boy's trolley up and stacked it on the back of our luxury coach. The journey back to Wigan was a real highlight of the weekend for me. It was great being with my loved ones, but being just with my mates who I'd won the trophy with, was brilliant. We had hangovers, we all had awful haircuts and we had a lot of alcohol to get through.

Stuart Jones, a young guy in our squad and one of the travelling reserves, was a cracking lad but he was so ill on the way back to Wigan. He was green, and sat at the back of the coach being sick. I really felt for him, but Andrew Farrell didn't share my sympathy, and he got his video camera out of his bag to capture the vomiting escapades.

Our team song was 'We Built This City' by Starship, and it was practically played on loop for the entire journey. We sang it enthusiastically each time it came on! Our conditioner Nigel Ashley Jones picked the tune, we all concede that it's not a classic, but it did the trick and got us going. When we reached Wigan, there were thousands of fans lining the streets for the customary open-top bus parade through the town. For about three or four miles into the town centre, the roads were blocked with jubilant fans. From the front of the open-top bus, I scanned the faces in the crowd, waving and smiling to the fans. I jolted when I saw my nan, sat in a wheelchair, next to my mum and Nicola. She was so happy, waving her hand frantically. I waved back, and then I took her photo from the top of the bus—a picture I've treasured ever since. We all went back to the town hall for lunch with the mayor, before we were allowed to leave and continue partying. We hit a few bars around town before all heading back to my house. One of my great friends came back with us that night. Christy Welland, the son of Oscar-winning actor Colin, could sniff out a party like no other. He was a Wigan fan whose nickname was Shamu, after the famous killer whale, as he's a big guy, about 30 stone. Like the game itself, the rest of the party was a blur, though I distinctly remember Gary Connolly and me trying to pull my match jersey over Shamu's massive frame! A few days after the game, I watched it on video. As I scrutinised my performance I realised I'd been running on adrenaline. Jonathan Davies, who was commentating for the BBC, actually laughed, saying that I had no right to make those tackles! I also realised just how well Adrian Lam played that day.

He controlled everything, and in my opinion, he was the best player on the pitch in the final. He could have quite easily won the Lance Todd Trophy, which is voted for by the rugby league press. To this day, I'm convinced that it was only the fact that I had spent a crazy week in hospital before the game that had swung the vote in my favour.

12

MATES, BEERS AND MAD MONDAYS

'Son, when you participate in sport it's not whether you win or lose, it's how drunk you get.'

Homer Simpson

SOME PEOPLE have to cut down their drinking when they make it as players; I was the opposite. Believe it or not, I'd never even been drunk until I'd started at Wigan—but it wasn't long before I was given an induction into how to celebrate a big win. After the Regal Trophy victory in 1995, we went back to Central Park for a Chinese banquet—the club always put on functions like that after a Cup Final, and they were good. I hadn't been there long when I ended up stood at the bar with Terry O'Conner and a couple of other guys. Terry suggested celebrating with a couple of shorts and, being young and naive, I succumbed to the peer pressure. So when the first triple Jack Daniels—diluted with a splash of Coke—was put in front of me, I duly knocked it back. The other three downed their drinks too, and gave the familiar exhale that follows a strong drink, before wiping their mouths and asking the barmaid for another round. For an hour, we chatted and laughed in between downing more and more—I was having a great time, getting drunk with my mates . . . until I realised that they weren't getting drunk. At first, I put it down to my own inexperience, but they couldn't contain their laughter and they confessed that, while I'd been drinking triple JDs and Coke, their glasses had just contained Coke!

I was too drunk to be angry, but I had to leave the bar and go outside for some fresh air. Until that point, I'd never realised that the car park at Central Park span around so quickly! I couldn't focus, I was in trouble. Somehow, I managed to flag down a taxi to take me home, a trip that usually cost about six quid; this time it cost me £26—I'd thrown up all over the back seat. It was early in the evening when I got home so my mum and dad were still up watching TV. I somehow managed to hide the fact that I was hammered, said goodnight and went up to bed. I blamed the vomit down my shirt on somebody throwing curry at me. I don't think mum believed that one but she let it pass.

My bedroom at home was a tiny box room that consisted of a bed, some shelving and a one metre square piece of carpet. I opened my door and shut it behind me, stood on the carpet and projected vomit all over my bed and the bedroom window. One of our neighbours, Maureen, lived opposite and saw the whole episode. She quickly got her slippers on and came running across the road to tell my mum and dad about it. They came running upstairs to find me lying naked in all the sick, the room like a disaster zone. They took care of me, a humbling experience for an 18-year-old—being bathed by my mum as my sister was changing the bed and my dad was cleaning the windows. I had just caused absolute devastation thanks to Terry O'Connor who, I am told, had an enjoyable evening at Central Park.

Fortunately, after that early episode in my career, I was a willing participant in nights out on the beer. As a player, my favourite time of week was always the hours immediately after each game. You could relax knowing you had tried your best and had a few hours of freedom until the morning after, when the analysis of your last performance would begin and the build-up to your next game would start. Over the years, a lot of routines changed; there would be periods were we would all attend a pub together with our partners, there would be times when we would go swimming straight after the match, but certainly my best times were when we just let our hair down and ripped into the beer for a few hours. It brought us closer and galvanised the team spirit.

Players can't absorb themselves into rugby league, they can't live and breathe the game as fans do because that puts them on edge all the time. Players need time to enjoy their lives and let their hair down, though I didn't like doing that after I'd played badly, or after a defeat. Whether I was in Wigan or in Australia, if I'd lost, I stayed in. I remember playing in the infamous game in Sydney when Great Britain were battered 64–10 by Australia, and I was amazed that some of my team-mates went out and had a drink that night. I was depressed, but you have got to have a degree of pride, so I just stayed in alone.

Rugby league certainly has its fair share of characters; and it's the richer for it. Every club will have stories to tell about weird and wonderful individuals that grace our game. I feel truly blessed to have played with some absolute nutters!

Take Wayne 'Wagga' Godwin, my former Wigan team-mate. The first time I took him to a gig, he asked if there was a dance floor! Every club needs someone like him. He is such a bundle of life—he walks into every room and asks enthusiastically, in a thick Yorkshire droll, 'Hiya how you doin'?' On one pre-season trip we went to Florida, and had three houses between the team. Coaching staff were in one and the other two housed 10 lads in each. Each house had a leader who had to develop rules and a code of conduct, giving each house member a role in the house. Wagga was our tea boy. Every time somebody wanted a brew, they just asked him and he had to make it . . . naked. That was the rule, and he never once complained; for 10 days straight, morning, noon and night, he got up as soon as someone asked for a drink, stripped off his clothes and brewed up.

Brian Carney is proof that not all rugby league players were thick northerners; he's from Ireland and he's got a law degree. But it's fair to say that not all players are renowned for brain power, and as a player, I always loved listening to some of the changing room conversations. I had to laugh one day when I asked Danny Tickle what he was doing after training. He told me that he was going up to Terry Newton's house for some mortgage advice. It makes me giggle now thinking about it. I would literally have bought a ticket to watch that event! Imagine listening to Terry explaining base rates and repayment options! I guess every sport has its characters but sometimes it is the little things that make me laugh more than anything.

Some of my greatest memories from rugby league aren't from the matches, but from the after-match drinks and end-of-season parties. One thing that rugby league players can do is put a few away. I think it stems from the training sessions; we are forced to push ourselves to the limit, and that same mentality applied to our approach to going out for a drink. We were never satisfied until we had gone as far as we could.

Players can't drink during the week, and the modern game is so hard that you couldn't possibly head out and train the day after a night on the tiles. But when the occasion allowed it, we made up for the times we sacrificed so much. For as long as I played at Wigan, and it's the same at other clubs, there's a weekend at the end of the season called 'Mad Monday'. This takes place the day after your last game, whether that's a Monday or not, and it doesn't last for one day, but rather for two or three. The players reflect on the trials and tribulations of the year by getting completely wrecked, and these sessions could begin as early as 9am with fines for latecomers, end at five the next morning and start again after four hours' sleep.

It was survival of the fittest; kill or be killed. Sometimes we celebrated our season and sometimes we said goodbye to team-mates who were moving on to other clubs or retiring. Either way they were the best parties you could ever think of with boys becoming men—granted, sometimes dressed in women's clothes—and players coming out of their shells. It's a tremendous feeling knowing you have just ended a season with a bunch of men, fought for each other, and then go boozing with them out of love and affection.

Everyone acted like idiots and played stupid games. I remember once we all sat in a circle and the game was quite simply to jab the bloke to your right in the chops, just for a laugh. Stupid I know. As it happens, I was sat next to Stuart Raper—our coach at the time—but the same rules applied. I apologised to him, then just gave him a little punch. He understood the situation and realised that if I hadn't punched him the lads would have ruined me. The days were filled by chilling out and having a laugh.

One year I found Denis Betts asleep in a corner, though that was far more pleasant than the sight of Brian Carney, completely naked, peddling a bike through the street, only to stop to climb a tree . . . and fall 10 feet to the ground. You would find lads singing karaoke or playing guitars, usually pretty badly.

Most times, we packed into a pub on the outskirts of Wigan

called The Wheel, downing pints for fun and then washing them down with a shot of some sort. There was no chance of getting kicked out as a relative of Terry Newton's was the landlord. I'd only had two drinks when I saw one of the most bizarre sights of my life—a local taking a mouse for a walk! He was dragging the rodent by a lead past The Wheel along the Worsley Mesnes street—honestly. When it came time to head into town, we all jumped on the bus outside the pub. It was the first time I had been on a bus since school and lads were wrestling in the aisles and singing at the top of their voices—I don't know whether or not the driver was enjoying it or scared for his life!

We would usually end up in the Stagedoor, which was run by my friend Wilf Roden, and he would let us have run of the mill as he did with players from St Judes, St Pats and Rose Bridge, the three big local amateur sides in Wigan. The lads partied like it was New Year's Eve, and we always respected the place.

The hangovers were incredible. I still smile at the memory of waking up with my head pounding. I'd lay in my bed, trying and failing, to remember the events of the night before. One morning, after plucking up the courage to get some aspirin, I walked downstairs, turned into the lounge and found a six-foot, wooden statue of an American Indian staring back at me! Then I remembered that, at closing, Craig Smith and I had borrowed it from the Stagedoor and squeezed it into our taxi home.

An hour later, feeling slightly better, a horn beeped outside; Craig was there to pick me up and take me back out to the pubs and I wasn't going alone—my new American Indian friend came back to the pub. In fact, the Indian came with us into every pub that afternoon before we made it back to the Stagedoor; Wilf hadn't even noticed it was gone. I think he was more concerned that his previous night's takings, a few thousand pounds, were missing—he'd put them in Brett Dallas' coat pocket instead of his own by mistake. BD handed them back the following night.

A lot of relationships were put to the test during Mad Monday celebrations as wives, girlfriends and mums had no idea where players were or when they were coming home. David Furner told me that, at the end of every season, his missus told him, 'Go out and drink for four days, I don't want to see you, but I know you will come home crying after three'. She was usually right.

We had some amazing end-of-season parties at Gary Connolly's house. He has a huge living room with a six-foot wide fireplace, which everybody danced on . . . and usually fell off. Gary is a neighbour of mine—he lives across a courtyard, we both have barn conversions—and you can see straight into his living room from my house. I woke up one morning, after a few hours' sleep following a great party, only to look across and see people still dancing on the tables at 10am! It was a legendary party venue. Gary and I also have the same music systems, and on the odd occasion that I have been out and had a few drinks and Gary has stopped in, I sneak across and turn his stereo on full blast through the window with the remote control! Gary always sees the funny side although his missus usually does not.

Gary is the kind of friend everybody could wish for. Nothing is too much trouble for him. For my 25th birthday party, we were given the weekend off and arranged to go to a school-themed disco party in Manchester, all dressed as schoolboys. Gary was playing for Orrell rugby union at the time, so a group of us went to watch him play in the afternoon and have a few pints of Guinness at Edge Hall Road before we caught a minibus to Manchester, where we met Brian Carney.

Brian was unaware that I was already pretty drunk, I was hiding it pretty well, and in the first bar we went into he bought me a customary birthday drink. I don't know what was actually in this concoction but I certainly regret drinking it—half an hour later it hit me like a steam train. I couldn't stand, focus or function. I sat on the floor outside the bar, dressed as a schoolboy with my head in my hands and, to this day, it is the most drunk I have ever been. Gary saw me and was obviously concerned, so he flagged down a taxi, ushered me to it and asked the driver to stop off for a few cans for him on the way to taking me back to Wigan. Gary put me in bed, got back in the taxi and made the 30 mile trip back to Manchester to carry on partying—I can't imagine what would have happened if he hadn't done that.

My friendship with Gary means the world to me, I spend a lot of time with him and his wife Kath and they are an amazing couple. When they had their son, Adam, a few years ago I started crying when I got the phone call. Adam has become one of my best pals—we occasionally go to the cinema together, and sometimes he'll call around to watch cartoons at my house—he'll go on to break a lot of hearts when he's older. Gary has a big lawn and therefore has a sit-on mower. Adam loves to drive it but needs adult supervision. One afternoon we were on it together and he shouted over the noise of the machine, 'I love you Rads'. I nearly crashed into Gary's apple tree, as I was very emotional.

Gary looked after me on my birthday, but I was normally the sensible one. I was the player who looked after the group. I can't tell you the amount of arguments I've had to defuse before they boiled over. I wanted a stress-free night. I was approachable and so people would always come to me to report any bother, and bouncers would always come to me if the lads needed to calm down. Some players act like idiots when they go out but, generally, rugby league players don't differ from any other bunch of blokes on a night out. They were just there to have a laugh;

unfortunately, sometimes drunk guys tried to make an impression in front of their mates and tried to start a fight. I did my best to put those fires out, I hated trouble, and I also knew that even a minor skirmish could be blown out of all proportions when it was passed around, from a few shoves and short words into a scene resembling a Hollywood fight!

I loved seeing the transformation of players once they let their hair down. Brian Carney lived his life in such a strict and disciplined way—his training habits and diet were impeccable—but when the season was over he would always be the life and soul of the party; and usually the messiest. One of his favourite tricks was turning up in strange clothes, or asking old men in a pub whether he could buy their jackets. He was well known in all the charity shops in his village as he spent so much time rummaging for the best gear from the sixties and seventies.

Brian is one of my closest mates, and people often ask me how I met him. It was in Edinburgh, during a game against Gateshead that had, for some reason, been moved to Scotland. But I only shook his hand after a disappointing game—we lost 20–16—and there was no inkling then of the friendship that would be formed in the following years. In fact, the only reason I remember our first meeting at all was because of one incident; our team coach was behind a bus for about two miles, and on the back seat of the bus, there was a young couple, half-naked, going at it! They weren't bothered that we—and anyone else nearby—could see them. As soon as they were spotted, about 20 blokes rushed to the front of our coach, all cramming for a glance of the Scottish exhibitionists! Fair play to the bloke, he gave her a fair seeing to!

Brian also shared my passion for travelling, and he was—as many know—a real prankster. One time in Prague, he got our great friend Lee Heaton (his nickname is Lee-thal) with a corker. The two of them were sharing a room; I roomed with another of my good friends, Wigan's former physio Rob Harris. We returned to our rooms after an afternoon stroll and Lee said he wanted a lie down, so Brian told him he would come to our room. Lee's head hadn't been on the pillow a few minutes when there was a knock at the door. He opened it to find the pretty Czech girl who we had seen at reception. 'Toilet, problem?' she said, in pigeon English. A few feet away, Brian's ear was pressed to our room door listening in, his hand covering his mouth to contain his laughter. 'Toilet, problem?' she repeated to Lee.

'Is there?' Lee exclaimed in surprise, completely unaware, and invited her in to inspect. Well, without going into too fine a detail, Brian had made a real mess in the bowl. The poor Czech girl discovered this when she lifted the toilet lid. The colour drained from Lee's face. So there was born the classic 'back to fronter'. You don't need to be a biologist to work out how it's done.

Brian seemed to have family everywhere. One year we made a trip to Florida with Andy Johnson, a former Wigan team-mate of mine, and after a couple of calls, Brian discovered that one of his uncles worked at an exclusive hotel in Miami that had actually featured in the film, *The Bodyguard*. He got us a great room there and our days were spent sipping cocktails around the hotel's gigantic pool. I mentioned before Brian's impeccable training habits; he wasn't always like that. When he first came to Wigan he pretty much ate what he liked and in Miami, he ate burgers non-stop. He put on weight by the minute. It was only when he saw the photos when we got home (and having endured the shame of being beaten by our prop, Danny Sculthorpe, on a pre-season training run) he changed his eating habits completely.

We spent our Miami nights hitting the famous South Beach bars where you would find the best-dressed, best-looking people. And they could all dance—really dance—salsa, tango and stuff like that. Here were three rugby players sipping pints at the bar, and if that didn't stick out, then our 'running man' dance moves certainly did! Andy and Brian were two good looking guys at the time but at this point my nose was all over my face, so Miami was not really good for my ego.

Brian's brother, Liam, worked in a restaurant in Key West, about six hours' drive from Miami. He told us to come down for a 'Fantasy Fest' that we couldn't miss, so we hired a car and drove down the beautiful Florida Keys. We broke up the trip by going snorkelling along the reefs and, when we made it down to Key West we met Liam on Duval Street, the place where it all happened. We literally turned into a street of madness—it was 11am and there must have been 70,000 people having a street party. We were speechless. There were musicians, street floats, people in fancy dress, women with painted bodies—and not a sober person in sight.

It was a hot, sticky day, and with everyone else practically naked, we saw no harm in taking our t-shirts off. It was the turning point of our day. After soaking up the atmosphere, we walked into a nearby bar and, amazingly, we were stopped by a burly doorman and ordered to put our tops back on. I say amazingly because everybody on the street was practically naked!

The guy told us that men needed to wear a t-shirt to get into any bar on the road . . . the only problem was I'd dropped mine in a puddle down the road, so I had to go and buy a new one. At the shop, we also bought massive foam cowboy hats to get into the party mood, but when I went to pay I noticed that a lot of people were buying necklaces of beads. Intrigued, I asked the shop keeper why the beads were so popular and, after convincing him that I wasn't winding him up, he told me the details of the party. 'Fantasy Fest' happened every Halloween and lasted day and night for a full week. Like most festivals, it had its own tradition which he outlined: 'You offer these beads to a woman whose breasts you want to see.'

'Do they not get offended?' I asked. The reply was the one I had hoped for.

'Hell no, that's why they're here.'

Brian, Andy and I left the shop with more necklaces hanging from us than Mr T. The next few hours were a surreal, hazy blur. I think we drank strawberry daiquiris out of two foot aliens and I'm sure there was a roller-boots incident and somebody with a shark bite. I know we handed out beaded necklaces like confetti. And I never laughed as much in my life as I did that day.

I feel blessed that I have had so many wonderful times in my life, so many great nights out. And when I am an old man, sat in my rocking chair, I will still chuckle at the dream-like memories of Fantasy Fest . . . and wonder just what the hell happened down there.

13

WANTING TO WIN FOR SOMEONE SPECIAL

'We're here for a good time, not a long time.'

Mike Gregory

OUR 2002 season had been enjoyable and pretty successful, but a raft of injuries saw our Super League campaign fade out. We lost five of our opening 29 matches, four of our final seven games, but it had still been a success because we had won the Challenge Cup Final at Murrayfield. In February 2003, we embarked on our next Challenge Cup campaign with the easiest of obstacles—a match against Widnes amateur side, Halton Simms Cross. After the euphoria of the previous season, it was an exciting time, but an early morning phone call instantly changed all that. Brian Carney phoned me at about 8am. I could tell from his tone of voice that something was wrong. He told he that there had been a car accident, and that two of Wigan's alliance players, Billy-Joe Edwards and Craig Johnson, had been killed. I was speechless. And numb. I knew both players pretty well; they both had promising careers ahead of them, but more than that, they had the rest of their lives to look forward to. Only the weekend before, Craig had been at my house having a few beers and a few laughs with us. My thoughts turned immediately to Paul,

Craig's brother and a team-mate of mine at Wigan since he came into the first team in 1996. I asked Brian if he knew how PJ was. He said that he was wandering the streets in distress, so he was going to pick him up and bring him to my house.

They arrived a few minutes later, and PJ was as white as a ghost. He was emotionless, in a state of shock, and I didn't know what to say to him. Craig and Billy-Joe lived their lives to the full, they were always happy and joking—I kept asking myself, 'Why has this happened?' PJ stopped for a while, but he was just not with it—it hadn't sunk in that his brother had died. When he went back to his mum and dad's, I sent a text to Giz—Shaun Edwards, Billy-Joe's brother—to tell him how sorry I was, though I knew no words could help him. I was so drained and disillusioned with the incredible injustice of what had happened, I couldn't imagine what their families were going through.

Our Challenge Cup game went ahead but it was a miserable affair; we had the minute's silence but rugby didn't mean anything that day. We just went through the motions, I scored a hat-trick and we won by more than 80 points, but it didn't matter. In the emotional week that followed, all the squad attended both funerals of these young guys. Both Shaun and PJ held their emotions together unbelievably well. Both lads were from great families, and to them, I'm sure it felt like their worlds had ended. I felt so helpless seeing the pain that Shaun and PJ were going through. There wasn't anything I could say, but a dip of the head, a firm handshake and a hug was probably the order of the day.

Their families visit their sons' graves daily, determined to let their spirit live on. I still have pictures up in my back room from the week before Craig died. He was in my house, unaware that his life was about to be so cruelly cut short. I'd never known anyone so young die before, and it taught me just how fragile life is. It also made me feel guilty, because I played a game I loved and got paid well for it and yet I worried about insignificant little things, while these two great, fun-loving guys had just lost their lives.

Despite the tragedy, the team started well but we were hit by an incredible number of injuries. Our 2003 Good Friday victory over St Helens when we won 24–22, is still talked about among Wigan fans as one of the most famous derby wins. It was certainly a great way for Kevin Brown to announce himself on the big stage. We'd lost our regular stand-off, Julian O'Neill; I liked Jules a lot, he'd coped with many tragedies during his life, but I'd be lying if I said I was surprised he was released. I think Wigan tired of making excuses for him; they'd been getting reports of him being drunk in pubs. I always knew when he'd been on a bender, because he'd arrive for training stinking of Jean Paul Gaultier cologne. That was his masking tool!

Browny made his debut in that match against Saints and a few weeks later produced a moment of genius—an audacious pass against Warrington that helped us to a thrilling 21–20 win. At the same time, Jamie Ainscough's career was brought to a premature end due to an arm infection caused when one of Martin Gleeson's teeth became embedded into his flesh. I was playing in the match when it happened and blood sprayed everywhere—it was like a scene from *M*A*S*H!* Jamie had come to Wigan to replace Pearl and, just like his fellow Australian, he sure ticked the box for being relaxed and laid back. He had ability, but I just wished he had a little bit more hunger. He was constantly tired, because he became addicted to those tactical computer games and would stay up late at night to play against people from other countries. He also spent a fortune on expensive *Lord of the Rings* statues.

The departures of a stand-off and a centre freed up at least one spot in our squad, but it was gruff—not grace—that our team needed, and they found the perfect man to provide it in Quentin Pongia. The former Kiwi captain was a big, mean, dirty player. He was coming towards the end of his career but he was still ferocity personified, and he would train every day as hard as when he was playing a game. He was the kind of player that the team actually lacked when he left. Q didn't say much, but he would observe who was not pulling their weight in the gym, and then question them why not. He toughened up our front row and made his close mate Craig Smith play even better, as they would try to outperform each other and they became real cornerstones of our team.

In mid-season, after a win at London, Stuart Raper told the squad that he would be leaving Wigan at the end of the season. Wigan didn't give him that long. He wanted to return home because he had a young family and he'd been in England for a few years. He wanted to leave on his terms at the end of the campaign, but I wasn't surprised that Maurice Lindsay decided to cut short his stay. Stuart was one of those characters who players would either love or hate. They either responded to his style, or reacted to it. I was one of those who enjoyed working with him, but I understood why other people did not like him. He was not at Wigan to make friends, he just wanted to be successful. Some may think that stance is admirable, especially in a cut-throat industry like sport, but it's impossible to be successful without the respect of others in your team. Even in the Wigan team I entered in the early 1990s, not all the players were the closest friends in the world, but they had that respect for each other. Stuart didn't have that from all his players.

In all my years at Wigan, I would hear fans speculating about a real 'player power' culture. I'm sure some players were asked by Maurice for their opinions about certain coaches, though I don't think anything they said would, on their own, have been enough to get a coach sacked. In Stuart's case, though, I think a few senior players had a massive role in his departure. He wound too many people up with his moody attitude. Maurice often sought the advice of senior players when he could sense there was a problem, and I have no doubt that he did that before he sacked Stuey. I was one of the senior players at the time, but I was not once asked for my thoughts on him. If I had been, I'd have said that I understood some players' concerns but I wouldn't have said it was time for him to go. Maybe a word in his ear, to see if he could change his ways a bit, would have been enough.

We trained in a gym under the East Stand, and famous motivational quotes from various historical figures and sporting greats were pinned to the walls, all mounted nicely on plaques with the Wigan logo on them. Above Stuart's office door was a quote by Stuart that read, 'Plan your work, work your plan'. The morning after he was sacked, I arrived for training to find his sign ripped from the wall and smashed up. That disappointed me enormously. Nobody knew who did it, though I've got a feeling it was a player who had a huge role in Stuart's sacking.

Stuart must have known that some players had been influential in his dismissal, and I didn't want him thinking I was one. I was still grateful to him for the faith he'd shown in me in the Challenge Cup Final a year earlier and, on top of that, I liked him. So a few days later, myself and Brian Carney went to his house with a couple of other lads for a barbeque and a beer—I think, I hope, that he knew from the fact I visited him at his home, that I had nothing to do with his exit. His departure allowed Mike Gregory to step up from assistant coach to head coach, which was a dream job for him. Though

Greg served Warrington with distinction as a player, he remained a true Wiganer and he was so happy to take charge of his hometown club. Not since Colin Clarke in 1985 had a Wiganer been in charge of Wigan, and Mike looked like he was born to do it. He was immensely popular around town; people warmed to his humour, honesty and integrity. Initially, he was only on a three-month caretaker contract, but he gave Wigan little choice but to keep him on. From his first game in charge against his former club, Warrington, he took us on an 11 match unbeaten streak.

Players hate to see former players who go on to become coaches, and forget what it was like to be a player. And let me tell you, there are loads of them, but Greg wasn't. He listened to his players, he had no ego and if you felt a little flat one day he would tell you to take a rest. He wasn't the greatest of tactical coaches, but that was over-compensated for by his methods and approach. He was a coach from the old-school who believed great teams were built on great defences, a policy I agreed with. 'Rip and tear,' was his favourite motto, and he'd yell it as he sent us to do wrestling drills, involving throwing around 30kg dummies; it's a similar skill-set to rugby league, in that it helps you turn a player on the floor. Greg would get excited on game day about the challenges that would be thrown at us that day, and it was infectious. He made you want to play for him. It's no surprise that blokes like Quentin, Craig and Andrew Farrell really took to his 'rip 'n tear' coaching style, but the backs liked him too. During his spell in charge, Brian Carney established himself as one of the top wingers in the world. I was blessed to play with Jason Robinson and Martin Offiah earlier in my career, but it was different playing alongside Brian and Brett Dallas. As a back three, we had an almost telepathic understanding—all we had to do was give each other a nod or a wink and we knew automatically what wavelength we were on, we knew we were ready to play.

Brian underlined his class when we played Leeds in the Grand Final qualifier at Headingley—it was one of the best games of the Super League era. The score see-sawed all game and there was so much tension as the prize was a final spot. Bri scored two incredible tries, the first of which I was involved in, as we combined from a kick return, Brian pinballed between defenders and scored a breathtaking try. The second try was all him—though Greg gave me a lot of the credit in the video review! Leeds put a measured kick into the in-goal, which was well chased, and I was about to get trapped which would have forced a drop-out, and obviously Leeds would have regained possession. But after regathering I just dived over the try-line, head first into the oncoming Leeds defenders. I got a real whip on my head, but it was worth it, because from the next play Brian picked the ball up from dummy-half and embarked on an all-action run to the line, in front of the euphoric Wigan fans. In a nail-biting finish, Danny Tickle kicked a drop goal to give us a 23–22 win—and make us the first team to reach the Grand Final from outside the top two.

Six days later, the day before the Grand Final, we all went to visit Old Trafford for a pre-game walk around and then into Manchester for a meal. On the coach, Greg collapsed in front of us. It was a scary sight—but none of us thought that it would be the beginning of the end for the champion guy. That incident, though, had nothing to do with our defeat. Lammy missed out through injury, which was a huge loss for us. That was my fourth Grand Final, my third defeat and definitely the most painful. After the game, I slumped to the ground, as if wanting the Old Trafford pitch to swallow me up. I was welling up, and I wasn't alone; Terry Newton cried his eyes out. Who said rugby players don't cry? Those tears showed just how upset we were. We hadn't lost in nearly three months, and it was a bitter pill for us to swallow. Bradford—coached by Brian Noble—out-scored us three tries to two, which suggests the scoreline was close, but Paul Deacon's kicking killed us off and with his six goals and a drop goal, they beat us 25–12. Some who aren't rugby league players think we hold grudges against opponents, but we don't. They're just like us—they want the same thing and, ultimately, there can only be one winner. Which is why winning is so enjoyable . . . and losing so painful. Deacs had been a mate of mine for a while and, when I held a party at my house a few weeks later, I invited him along. It proved to be a milestone decision in my life—he introduced me to my future wife.

People always wondered which girl I would end up with. Whoever she was, she would have many hurdles to overcome and tests to pass before she was given the nod of approval from my mum (the Mrs Rad test I liked to call it). Every mum wants the best for their son, but it seemed more important to my mum because she needed to make sure that whoever I ended up with was with me for the right reasons. Rachel was lucky— she didn't have to sit the Mrs Rad test!

I met Rachel in Wigan after an end-of-season drink with the Great Britain team. Her brother, Ian, is best friends with Deacs, so he knew her very well. I was attracted to her from the start and so, at the end of the night and before the party moved to mine, I asked Deacs who she was. He filled me in on how long he'd known her and gave her a glowing endorsement, saying she was a lovely girl and she was interested in me. 'Is she?' I asked. I wasted no time in seizing my chance; I approached her and, having had a few beers, I must have laid it on thick but she seemed impressed enough to swap phone numbers.

All the GB boys were coming back to my house, and I invited her along, erasing any reluctance or reservations she may have had by pointing out that Deacs was coming. We had a top night, and I hit it off with Rachel straight away. The following day, I was heading off to Miami with a couple of pals, but before I left I asked her if I could see her again when I got back. She agreed, and I texted her a few times while I was away. Two weeks later, I was at my mum's house, when mum said she had found the perfect girl for me. Mum told me that this mystery girl worked at her fitness class and even lived on her estate, and she was very chatty and pleasant. I asked mum her name and she replied, 'Rachel'. I knew straight away it was the same Rachel I had asked out two weeks earlier. Mum was well pleased—that was one less challenge to worry about!

Maybe it was fate, I don't know. All I do know is that when I did go out with Rachel again we got on really well. It was natural, the conversation flowed effortlessly and I was at ease with her. She is an amazing girl, with honesty and morals; she'd obviously been brought up very well. Everybody I introduced her to fell in love with her. My mum and Rachel became good friends, and she bonded with my sister, Nicola, who was always very protective of me. After I'd introduced her to my dad, he sent me a text as soon as we'd left him to say she was nice and asked where I found her. Rachel seemed to understand me very well. She has a laid back approach to life but also the ability to stand up for herself, and I think mum liked that in her, as she would never let me have my own way all of the time! On top of that, Rachel is stunning, and I know how lucky I am.

Her family took me in straight away, which was a relief. I knew Deacs would have put in good words for me with Rachel's brother Ian, and those reports would have filtered through to her parents Frank and Sharon. I was still conscious of the fact that some rugby players—and I'm trying to be diplomatic here—can have a reputation with girls, especially with girls a few years younger than themselves, which Rachel is. Frank and Sharon were great with me. As long as I was treating her well, they were fine with the situation.

Rachel and I were good friends initially, before our relationship got serious; we both had a lot going on in our lives, and I think the fact we were mates first really helped us.

The year 2004 proved to be an emotional year at Wigan, too, for sad reasons. Greg was getting worse, his disease was eating his body, though he hid his deteriorating condition as best as he could. He didn't want the players focussed on him, he wanted us focussed on the team, and while we never told him, our player talks were all centred around, 'Let's do it for Greg'. It must have been really difficult for him. Several times, he would be addressing the team and he'd well up, or struggle to speak. At that point, we didn't know how serious his illness was—as silly as this sounds now, we actually thought that he was just drunk on the emotions of coaching his hometown club. Coaches tended to fall into two categories, either the tacticians who over-analysed a game, or those who were great motivational speakers. Greg was in his own category.

All he had to do was look at you and ask you to do something on the field for him, and you would promise yourself that you would do the job. He could coach, too—of course he could—but his big strength was in getting the players to respect him. One example; players who have been dropped normally fall out with their coach. It's natural for them to be disappointed—they would be angry with the coach. But with Greg, even the guys who weren't picked loved him and respected him.

He introduced Filofaxes, to make sure all the players were

organised. Before we played Warrington in a Challenge Cup semi-final, I had a famous quote by Vince Lombardi, a former American Football coach, printed onto A5 paper with the Wigan crest in the background: 'A man's finest hour, his greatest fulfilment to all he holds dear, is that moment when he has worked his heart out in a good cause and lies exhausted on the field of battle . . . victorious.'

I gave a copy to every player to put in their Filofax. We won the game 30–18—Brett Dallas scored a hat-trick—to set up a final date against St Helens, two years after I'd beaten them in the Challenge Cup Final. Greg's condition was gradually but noticeably getting worse. His hands could not operate as they should, and he was taking more time to think about what to say and deliver his messages. Wigan made the decision that, after the Cup Final, he would leave to go for treatment in America and I knew he wouldn't come back to the club.

I knew it was going to be his last game in charge, and I wanted to win it for him. I always enjoyed playing rugby in Wales, even though union was the national sport, they always respected us and many of their fans had heard of the massive Wigan club. I thought we had prepared as well as we could for the game. I thought it was written in the stars that we would win it for Greg. I'd reached the stage in my career when I didn't get nervous before games, I'd get excited about playing on such big stages. The day before a final tended to be a tiring affair; the players would just sit around the hotel, killing time by drinking coffee and playing cards.

And so it was on 14th May. Seven of us lazed around the lobby, filling the time with small-talk and playing cards, when the Hollywood star Jennifer Love Hewitt walked in. I'm surprised she didn't hear our jaws all hit the tiled floor at once. She was gorgeous, absolutely stunning. We sneaked glances at her, ensuring we weren't caught, while trying our best at least to look like we were interested in our card game. To our amazement, Jennifer and her mum glided over, pulled up chairs and introduced themselves! Incredibly, they stayed with us for about two hours. She enquired about our game but for the rest of the time, different lads tried to impress her. Amazingly they tried the same chat-up techniques they used on Wigan girls in an attempt to impress one of the most beautiful and celebrated young actresses in Hollywood! Brian Carney tried the hardest, turning on the Irish charm, shooting down other players' advances and trying every trick he knew to make an impression. It was hilarious, and she seemed to enjoy herself. She was adorable and she made the boring afternoon pass a lot faster. She certainly provided a topic of conversation for our evening meal, with seven blokes each debating who she liked the most. The heated conversation was quite pathetic, really; she definitely only had eyes for me!

I always hated the morning of a big game. The minutes would drag. After a lazy breakfast, we'd go to our rooms to shower and put on our Cup Final suits. After we did that, we all met and Greg addressed us all. Just listening to him speak about his love of our club and of each of us was very touching, he could make the most unemotional player well up. I was convinced we would win. Hours later I stood in the tunnel of the amazing stadium thinking, 'How good is this?' I felt like I was born to play on these occasions, and when the beautiful Katherine Jenkins sang our national anthem it was everything I'd dreamed of. It didn't take long for my mood to change. After about 10 minutes of the game, the ball came to me on the last tackle and I attempted to kick the ball down field. As I did, Jason Hooper, the Saints stand-off, came from nowhere and charged my kick down, Saints re-gathered and scored the first try. Now I'm an honest guy, and when I made a mistake on the pitch I was the first to put my hand up and say, 'sorry'.

But on this occasion, something was wrong. There was no way Hoops could have got to me so quickly. I was standing 10 yards behind the play the ball and the Saints defenders were another 10 yards back—that means he ran 20 yards in about half a second. He must have been a few yards offside but, to my disgust, the try was given. I have looked back at the video since and my original thoughts were correct, he was a country mile offside.

From then on, the game ran away from us and we were never in it. My good friend, Paul Wellens, scored a good try on the stroke of half-time and we had a lot of work to do. The second half started pretty well for us and we should have scored early on when Kevin Brown made a break, but we never capitalised, and soon Saints made us pay as they made a break and unleashed their Australian winger Darren Albert towards the corner. He was quick, and running flat out, but I pumped my legs as hard as I could and dragged him down before the try-line. Somebody later told me that the tackle would go down in Challenge Cup history; I should have reminded him that losers rarely get remembered from Cup Finals. That tackle wasn't enough. A few minutes later Sean Long chipped over and re-gathered, and—just as I shaped to tackle Longy—he fed Willie Talau who scored a try that sealed the game. I just patted Longy on his head and told him, 'Too good mate, I can't stop that'. It was a brilliant play that probably landed him the Lance Todd Trophy, as Saints won 32–16. In 10 months in charge, Greg had led us to two finals but we'd lost them both. I felt awful for Greg.

I thought a win would have been a great tonic for him, and I felt that we had all let him down. Of course Greg did not view it that way. He thanked us and told us all that he loved us. It was just so typical of the man. After the game, I was picked for a random drugs test, and as our hotel was about 400m from the ground I told the team to go on in the coach and I'd make my own way back when I finished. That proved to be a mistake. I thought every fan would have gone home by then, but every pub had fans from every club pouring out of the doors. The Millennium Stadium is surrounded by pubs, and the fans were chatting on the pedestrianised streets. I sweated cobs as I walked through them all, my head dipped and my eyes scanned the crowd without making eye-contact. A drunken Wigan fan approached me and, for the only time in my career, gave me a heap of abuse. He said the loss was my fault, and that I'd messed up by gifting Saints the opening try. I was about to point out that Hoops was a mile offside but then I thought, 'Just take it on the chin son', so I turned and walked back to the hotel.

Denis Betts took the reins while Greg was away and to his credit, he didn't change a thing, continuing Greg's ethos. It must have been difficult for Denis, especially considering we all knew that there was a real shit-storm going on over Greg. He wanted to return to work but Dave Whelan and Maurice Lindsay didn't want him to. It was tough for the players. Mike's condition was getting worse, his hands didn't function and his speech was a little slurred, but he still had ideas and he and Denis worked brilliantly together—as well as any head coach and assistant coach I'd known. I thought he should have been allowed to come back. I couldn't understand Dave's logic. Maybe he didn't know just how popular Greg was, but he could have made so many friends instead of enemies by supporting Greg. Knowing Greg, he would have put the team first, and he wouldn't have wanted to come back if he didn't think he could do the job.

That summer, I finally discovered what had been giving me back problems for a few years. I'd been to various specialists, even those on Harley Street, and undergone various programmes and tests, but no one could tell me why it caused me so much grief. My mate Rob Harris, a physio, discovered that I had two broken bones at the bottom of my back. He put me on a core programme to fix and support my back, a programme that I stick to even now. I was in a hospital in Manchester on a Thursday, and the surgeons decided to try some injections into the lower back. I was handed a robe and asked to get changed, which I did. 'Just stay there for a minute,' a nurse told me. 'There's another patient, I'll walk her down to surgery too.'

A minute later, she knocked on my door and I went out to see her with a female patient, about 50, dressed in a similar robe. She told me she was a Wigan fan, but she didn't need to—her eyes had already told me that she recognised me. She asked me if I was playing against Bradford two days later and I said, 'Yeah, I think so'. She couldn't believe it! She loved it . . . strolling to surgery with a Wigan player, who was going to play two days later. I don't think a woman has ever gone into back surgery as relaxed and confident as she was.

As for me, I had 14 injections into the bottom of my back, and I did play two days later (we won, 32–16). Jamie Peacock was about to score and I managed to stop him, and he said, there and then, 'Some bloody tackle, that, Rads'.

I chuckled, but not at what he said, but at the thought that on the terraces or at her home or even maybe on a hospital ward, there was a 50-year-old Wigan fan with a sore back, boring her friends that she walked to surgery with me two days earlier!

I was plagued by injuries throughout 2004, and even missed my own testimonial game against Huddersfield at the JJB Stadium because of a knee problem, but it was still special to celebrate my 10-year milestone. Staying at one club throughout a career is not very common in modern day sport and it's something that I am proud of. We had events all through the year, all run by the diligence of my dad; he worked his socks off with my committee planning every detail. He spent hours putting together my testimonial brochure and the end product was a professional-looking publication. I wanted my testimonial to be a celebration of my career at Wigan. I only had about five events and they were such rewarding nights for me—not necessarily financially, but emotionally. One event at a hotel in Wigan was a special affair. It was a dinner with music based on songs from the movies, and we had a band called 'The Diamond Girls' sing and serenade me, which was incredible. The only sour note was that somebody bid for my Super League Dream-team shirt and took it home without paying for it! To this day I've no clue who did it. Humphrey and Dorothy Moon who own the local Toyota dealership in town sponsored the whole event. These two incredible people have helped me all through my career and I have much to thank them for.

14

RETIRING

'Rugby league is my oxygen. Without it, I can't exist.'
Adrian Lam

IN THE YEARS I'd played the game, I always got on with my coaches. I always felt wanted and respected. I became one of the senior players, but I'd never stopped wanting to learn. At 29, I was as hungry and driven as ever, and though the team struggled to recover from the loss of Andy Farrell to rugby union in 2005, I was determined to step up and help smooth the transition. With the team hitting a sticky patch, Ian Millward was brought in as the new head coach, but with Denis Betts working as his assistant. I was excited about Ian coming in. I'd respected him for years, he was an awesome coach and he'd achieved tremendous success with Saints. I'd only met him fleetingly, and we'd always got on, although I'd seen comments that he'd made about me, basically saying that other players were better and that I wasn't in the same league as some other full-backs. I brushed that off—everyone is entitled to their opinion—and when he came to Wigan, I wanted to change his opinion of me. It wasn't long, though, before I realised it was going to be difficult working together. As much as I respected him, I didn't feel I got any respect back.

I only played two games with Ian in charge, my hopes of making an impression on him coming to an abrupt end at Wakefield at the end of July. On the stroke of half-time, Wakefield stabbed a kick through for their winger, Semi Tadulala, to chase. A big and pacey Islander, I sprinted across and threw myself at him as he re-gathered the ball. That's when I felt my knee go. It wasn't that painful, but something had given way—it didn't feel right. The half-time hooter sounded and I limped off, into the dressing room. I'd only been back from a knee injury a few weeks, this was the last thing I needed. I iced the joint at half-time and struggled through until the end of the match, which we lost.

After the game, I didn't get my knee seen to immediately. We'd all been given four days off to go away and recharge the batteries. I'd booked a trip to Rome with Rachel, and I was going to propose to her. The next morning, as we waited for our flight, I looked at my knee and it was huge—it had swelled so much—but I thought, 'I'm going to ask Rachel to be my wife and everything's planned out, I can't call it off now'. When I got to Italy, I tried to nurse the injury, applying plenty of ice and spending free time in the hotel pool. I had a great time exploring an incredible city, but my knee was in a terrible way. I knew I'd done some damage, but there was little I could do, so I tried my best to block it out of my mind and enjoy myself.

On the Sunday night, we went out for a meal outside the magnificent Pantheon—it was a perfect setting for a proposal. I'd been calm in all the planning, and given I'd played in front of thousands of people and hundreds of thousands more on television, I didn't think I'd have any problems. But I was more nervous than I thought I'd be, and Rachel was probably wondering why I was going through so much red wine! After the meal we strolled to the amazing Trevi fountain, where I planned to pop the question. I had bought the ring three weeks earlier, but it was hard to hide the box in my jeans— especially considering I was already drawing attention to myself with my limp. We arrived at the fountain, which I imagined would be deserted, but it was bustling with couples and families. 'There's no way I can go down on one knee here,' I thought, so we carried on strolling and I made a quick decision to do it on our way back when, hopefully, the crowd had dispersed.

We walked back to the fountain around midnight and I couldn't believe it, it was still packed! I knew there was no turning back, it had to be done. So we made our way down the steps and sat on the wall near the bottom. It was a beautiful sight, all lit up, and I was about to drop down to one knee when I realised with one knee so knackered, there was no way I could! A big crowd, unable to bend on one knee . . . hardly the dream proposal I'd planned. So instead of doing the traditional proposal, I turned myself to face her and asked her if she would spend the rest of her life with me. I opened the box containing the ring, she looked down and burst into tears. 'Yes,' she sobbed. I was conscious that there were people around us, all staring, though I was surprised when they started taking photos of us! I didn't care, I was lost in the moment. I became emotional and, within a minute or two, we were both on our phones to break the news to our parents.

When we returned to training, Wigan had arranged a couple of days away in Bangor at a university, a chance to torture us for having some time off. Still in a lot of pain, I kept news of my knee injury to myself and decided to try all the training. One part of the training was the dreaded five-minute run, which is basically a test to see how far you can run in five minutes with a minimum pass mark of 1,300 metres. That's an achievable standard for most but, after a few days off, still quite difficult. Even though I was in pain, I did the run and actually made the pass mark. I was pleased I'd made the mark, but I knew things weren't good—my knee was enormous. I showed Emma, our physio, and she said I needed to see a doctor.

After numerous scans, I visited the renowned knee specialist Dai Rees, down in Crewe. He told me that my meniscus was spilt but in a strange way, it had twisted under itself. He recommended surgery immediately, and my season was over. The team were struggling on the pitch and, unable to help out, my mood darkened. It was at this time that rugby union approached me for a second time, and my head was a mess. I was injured, the team was struggling, I wasn't wanted by my Wigan coach and I was wanted by union. Sensing I needed to clear my head, Ian allowed me to have a few days off, so I booked a flight to Barcelona and flew out on my own.

On my second night, I walked out to get something to eat when I saw a billboard outside a bar: Sky Sports, Super League, Leeds v Wigan. 'Why not?' I thought, and walked in. I sat at the bar, ordered a beer—which was the first time I'd ever watched Wigan on TV, with a beer—and waited for kick-off. An American businessman was next to me, alone. We got chatting, and—when the game came on—he took an interest in it. I explained the rules and the basic principles and the differences between league and union, and he enjoyed the collisions and the tries . . . though, unfortunately, Leeds scored them all. Wigan tumbled to a 70–0 defeat, a league record, and I was watching it in Barcelona with a beer and my new American friend. He never knew that I was a player, he just thought I was an English guy who knew the rules, and he listened intently to the commentary throughout the game, pausing only for small-talk and to order more drinks. What made me laugh was when Eddie and Stevo, the commentators, began discussing the speculation about me possibly moving to rugby union. 'I got to tell you,' the Yank said to me, 'that Radlinski fella would be mad not to leave that joint if they're getting beaten 70–0 all the time.' I laughed my head off, and he asked what he'd said that was so funny—I was going to tell him that I was 'that Radlinski fella', but I couldn't bring myself to it. An hour later, I walked back to my hotel, depressed but still laughing to myself about what the American had just said.

My only ever argument with Ian Millward came the following week, after their 75–0 mauling by St Helens. I'd not played, though I felt for the players who had. There were some decent players in the squad but there was a desperate lack of experience. Dennis Moran, who I'd always rated highly at London, was struggling because he'd gone from being a free-spirit there—and a prolific try scorer—to a chief organiser at Wigan, and it wasn't his fault. He wasn't that sort of player. The night after their 75–0 defeat, the club arranged a meal at a Frankie and Benny's restaurant. At those official functions, when players are told that attendance was compulsory, the club always paid but, because of the bad result, the lads were told after they'd eaten that they had to pay themselves. Quite a few kicked off about it, saying it was unfair. I didn't complain, I couldn't find the energy to worry about it, but the next day Basil—that's Ian Millward's nickname—pulled me into his office and had a go at me, saying I was one of the senior players and should have helped calm them down.

He'd just led a side to a 75–0 hammering by Saints, and in doing so ensured Wigan fans would suffer a lifetime of taunts by their rival fans, and he was having a go at me for other players complaining about a restaurant bill! I couldn't believe it. Fortunately, Wigan managed to turn it around—Lammy came within a game of coming out of retirement—though another of my close friends left at the end of the season, when Brian Carney joined the Australian side Newcastle Knights. My relationship with Basil continued to be frosty, at best. Four days after my second knee operation, in December 2005, I was made to stand out on a field on an icy Wigan day and watch the team train for two-and-a-half hours. I was shivering away, and team-mates kept coming up to me to tell me to go inside—maybe they thought I was watching them through choice. The coaches, though, knew Ian had told me to watch the session, and one of his own staff even came to me and said that how he was treating me was disgusting.

Two months later, as my team-mates were preparing for the new season, my knee had still not responded to treatment. I'd seen various people about it, completed numerous training programmes, and even spent hours in a hyperbaric oxygen chamber which, like a submarine, decompressed my body to 45 foot to try to aid the repair of my knee. Still there was no improvement. I was stuck in a rut. The surgeon was reluctant to operate on the joint again as he said it would almost certainly lead to arthritis later in life. And on top of that, I didn't feel wanted by Millward. Eventually, reluctantly, I called my advisor, Andy Clarke, and asked him what options I had.

Mark Leather and Emma Fletcher, Wigan's physios at the time, were helpful and tried to keep my spirits up, but they were up against it—I was doing little more than wandering around the stadium, doing the little bits of training that I could. I put on a brave face, and told anyone who asked—and living in a town like Wigan, there were a few—that the rehab was going well, but privately I was becoming more and more depressed.

On the night of my testimonial game in February, Maurice

Lindsay called me into his office at the stadium for one of his chats. Maurice was well known for these pep-talks, and he was usually good at them. He had an uncanny ability to say the right thing, and could charm even his biggest critic. His office was filled with pictures of his most memorable times in the game, and he would often bring the pictures into reference when he was speaking to you.

That night he told me that my surgeon had called him and said that it was now time to pick up my training, and suggested that I picked a game in about four weeks time to target as my return. He felt, Maurice told me, it would be better to have a goal to aim for, and suggested that I did everything I could in order to be fit for that game.

Maurice made me feel good about myself. He told me that I had been his favourite Wigan player for the last decade, which meant a great deal considering the awesome players who had played for the club. I left his office feeling refreshed, and wanted. My knee still hurt, but he'd told me what I wanted to hear.

Desperate to sort the problem out, I made a trip up to Middlesbrough to visit a knee specialist for a second opinion. Mark, our physio, drove me up there. I liked Mark, he had joined us having spent most of his career in football but our coaches—in particular our conditioner, Steve Walsh—felt he was treating us like footballers, and that he needed to toughen up. It was hard on the players. They would see Mark, and he would advise them on their course of rehabilitation, and then they'd leave the physio room to be told by Walshy that they should be doing something completely different. That really annoyed me, because Walshy was undermining Mark's experience when really he should have been sticking to his own job and letting Mark do his. It was difficult for me, because I enjoyed the company of both, though I sided with

Mark. Even so, it wasn't the best working environment especially for the injured players, and all the other players were picking up the awkwardness.

The specialist in Middlesbrough injected dye into my knee and sent me for a scan so he could see what was happening. After reviewing the scans, he said he would recommend surgery in a few weeks time—I'd only had an operation a few weeks earlier and he said it was too soon to go into the joint again. My cartilage was still split on the lateral side, apparently the worst side to do it on, and my first surgeon had left it there to act as a shock absorber; basically, he felt it was better inside the knee than out. But with no sign of improvement—the knee was still painful and swollen—I was running out of options. The journey back from Middlesbrough was a long one, with Mark and me weighing up all the options. If the pain in my knee was not manageable, and it appeared it wasn't, we came to the conclusion that surgery was really the only option. Surgery never scared me, but I was paranoid about people rolling their eyes and thinking, 'He's out again'. I was conscious of what the fans, my team-mates and my coaches would think.

Still unsure about what to do, a few days later I got a call from my friend, Rob Harris, the physio, asking if I'd meet him for a brew. Rob had been Wigan's physio a few years earlier before moving on to Manchester City and then to his own practice in Manchester, and his knowledge of physiotherapy was incredible. He is a Kiwi lad, about the same age as me, and was one of my neighbours for quite a while. On top of that, I knew he cared for me as a friend, because he'd gone out of his way to resolve my back problem years earlier. I met him on a Saturday morning, a few days after my meeting with Maurice, and he asked me to tell him everything about the situation: the pain, the restrictions, the treatment, the operations, the dates, everything. He asked me to do a few exercises, then he asked me to sit down. 'I'm going to tell you something, and you're not going to like it,' he told me. I gulped, my eyes focussing on his.

He confessed to knowing everything that was going on with the knee. He was good friends with the surgeon who had done my operations and had spoken to him out of concern for me, my injury and the treatment I was getting from Wigan. Rob told me just how serious my knee problem was. He told me that I shouldn't even think about running for another two months, and even then, he told me bluntly, the problem may not be fixed. I was overcome by worry. I had that surreal feeling you get when hearing bad news, as if you're waiting for someone to say, 'No, I've made a mistake . . .' but in your heart you know that admission is not going to come.

I told him that Maurice had spoken to the surgeon and he said that I was okay and suggested that I played in four weeks. Rob told me that the surgeon didn't phone Maurice, in actual fact, Maurice had phoned him. Maurice had just picked little points out of their conversation and put together his version of events as to what should happen next. I was shocked by that. Maurice hadn't lied, but he had added things to the story. Yes, it was time for me to pick my training up and see how I responded, but it seemed the surgeon didn't say that I would be ready to play in four weeks' time. Far from it.

My good mate, Andrew Pinkerton, had accompanied me to meet Rob. I trusted these two guys with my life. I could tell that Rob felt guilty about being so brutally honest with the truth, but he did it out of friendship. I left that meeting feeling confused. I was angry with Maurice, but I didn't really blame him for what he had done. I was getting an awful lot of money from Wigan, yet I had not played for six months and there was no clue as to when I would be fit. He just needed answers and the only way he was going to get them was by seeing me play.

I was already depressed, and this news just made me feel worse. I wasn't used to feeling like this—I'd always been a happy and positive person—and these emotions were unusual for me. There were plenty of people I could trust, but I didn't know who to confide in because I'd never really had to do that before. I spoke to those closest to me—my mum, dad and Rachel—and asked them their thoughts. They all said that the only thing that mattered was my happiness. They hated seeing me like I was. In the past, when players had problems—professional or personal—I'd seen them seek help and advice from their coach. But I didn't feel like I could do that because I never felt completely comfortable around Basil. He never made me feel wanted or needed, and when we were together there would be uncomfortable silences. It was strange. I'd never felt that way with anybody else before—I'm the type to get on with everyone—but in the few months I'd been injured he never once asked how my knee was, or how my progress was going. Not once did he come over with a few words of encouragement and tell me to keep my chin up. Instead, he asked the physios for progress reports. When a player is in a bad place, they want help, an arm around the shoulder or a word in the ear. He didn't show me any respect.

I remember one weekend, being full of the flu, a few of the lads went out for a drink while Rachel, my mum and my sister, went out for a meal. I went to neither, and stayed home alone. That night, my family bumped into the rest of the lads and they all had a drink together. When Rachel got home that night she said that some of the players had told her that they couldn't understand why I was being treated so badly by Ian. She said they were all talking about it. I had sensed as much, but I dismissed it as paranoia—it seemed my first instinct had been right, after all. It all came to a head in the middle of

February, 2006. Each morning, I was making an 80-minute trip—through the madness of the rush-hour traffic—to the hyperbaric chamber, just outside Liverpool.

I was in the chamber with five or six other patients, all of whom had cancer or other serious illnesses. There was little to do, so I did a lot of thinking and a lot of soul-searching. I was unhappy, but I felt guilty, too, as I sat there with patients who had greater problems than I had. Each one of them would have given anything to have been in my shoes, but I couldn't help how I was feeling. My spirits had been broken, which was something I could never have imagined. I needed to do something about it, so I called Andrew Clarke and met him at his office later that day. I told him how I was feeling, and he said he had a meeting with Maurice later that week about another issue, and that he would test the water to see what his thoughts were about me.

I was quite surprised when Andrew phoned me, soon after his meeting, to say that Maurice was prepared to come to some kind of severance pay and end my association with the club. It seemed so quick and easy, but so strange. I was sad at the prospect of ending my career that way. But at the same time, there was an enormous sense of relief. People use the saying 'a weight off my shoulders' and I'd never truly understood it until that day.

His seeming willingness to let me go made me see events clearer. Everything made sense. The paranoia I'd been getting, Maurice trying to rush me back . . . I then remembered Maurice telling me that Ian had suggested they could go to Australia and pick up a new full-back easily. Maurice also said to me that he sensed Ian's disappointment when I agreed to stay with Wigan and turned down the chance to move to rugby union, saying that it would have freed up some cash had I switched codes. I learned there was little loyalty in sport. It's a business—Maurice needed to run the club efficiently and Ian had to produce a winning team. I was no good to either of them injured.

Maurice had been fantastic to me over the years. I can't count all the issues he'd helped me with. I had my final meeting with him to agree my severance pay, and while he was usually the one to deliver the emotional speeches, I wanted to let him know how grateful I was for all his help. I told him that, when I was growing up, I had four heroes—Dean Bell, Joe Lydon, Steve Hampson and Ellery Hanley. Over the years, I'd become pretty good mates with Dean, Joe and Hampo, but I'd never met Ellery. And, the truth was, I never wanted to. Because I knew my other heroes personally, I wanted to keep the aura surrounding Ellery that he'd had when I was a kid. He was a God to be worshipped. He wrote a piece for my testimonial brochure in which he described me as being alongside Andrew Johns as one of the very best players in the world, which blew me away, and made me hold him on an even higher plateau than I already had. I told Maurice this story, and then I said, 'Maurice, I place you alongside Ellery on the same plateau'.

He was really touched that I'd compared him to Ellery, because he loved him as much as I did. Maurice is the kind of guy to polarise opinion, and as the man who made the signings and released players, he was never going to please everyone. But I always think the fairest way to judge people is on how they have treated you, and I can't say a bad word against Maurice. As I stood to leave his office, I turned at the door and said, 'Can I please have two season tickets, for my mum and Nicola'. We both had tears in our eyes.

I saw Ian the following day at a press conference that the club had arranged to announce my retirement, at the age of 29, because of a chronic knee problem. Ian actually wished me well, and said that he was sorry he hadn't had the chance to coach me for longer. I shook his hand, thanked him as warmly as I could and walked out of the JJB Stadium with my head held high, my integrity intact—and my mind clear of any problems for the first time in a long time. The response I got when my retirement was announced was overwhelming. It made the national TV news, rare for rugby league, and every newspaper ran the story. I received so many e-mails, letters and cards from all over the country, it was really heart-warming. What surprised me most was that I got nearly as many letters from St Helens fans as from Wigan fans! They all said that I had been their favourite ever Wiganer, which was a great, if unexpected, compliment. Many players from other teams sent their best wishes, thanking me for helping them in their careers. Brian Carney sent me a message from Australia saying that I didn't realise the effect I had made on so many other people's lives. Then, the biggest compliment of them all, Shaun Edwards phoned me to tell me I would go down as a Wigan legend. Imagine hearing that from him! Personal tributes flooded in from blokes I'd played with and against. I also received a card from a 72-year-old fan, saying that she had been watching Wigan since the 1950s and that I was her favourite player. She even put a £10 note in the card and told me to treat myself!

I was disappointed that my Wigan team-mates didn't arrange a team drink for me to say goodbye, like we had always done in the past for players who left, but my mum reminded me that I was usually the one who arranged those send-offs so I didn't take it personally.

Unfortunately, the week I left Wigan, we had to put down our beloved family dog Kodie. He'd been battling cancer and was so ill, we knew it was for the best. The day was not one of my best, because as I turned left into the street where the vets' surgery was based, a car cut past me and smashed into our side. It was the other driver's fault. His car was sent spinning. We were shocked, and it took a few seconds for us all to gather our thoughts, by which time the other guy had driven off. On any other day, I would have pursued him—an idiot had just trashed my 4x4—but on that day, I couldn't care less. We were all in pieces about saying farewell to Kodie. We went into the vets, everyone kissed the little fella on his forehead and my dad carried him through in his favourite blanket, and snuggling his favourite toy. That dog was a Radlinski, he was like a little brother to me—he left a gaping hole in our family but, as I walked the street with my dad later that afternoon, we reminded each other that we'd been lucky to have him enrich our family.

In the days after I'd retired, I had no regrets, no second-thoughts. I was completely at one with myself. My eyes welled when I read some of the tributes to me from great players, I felt humble and satisfied with what I'd achieved in the game. Sport has more rewards than other jobs—both financially and personally—but it is far more ruthless than most industries, and it carries greater pressures. I'd played at the highest level in arguably the most competitive era, and done so with honesty. I felt content and proud of what I'd done, and I was happiest for my family. They deserved the credit, because without them I would never have enjoyed such a successful career.

I'd left happy, but the club I left wasn't in such a healthy shape. Some people wouldn't believe this but, when I left Wigan, it was costing players to play for 'the world's greatest rugby club'. Wigan were taking £20 a month out of every player's monthly wage to pay for the club suits. Players had to join the JJB Heath Club, even though Dave Whelan—the club's owner—also owned Wigan Warriors, and we were also given a list of equipment that we needed to buy at the beginning of pre-season training. It included a bike, weightlifting shoes, goggles, flippers, sunglasses . . . the list was quite extensive. Players were given training gear, but if any didn't fit, they couldn't swap it for a different size, they had to go to the shop and buy themselves new gear! I can only imagine what would have happened at the start of my career had the club presented Kelvin Skerrett and Neil Cowie with a list of equipment that they needed to buy and pay for! Young lads told me that they couldn't afford all the equipment, and that a quarter of their yearly wage had been spent on buying it. When I'd first got into the first team, there was prestige about it. A kudos. We got everything given to us and all our needs were looked after—the club realised that a happy player was a better player. When I left Wigan, players had to buy their own boots and trainers—even though JJB Sports, the country's biggest sports chain, were our main sponsors. I left an unhappy club, players with little confidence. Wigan with no magic.

When they started the 2006 season and lost six out of their first seven games, players phoned me up on the way home from games asking if I could speak to Maurice about how bad it was, even though I wasn't there anymore. I didn't, because it wasn't my area, but the players I spoke to weren't enjoying their jobs. I understood them completely, as I had not been either. In some respects, my injury had given me an exit route—I don't know what I'd have done had I been fit and in the team at that time. The players had no way out and had to tolerate a regime that they couldn't confront because they knew it would cause greater upset.

Ian was a very good coach, his track record proved that, and some of his ideas were great. I remember once he did a tackling drill in which he made players hold tennis balls to

Me, Gary Connolly and Andrew Johnson on a boxing night in Wigan

Every boy from Wigan's dream

On the open bus tour after the 2002 Challenge Cup Final victory—I was shattered but a happy man. Note Ricky Bibey's underpants destroyed and wrapped around his head. It's a tough school

This is me scoring a try in the semi-final of the Challenge Cup in 2004 against Warrington

Rugby league is a tough game but wearing the GB Lion makes it worthwhile

Scoring my first try against Australia at the KC Stadium, Hull 2003

Scoring a try off an Andrew Farrell kick. He set up many a try for me

Me and Rachel in the Coliseum in Rome the day before I proposed

Losing hurts. Me after the 2003 defeat to Bradford in the Grand Final

The last ever game at Central Park. A poignant and special moment with Gary and Simon

Catching squid in Australia. Craig Smith cooked the squid later that night, and we shared it with Brian and Furnsy—great friends and memories

The church in Warsaw, Poland where my dad and I found his dad's grave. It was an emotional day

Mum, Rachel, me and sister Nicola at Buckingham Palace after receiving my MBE

Dad and me outside Buckingham Palace after I received my MBE—you've never seen a prouder man

All the family on our wedding day

Mum, Nicola and me in our favourite restaurant in Florida

encourage them to use their shoulders in the tackle, rather than their hands. It was a great drill, and one I'd never done before.

But players need to want to play for the coach to be successful, and Wigan didn't feel that way. Having a coach humiliate some players wasn't going to win any games, or friends. Some fans would say that if the players didn't want to play for the coach, they should have played for the fans and for the badge, but it wasn't that easy. The lads thought about the fans frequently, but our supporters didn't realise how bad the situation was. Basil took the praise when the team won, but when they lost it was the players' fault, and that created a bad vibe. Players were suffering from a lack of confidence and, with the fans' pressure too, it was a horrible position to be in. At the start of 2006, when I saw the players taking the field to play for Ian Millward's Wigan, people asked whether I envied them. I didn't.

I felt sorry for them and, worse still, I feared for them.

15

THOUGHTS ON THE GAME

'I'm tired of hearing about money, money, money, I just want to play the game, drink Pepsi and wear Reebok.'
Shaquille O'Neal

I LOVE rugby league. I love the life it has provided me, the friendships it has given me and, just like when I was a child, I love the game itself. It's an amazing game, fast and ferocious, and one we should celebrate more often. Aside from potentially reducing the number of substitutions, there's nothing about the game itself that I would change. It's a great product. But, with a little more common sense, I believe the sport could be improved and ultimately strengthened.

Jack Gibson, the Australian coaching guru famous for his pithy one-liners, once said that rugby league must be a great game to survive the people who run it. I think he had a point, and that's what this chapter is about—why I think our game is so great, and why those in charge so often ruin it. Here are some of my thoughts on rugby league. They are wide-ranging, from my respect for players through to sponsorship, expansion, the salary cap and the international game. Gibson was right, rugby league is a great game. And it could be made even greater.

I respect anyone who plays, or has played, rugby league. It doesn't matter if they play for Cronulla Sharks in the NRL or Shevington Sharks in North West Counties amateur league, they still have the guts to pull on a rugby jersey, take to the field and put their bodies on the line. That deserves respect. Players of our game need to be fit—just retreating 10m in defence for repeat sets can burn your lungs—as well as strong, fast and skilful. Professional players are usually the ones with higher levels of these qualities than amateurs; great players are usually those who can perform under the highest pressure, but everyone deserves applauding. In my mind, no other sport demands more from its performers.

Rugby league is one of the toughest sports in the world, that's plain for everybody to see. There are other tough sports—I've got immense admiration for boxers and their punishing training regimes—but I think our game is the toughest, because of the amount of pain tolerance players have. Rugby league is often described as a contact sport. It's not, it's a collision sport, and some of the hits are brutal.

Players will often say they're 'fully fit' but they're not. Not really. What they mean is they're fit to play, but every player at the top level will be carrying an injury of some sort. It might have been picked up the week before or in training that week, and they won't moan about it, or allow it to prevent them playing unless the physios, doctors and coaches say so. It might take strapping and padding and even a few pain-killing injections, but if a player can take to the field, they will. Not only do they want to play, but they want to satisfy their own pride, and they know that playing through pain earns respect from their team-mates. That's why, if you see a player get smashed in a tackle, you will see him bounce up straight away if he can. He does not want to let the guy who has tackled him know that he is hurt. His pride won't allow it.

It's also why rugby league changing rooms often resemble a scene from *M*A*S*H* after a game. The floor will be littered with used strapping and puddles of blood, and doctors and physiotherapists will hand out pain killers and anti-inflammatory pills. Many of the injuries that blighted the end of my career were niggles—muscle strains, cartilage tears—and they're the worst type because they're impossible to overcome or shake-off. They're the injuries that are the most frustrating. There are many instances when the bravery of players has been well-documented. Remember Shaun Edwards playing in a Challenge Cup Final with a smashed cheekbone? Or Andy Farrell returning to face Leeds with his broken nose heavily strapped up? My foot infection during the Challenge Cup Final in 2002 was also in the public domain, but these aren't isolated instances. Every week, players show courage by taking to the field with various injuries, wanting no fanfare or fuss; self-satisfaction is ample reward for them.

I once played for eight weeks with injections in a broken bone in my hand, which still gives me grief now. It was only discovered while I was getting X-rayed for another hand injury! It didn't stop me playing; five minutes before each game, I saw the doctor to get it needled, which hurt like hell. I did that for as long as I could, but I couldn't operate my hand fully, and when I knocked-on against Widnes and got a huge bollocking from Andrew Farrell I knew it was time to get it sorted out!

Two days later, I went under the knife, had a metal plate inserted and missed the next three months. Such stories are not unique, every player has their own stories to tell about injuries. That's why, by the time I'd retired, I'd had stitches all over my face, three teeth knocked out, my nose broken nine times, broken my wrist, dislocated several fingers, torn hamstrings and had surgery on my ankle, knee and back. That comes down to mental toughness and, while I was playing, if I saw a team-mate struggling I would look him in the eye and tell him that he was doing a good job; that usually helped him find the inner-strength to carry on. In the American Football film, *Any Given Sunday*, Al Pacino plays a coach who delivers a brilliant speech called 'Peace with Inches'. It's inspiring. It's about going that extra inch for your team-mate because he'll be going that extra inch for you, and when you add up all those extra inches it makes a difference between winning and losing, between living and dying. Just writing about it now is stirring something up inside me.

I always made it a personal goal, before every game, to out-play my opposite number and the player who persistently proved challenging was Paul Wellens. I know a lot of fans compared us and debated our strengths and weaknesses; sport thrives on such healthy debate, though it used to annoy me when—two years after I'd retired—comparisons were still being made between us! That wasn't fair, because the guy still playing would be naturally fresher in the memory, but I found it a compliment to be mentioned in the same breath as Wello because he is a wonderful player. He's also a better bloke than he is a player, which tells you how highly I regard him. I've got a high regard for many people in the game, who I've listed below, but none more so than Keiron Cunningham. He is a world-class player, and it would be a small tragedy if he does not win the Man of Steel before he retires because his St Helens team-mates Sean Long, Paul Sculthorpe, Wello, Jamie Lyon, James Roby and James Graham have all won that coveted prize. Keiron deserves to be among them. For such a powerful man, he has got tremendous speed and agility, and I regard him as the best player of the entire Super League era.

I have tremendous respect for Jamie Peacock. I love how much he puts into every game. Sometimes they have to drag him off the field and you can see that his lungs are physically burning—athletes in other sports must look at him and think that these rugby league guys are crazy. It's hard to disagree. Mick Cassidy pushed his body to the limit for years, playing above his weight, while Sean Long always had the ability to control a game completely, which is a rare skill.

I think Leeds have two real superstars of our game in Rob Burrow and Danny McGuire. Not only are they exciting and dynamic to watch, you couldn't wish to meet two nicer guys. It is no wonder they are successful, they work hard and do it in such an unassuming way. They're the kind of guys I like to see winning trophies. I love people who work hard at their game, but it annoys me when they don't get what they deserve. Micky Higham was a classic example at Wigan, he just came in, never moaned and worked his ass off but never got the credit he warranted. The fans were right to be outraged when the club allowed him to leave, because good teams need to be built around players with good habits and work ethics. They are the backbone of a team and the key to success.

As a sport, rugby league is in its own class as far as respect for opponents is concerned. Players spend 80 minutes bashing each other and the next 10 minutes catching up and congratulating each other on how they've played. It's part of the game we should be proud of. No matter how heated the game might be, the sound of the final whistle instantly changes anger and conflict into concern for opponents' injuries.

There were times when, during the game, I was pushed, tackled high or hit, but when it came to shaking hands after the full-time whistle, those instances were forgotten. They weren't even mentioned—just a raised eyebrow, a shake of the hand and a 'well-played' usually sufficed. It's the old cliché about 'What happens on the pitch stays on the pitch', and it's dead right. Well, most of the time. The only player who really stung me with his actions on the pitch was my old Wigan team-mate Terry O'Connor.

I'd always got on well with Tez, he is a likeable bloke. After his switch to Widnes, we played them in a game at the Halton Stadium, and an incident occurred. I can't remember the details, but as captain that day I was allowed to approach the referee to ask for an explanation about his decision, and after I did that, Tez gave me the biggest mouthful ever. He told me where to go and started calling me a ginger this and a ginger that, among other things. It was unnecessary, and it upset me because I valued our good times at Wigan together. After the game, I showered quickly and sat on the coach on my own whilst the rest of the team were in the bar greeting their families. As I sat there, I couldn't get the incident out of my mind: how could a mate act that way? I know it was in the heat of the battle, but it was so out of order. We didn't speak for months until, when my retirement was announced, he sent me a text message apologising for the day he abused me. I accepted his apology and there's no problem there; perhaps Tez didn't know that I always found the need to defend people who got abused for having red hair. To me, it's a form of racism. What is the difference between having a go at the colour of someone's skin and having a go at the colour of their hair? It wasn't really an issue when I was growing up, but these days it's become a social joke—it's almost acceptable to make fun of it—and I'm sure there are kids with ginger hair being bullied because of it. That's why I'll do my bit to try and stamp it out. A few years ago I was watching the golf Open on TV and Gary Lineker was interviewing radio and TV personality Chris Evans. Chris commented that Gary was going grey, to which Gary replied, 'It's better than being red'. Within five minutes, I'd fired off an email of complaint to the BBC. They replied, conceding that he shouldn't have made that remark, though I doubt he was ever told.

Ironically, Lineker was one of the footballers who I loved watching when I was a child though I was never the biggest football fan. I only learned to appreciate fully the round-ball game in my late teens, and now I love watching it. Perhaps inevitably, my admiration leans towards those players who show their battling qualities—Steven Gerrard and Ryan Giggs are both skilful, and not afraid to roll their sleeves up—while I'm convinced Wayne Rooney has the attitude that would make him a star in rugby league. He doesn't dive and milk injuries, unlike many other footballers. In that respect, they could learn from rugby league but our game could take plenty from football, and other sports.

My good mate Brian Carney once told me that anyone can come up with problems, but it's far more productive to offer possible solutions too, so here goes.

Rugby league players crave respect, not recognition, but it really frustrates me that the profile of the top players is not very high. It's embarrassing, and the game's governing body, the RFL, should address this and try to turn the stars of our game into celebrities like they do in other sports. I would love nothing more than to see the likes of Danny McGuire on billboards advertising various products. I have met so many stars over my career from every sport, and one thing they all have in common is a great love and respect for our game. Many top footballers and big rugby union names can speak with authority about rugby league because they follow it, yet the RFL doesn't do enough to promote our sport. In my career I don't remember any players turning down promotional shoots or appearances; they're more than happy to do it, yet they are seldom asked. I'll give you an example: I became the first man to score 100 Super League tries and the

RFL never even recognised it. It didn't bother me at the time, but imagine that happening in other sports? I'm sure I remember a fuss being made when Alan Shearer became the first man to score 100 Premiership goals—it's a great opportunity to generate some positive publicity for the sport, yet in rugby league such milestones often pass with little mention.

Rugby league players are put through hell but, unlike other sports, they get few perks from the sponsors of the game. Now don't take this the wrong way and start thinking, 'Here's Rads, moaning that he didn't get enough freebies . . .' That's not the point. D'N'B is the official soft drink partner of the RFL. I love Dandelion and Burdock and can afford as much of it as I want, but why not have players marketing the product? engage Mutual Assurance sponsor Super League—why aren't players offered pensions or investment advice? Players are Super League's most important commodity and little gestures go a long way to making them feel treasured. Jason Robinson has told me about some of the perks on offer in rugby union— they're very attractive—and they put rugby league to shame. Union players, generally, earn a lot more than league players, while footballers, cricketers and other sports stars command wages that put rugby league players into shame. I was well paid throughout my career, but when I hear of footballers earning £100,000 a week, it kills me. Rugby league players are just as committed and dedicated to their sport as footballers are to their sport, and I know footballers have far more income from TV revenue, sponsorship and gate receipts, but we also have a salary cap in our sport that puts a wage ceiling on players' earnings. That means even if clubs could afford to pay players more money, they are prevented from doing so.

One of the positives of the salary cap is that it has levelled up the competition—something needed to be done to prevent a club emulating Wigan and buying all the best players. But it's the players who have suffered. As I said, I was well paid throughout my career and I'm not complaining about the money I earned, but I trained and played with blokes on far less money and I feel obliged to fight their cause, because the salary cap is not fair on many rugby league players. Those who reach the top of their game by becoming professionals, and then risk their long-term health by playing the game, should be able to earn their true worth. They often only play the game for 10 or 12 years; of course they want to earn as much money as possible. I know some fans would say, 'Many guys would play for free', but they miss the point. Players need money to pay the bills, and they also deserve it. Clubs make a lot of money from gate receipts, sponsorships and from television income. Surely the players, the very people that fans tune in or turn up to watch, should get their fair share.

How many other industries have a ceiling on wages? None. People in some jobs get bonuses if they perform well, yet rugby league players can't. And consider this—pay usually rises in line with inflation, which means most people get a pay rise each year. Teachers, nurses, journalists, taxi drivers . . . whatever the profession, they are earning more money than they were a decade ago. Yet in rugby league, because of the introduction of the salary cap, our top stars are probably earning less now than the top stars a decade ago. No matter how well they perform, there's no bonus as the salary cap will not allow it. If other workers had to put up with those conditions, I dare say it wouldn't be long before they jumped ship to other professions where they could earn more money. Well, rugby league players work under that strict pay criteria, and some have jumped ship to the only other industry open to their skill-set—rugby union.

I'm not a marketing expert, but I'm convinced one area

they could really strengthen the profile of rugby league is through bigger, better-known sponsors—even if they don't get as much revenue. Forget the engage Super League—why not take the hit and have Coke Zero, Pepsi, Nike, PlayStation or Sony sponsoring our competition? Even if they only offer a fraction of the memory that smaller companies give them, the fact that the competition would be called 'X-Box Super League' would tell the world that rugby league was big time.

It looks like rugby league will always be confined to the M62 corridor and that angers me. I know many people from all over the country who will stay in and watch the games on a Friday and Saturday night but that's not enough. We need more people through the gates to expand the sport. We have tried on numerous occasions to expand our game into different regions but none have really worked. I know the Catalans Dragons have done very well in the last couple of Super League seasons but has our game benefited from it? Their team was mainly built on Australian exports, so it's not helping the French game much—as their performances at the 2008 World Cup showed. Eyebrows were raised when the Celtic Crusaders were invited into Super League. If this takes off over the coming years and they do reasonably well, they could be a sleeping giant as the Welsh people love their rugby. I do think that they should be given a limited number of imports, though, and local young Welsh guys should be drafted in.

Such expansion shouldn't be at the expense of weakening the rugby league heartland. Widnes, for example, are a Super League outfit in the making, with a potential following of thousands. They have played a huge part in the history of our sport and this should not be forgotten—they deserve their place in the top-flight. I would also love to see a Cumbrian Super League side. They absolutely love the game up there but, sadly, they are too stubborn to combine their two biggest teams, Whitehaven and Workington. These two towns hate each other—and knowing the feeling between Wigan and St Helens, I know why they want to keep their own identities—but combined they would be a real strength. The RFL should play to their strengths and try and make the game in the heartland even stronger. They need to realise that Cumbria has a huge rugby league following. Forget taking the game on the road to Scotland—if we had a weekend in Cumbria with all the teams up there, it would be an overwhelming success, and the fans would love staying up in the Lake District. Gary Connolly and I went up to Barrow last year to present their end-of-season awards and we were treated like Gods, we felt like Ant and Dec on stage, posing for photographs and signing shirts and even women's breasts! The people at the RFL are sometimes blinkered and need to listen to what the supporters, and players, of our game want. Without the fans, and the players, our game is nothing, yet sadly neither are treated as well as they should be.

I, like everybody else, was hugely disappointed with our 2008 World Cup campaign. I genuinely felt that we could go down under and push for the title. How wrong I was. The Grand Final between St Helens and Leeds was one of the toughest and most exciting games I've seen, and I'm not sure why that intensity could not be replicated on the international scene. After the World Cup fiasco, people began to question whether we had too many overseas players in our competition and if it was weakening our international side, but of the 34 players that were on display in the Grand Final, only seven were overseas. St Helens and Leeds, our two most successful sides, are also the two sides with fewest overseas players. I think the players involved in the Grand Final—and subsequently, many England players—saw Old Trafford as the pinnacle of their season and careers. That may sound strange, considering there was a World Cup at stake, but in the back of their minds they'd have known that nothing would have changed even if they'd won the World Cup. There wouldn't have been a homecoming or a heroes' reception like the Olympians received. The guys would not have been the focus of huge advertising campaigns. 'World champion' . . . it would sound nice on any player's CV, but of the two I can't help wonder whether they'd rather have a Grand Final win and be a big fish in a small pond. There is no doubt that the profile of the game in Australia is far superior to the game in our country. Rugby league is front and back page news in the newspapers, similar to football in our country, and that increases the pressure on the players as they are constantly scrutinised. Maybe that's why they perform, as they know that a much wider and more critical audience will judge their performances. Australia could have turned out maybe five teams that had a realistic chance of beating England.

With so many more players in the game, at any level, then it seems quite logical why they're capable of producing more truly great players. With drier conditions, a stronger competition and more bodies, their talent pool is much deeper. Let's be honest, the only real superstars that the English game has created over the last couple of decades have been Martin Offiah, Ellery Hanley and Jason Robinson. And without those home-grown superstars in our game, there are no players for the children to want to emulate when they're older. We need to make the game more attractive to young guys by saying it opens just as many doors as other sports. There is no way that Austin Healy, Darren Gough or Kenny Logan, for example, were the best at their chosen sports but they are now marketed as though they were world champions. Maybe they deserve credit for having the guts to try something else. Maybe they had great management. But the truth of the matter is that whilst these all-singing, all-dancing sportsmen/celebrities are doing great, our sport is getting a smaller profile by comparison.

I've always championed rugby league. And it's not through bitterness that I make these points, but through genuine love of the game. It's a great game, and I think with better management and more common sense, it could be made even greater.

16

BEST OF THE BEST

'Perfection is not attainable, but if we chase perfection we can catch excellence.'

Vince Lombardi

IT'S A QUESTION I get asked all the time: who was the best player I played alongside? I can see why people are intrigued. From Robinson to Offiah, Edwards to Farrell, Renouf to Connolly, Lydon to Bell, I know I am blessed to have played with some of rugby league's true greats. When I'm asked who was the best, my answer is always the same, and it's often unexpected: Adrian Lam.

Of all my team-mates, through all the years, he stands out as being the best of the very best. He made the game easy for me, he was a dream to play with. If you couldn't play well as a full-back with Lammy in your team, then you shouldn't be playing the game. He joined the club at the start of 2001 and our first training session was hill runs at Haigh Hall. It was freezing—he must have wondered what he'd let himself in for! We'd already played against each other, he was always a class act, but it's only when you play alongside him that you realise how great he is during games.

As the forwards were driving the ball up, gaining us field position, he constantly talked to me. He'd ask where I was, if

I could see any gaps in the defensive line opening up . . . his mind was thinking two or three plays ahead, yet he was still alert enough to react to the unexpected. I played the best rugby of my career with him in control. His outlook on life was so positive, it was infectious—he breathed confidence into the side. He played rugby with a smile on his face and lived for the game. He lived next door to me, and he had a large trampoline in his garden. We would spend hours lying on it, looking up at the sky, and reviewing and analysing games in our minds.

I'll never forget the training session when he finally broke down with his knee—we all felt his pain, not only for his agony at that moment but because we knew he'd be sidelined for a few months—and later that night I sent him a text to ask how he was. He replied, 'Rugby league is my oxygen, without it I'm nothing'. I've never known anyone love the game as much. He loved Wigan, too, and the day he left he wrote me a letter and gave me one of his beloved Papua New Guinea jerseys that I treasure, though not as nearly as much as I treasure our friendship.

Lammy, of course, was one of many greats I played alongside. It took hours of agonising thought in compiling my Wigan dream-team. To those I left out, I apologise; there were many tough calls to make. I will say that some were selected not only on how they played, but on how they influenced and shaped my career. So without further delay, here is my Wigan dream-team from the players I played alongside during my career.

1. Full-back: *Kris Radlinski*—I have to pick me, I would have loved to have played at the back of this team!

2. Winger: *Jason Robinson*—Jason was so dynamic and

powerful, he could do things that other people only dreamed of. We used to laugh at the tries he scored in training. I'd feel sorry for the poor guy marking him because, one-on-one, he was almost impossible to stop. We might have lost the Grand Final in 1998 if it was not for his piece of brilliance in the first half. His work rate was phenomenal. As players, we were in as much disbelief as the fans at the things he could do on a pitch. He was rapid—nobody could touch him over 20 yards—and also had tremendous power and tenacity, traits that were often overlooked due to his jet-heeled running style. Jason is also a true friend of mine, and even when he reached the heights of superstardom in rugby union, he would still phone to check how I was doing. Fame didn't change him one bit.

3. *Steve Renouf*—The Pearl was so calm and relaxed, but he had that killer instinct. He didn't run through defensive lines as much as he glided through them, and found space that others couldn't. Opponents would line-up their defence and think their line was water-tight, but Pearl would flash through it. He set up the favourite try of my career, against Bradford at the JJB Stadium in 2000, when he made something very difficult look tremendously easy, timing a pass that sent me over for the match-winner with seconds to go. He also gave me his last ever head-guard, which is proudly displayed in my house. Before he left, he told me it was an honour to play with me, and for my testimonial brochure he wrote a piece saying that I was as good as Darren Lockyer. He was wrong, but it was still nice to read! Had I played more games alongside Dean Bell and Joe Lydon, two boyhood heroes of mine, then I'd have had a real headache picking my dream-team back-line. But I only played one game with Dean—my debut—while Joe was at the end of his playing career when I came into the side.

4. *Gary Connolly*—he is a close mate of mine, but our friendship has nothing to do with how highly I regarded him as a player. He was a genius of a centre. Because he started his career in the 1980s, he was old-school to an extent, as he was nurtured by the likes of Kevin Ward and his all-time hero, Paul Loughlin. He has freakish strength, especially at arm wrestling which is legendary in the pubs of Wigan.

He was probably better known for his defensive qualities—one-on-one, there was no one stronger—but he produced pieces of skill that nobody else could perform. And he had the knack of doing it when it mattered most; in tight situations and in the big games. I loved his relaxed approach to games, which differed to mine. He would sometimes sleep in changing rooms before games, or play little jokes with the linesman by hiding scissors down his shirt . . . just before they came to carry out a kit inspection! His laid back attitude and love for life—he's not nicknamed 'lager' by mistake—often masked just how knowledgeable he is about rugby league, and people often laugh when I tell them that, but he read a game with ease. He was a winger's dream to play alongside, often capable of creating something out of nothing. One of my most memorable tries was in the 1997 World Club Challenge against Canterbury at Central Park. Gary collected a high ball in the corner but he knew—in a split-second—he would be bundled into touch, so he passed the ball behind his back to me, a move the Harlem Globetrotters would have been proud of.

5. *Martin Offiah*—possessed speed that scared the living daylights out of everyone, including me. But he wasn't just a speed-merchant—he could swerve, he had great anticipation, and his skill level was under-rated because he created so many opportunities for people running off him. His slogan for Nike was 'Your hands can't catch what your eyes can't see', which was fitting, because over any distance beyond 30 metres, he was by far the quickest. Martin was the best winger rugby league has ever seen, bar none, a fact which eased my frustration that I couldn't find places for Brett Dallas and Brian Carney in my dream-team. Both were powerful and had blistering pace, and they were—and are—great mates. The best years of my career were playing alongside BD and Brian. A full-back has to develop a good relationship with his wingers, primarily to deal with kicks; Brian would sometimes field deep kicks and do these long, floated passes to me. Passing, though, was never his strength— I would shout obscenities as the ball was mid-air, nobody else knew or heard, but we would laugh about them afterwards!

6. Shaun Edwards—was the master, such a dedicated individual who demanded the respect of his team-mates. It's hard not to be successful when you have his strength of mind. He was a winner who did not know how to give in. His energy and intensity were 100 mph, and infectious, and more than compensated for his relatively small stature. Playing with Giz was like having a coach out on the pitch alongside us—he controlled a game like a puppeteer. His handling and kicking were good, but his ability to read a game and call the right play were the hallmarks of this champion.

7. Adrian Lam—even accounting for my glowing appraisal at the start of this chapter, it's hard for me to over-state the impact Lammy had on my career and also how he affected my outlook on life. He talked a beautiful game of rugby league, and he managed to play it that way too, but he was also tough.

8. Kelvin Skerrett—Super Kel, a true, old-fashioned, hard as nails prop. I loved the fact that he would not think twice about throwing a punch if somebody was annoying him. He excited the fans and had a cult following. It was good to play alongside him as he always looked out for his team-mates, and I always enjoyed going for a pint with him because no one would mess with us! The game needs characters like him.

9. *Terry Newton* — on his day, he was unstoppable. When he was enjoying his rugby and playing the game with a smile on his face, he produced some brilliant rugby. He was enthusiastic and hungry for the ball, looking to create chances on the field. He was another player I would pick to go to war with.

10. *Craig Smith* — an animal of a player, with a work ethic like no other. He put his body through so much and it worked . . . he looked like a Greek god when he took his top off! He was a brilliant leader, and had such an imposing presence in the changing rooms that everybody felt ready for the game after he spoke. He was one of the great players of the Super League era, and I missed him terribly when he left.

11. *David Furner* — he was built to play rugby league, he was simply an all-rounder who could do anything on a field. His approach was meticulous; he worked on every single aspect of the game: tackling, carrying, passing, fitness, kicking. Tough as teak (he's an awesome boxer) and enthusiastic, he threw everything into the game, and you always felt more confident going into a game when Furnsy was on your side.

12. *Denis Betts* — trained hard and played hard. The sign of a great player is consistency and he never let his standards slip. Denis always considered his team-mates, and put so much time into developing young players and improving their mentalities. He was an 80-minute player, who had a huge work rate and a great try scoring record for a back rower. He was probably one of the first modern day back rowers because he was quick as well as tough and strong.

13. *Andrew Farrell*—a giant of Wigan, and of rugby league. He wanted to win everything he attempted, no matter what the game was. All professional rugby league players are competitors; but then there are very competitive players, and ultra-competitive players. Faz was another notch above that. He was a real winner, who didn't think twice of swearing or speaking his mind on the pitch if you weren't doing your job. He would shout at his mum if she dropped a ball! I was once tackled and broke my wrist. I was on the floor in quite a bit of pain, but I didn't get any sympathy from Faz—he yelled at me to get up and play the ball, even calling me a soft so-and-so! He was one of those players who had such an imposing presence, and when he spoke, everybody listened. He was a year ahead of me at Wigan, so I played alongside him for most of my career and he was an awesome athlete. Playing for Wigan meant so much to him that he always looked for ways in which he could improve himself. Fans would see his aggression—his face was so animated during the match—but they often didn't realise when he was playing through the pain-barrier, simply because Faz refused to let his standards slip. For such a big man, he had great skill, and the ability to fire out passes like bullets.

As a player, you often get an inkling about which players will make good coaches when they retire. Lammy and Dave Furner both went on to success in Australia, which didn't surprise me one bit because both were not only knowledgeable and passionate, but they were excellent communicators. I would have loved to have been coached by Shaun Edwards. In some regards, I was, because he was such an influential player who would often take the reins during training sessions, but it would have been awesome to have him as my head coach. Who, though, would I choose to coach my select XIII? What makes a great coach? Who was the best? I intended to name one to coach my 'dream-team'. I agonised over these questions for hours; they're difficult to answer, as coaches need to wear different hats for different players. Somebody who I thought was a great coach could easily be someone else's worst coach, and vice versa. I feel I'm qualified to talk about varying coaching styles—one thing I had a lot of over the years at Wigan was coaches! It seemed every 18 months or so one departed and a new one came in.

Each one had their strengths and weaknesses, and if I could compile the ultimate coach—in some rugby league Weird Science kind of way—he may resemble something like this: he would have the man-management of Frank Endacott, the passion of Mike Gregory, the technical knowledge of Stuart Raper, Denis Betts and Andy Goodway, a sprinkling of the enthusiasm of Brian Noble and the integrity of Graeme West and top that off with the legend and aura that is John Monie. Phew, there you have it, Wigan's perfect coach, at least from the decade-and-a-half I've known. I never met a coach who had the lot. But by process of elimination, you'll notice the coaches who I didn't regard as highly—John Dorahy, who I only worked with fleetingly, Eric Hughes and Ian Millward. But just to reiterate, these are subjective, and other players may say the complete opposite of me.

I think a coach should be as willing to learn as the players, but I found that sadly that was not always the case. Some coaches seemed to think that, once they had the title of head coach, they knew everything about the game. I was always hungry for tips and advice to improve my game, even at the end of my career, but I soon learned that I knew more about playing full-back than they did. Not once did I have a coach who had played full-back during their playing careers, so how could they know how to play that role if they hadn't done it themselves? Especially when the position of full-back has so many intricacies you can only learn through trial and error. I think Wigan should have had specialist coaches specific to different positions—here's one example that, hopefully, illustrates why players would benefit.

Playing full-back requires a completely different kind of fitness than any other position. Whilst the rest of the team are going up and back 10 yards at a time, a full-back may be relatively dormant and then have to run 30 or 40 yards, at full speed, to catch a high ball and return it as fast as they can. I could go on a field and, if 100 kicks were put up, I would catch 100. But if I was tiring, it could be different, which is why skill work should be done when you're fatigued—the first thing to fade is your skill level. I never understood why I was never conditioned any differently to any other player. I discussed that with Nigel Ashley Jones, a great conditioner Wigan had from Frank Endacott's time to Denis Betts' time, and we designed drills specific to me, which I would do separately in my free time. And that's just one example of what a specialist coach could have done.

Of all the coaches to depart Wigan when I was playing, I was saddest when Denis left. I wish Wigan had persevered a little longer with him and given him a real chance, because he was a good coach and a real student of the game. Denis's biggest problem was bridging the gap between being a player and being a coach. You know the saying, 'familiarity breeds contempt'? I think everyone was a little guilty of that, myself included. I had played alongside Denis for nearly 10 years and considered him a real friend; I remember going to watch U2 with him, we had a few beers with Wayne Godwin and Brian Carney, and before long Denis was sat on Wayne's shoulders singing 'With or Without You'. We saw him as our team-mate, our mate, but in reality he was our coach . . . and there he was, sat on Wagga's shoulders! Looking back, I could have helped him out more. I should have kept some distance from him personally, because I truly believe that had Denis left Wigan for a couple of years and then returned as head coach, he would have been there for a long, and successful, time.

Frank knew how to get the best out of me. He was so positive and full of life, and he would walk through the door in a morning and hug me, and make me feel so good about myself. Frank kept a little book and in it, he would mark every player out of 10 in every game. He once pulled the lads together at training and told us all that the day before—I think we'd played Wakefield—he gave me 9.75 out of 10. That was the highest score he had ever given anyone in his entire career. I was really chuffed, because Frank had coached hundreds of games, and nearly as many New Zealand legends.

When Frank left, and I've mentioned elsewhere how heartbroken I was, Stuart arrived and I enjoyed my rugby league under him too. Stuey wasn't everyone's favourite, and he created a few enemies with his combative, moody style. For example, sometimes he would come into the gym in the mornings and walk straight past players, not even acknowledging them. But I never took it personally, it was just his way, and he allowed me to play my style, which I appreciated. Brian made me feel good about myself, he was very much a forwards' coach but his style of man-management gave me confidence. It was the same with Andy Goodway, who took over from John Monie in 1999. I got on brilliantly with Andy, and he respected what I did.

Mike Gregory was different again. He just made you want to take to the field and play your heart out for him. Quentin Pongia said he'd run through walls for that man, and I know what he meant. Greg was so proud to coach Wigan, and what followed in the months after he left the club was horrible, and made me really appreciate how fragile life can be. He was a bear of a man physically, yet his debilitating disease left him a shadow of his former self, and that tore me apart each and every time I went to see him. He remained so strong through it all, as did his sense of humour—and that distinguishable, lopsided grin—remained perfectly intact. And when he died, it hit me pretty hard—I'm sure other players will say the same. I'll never forget him, and I'll never fail to be astonished by his character. The way he conducted himself, without a shred of self-pity, eclipsed any deed of bravery I ever saw on a rugby league pitch. He was unable to move, yet he never once complained; instead, he'd ask how my family was—and he was genuinely interested. That's just the guy he was. The year he died, in 2007, I ran the Great North Run with his wife, Erica, and a team of others to raise money for Greg's charity. Erica is one of the most remarkable people I have ever met. She showed so much strength and courage through Mike's illness, and fought everything that came her way, that it taught me what unconditional love was all about. I drove her up to the North East for the run and, in the six hours we shared in my car, I learned so much from her. Mike was a popular coach, and it's not hard to see why. He was successful, sure, but fans could see how proud he was to coach the club. He had so much integrity and enthusiasm—he always used to say, 'Rip and tear, rip and tear' . . . it was an honour to play for him.

Another question I often get asked is who was the greatest player I ever faced. I have two contenders, both Australians, and it's impossible for me to split them. They are Darren Lockyer and Andrew Johns. They were different styles of players but equally as incredible, who performed magic tricks on the pitch. As with my Wigan dream-team, I've compiled a line-up of the greatest players I ever faced.

1. *Darren Lockyer*—is absolutely mercurial, he makes difficult things look easy. He never takes the wrong option, which in itself is such a sought-after trait. There can be periods of a game where he can go five or 10 minutes with no involvement, but he is just weighing up the game. Then he will inject himself into the game and produce a massive play. He has played at the top of the NRL for a decade—a true sign of a champion. He plays the game at such a high intensity and produces some consistently unbelievable performances.

2. *Lesley Vainikolo*—is a monster of a man, so powerful and surprisingly fast for such a big guy. He caused Wigan numerous problems over the years, scoring so many tries and producing powerful runs from his own half which would attract so much attention and drag the defensive line out of shape.

3. *Mark Gasnier*—is a brilliant modern day player, and a loss to the code following his switch to rugby union. He makes the difficult look easy and constantly finds himself in acres of space. That's not luck, that's talent.

4. *Paul Newlove*—was so light on his feet for such a big guy, he must have been a dream to play outside of as he created so many opportunities for his team. He never looked interested yet always came up with the goods.

5. *Wendell Sailor*—we had a few run-ins during our career. I don't know what I'd have done if he had hit me! Every time we played each other, it seemed he'd have a niggle or a push, but there's no denying his quality. He could easily play in the forwards as he is massive and so strong. He has a great work rate, and usually takes a drive every time his team has the ball.

6. *Laurie Daley*—was a genuine superstar of the game. Before a match, when I looked at the team sheet and saw he was playing, I could never believe I was playing against him. He was a tremendous defensive player for such a creative one, and a great bloke as well.

7. *Andrew Johns*—was such a talent. He was born with a ball in his hands, and had an amazing kicking game. He always produced on the biggest of occasions, and read the game like no other. He used to buzz on the field and probably the only place where he was truly comfortable was on the rugby field.

8. *Quentin Pongia*—it was awesome to have him in my team at Wigan for a spell, but to play against him . . . he was ferocious. His body was like granite, and when he hit you, you remembered! One of the most fearsome sights I've ever seen was watching Quentin do the haka before I played against him.

9. *Keiron Cunningham*—produced a high level of rugby league for well over a decade. He is a great athlete for such a big man, very light on his feet and can really move. He is a vital ingredient in the Saints machine, when he does not play, he is seriously missed.

10. *Jamie Peacock*—is an awesome rugby player. You have to scrape him off the field at the end of games. He throws his heart and soul into every performance. He has a phenomenal work rate and desire to succeed.

11. *Stephen Kearney* —when Stephen was on his game, he was the best in the world. He was the last, great 80-minute player. He was a true leader of his troops who, just by his presence, would take the Kiwis to higher levels.

12. *Adrian Morley* —is one of the toughest, yet nicest, guys you could wish to meet. Once, he smashed me in a tackle, deliberately standing on my hand and then—after I played the ball—asked me if I wanted to go to Tenerife with him! He enjoyed a great career on both sides of the world and is a massive addition to any squad, on the field and socially.

13. *Brad Fittler* —is yet another superstar Aussie. I can put my hand up and admit 'Yes I fell for the Brad Fittler sidestep'. I knew it was coming, I knew which foot it was, but he still made me look stupid. I consider myself a good defender but you can only fully appreciate the talent of the man when he performs his moves on you. A lot better players than me fell for that step and he did it for over a decade in the toughest competition.

17

COMEBACK KID

'By making a comeback, I'm changing the attitude of people towards me. If I'd have known people would have reacted so enthusiastically, I'd have done it years ago.'

Mark Spitz

I'LL NEVER forget the day I was first approached about coming out of retirement—and it's got nothing to do with the fact that it became a landmark in my career. No, that day was one of the most painful days of my life, a day I suffered agony I had never endured before.

I was in Gran Canaria with my girlfriend, Rachel—I know you're thinking that this was hardly a nightmare, but bear with me. I'm not really a sun man, never have been, never will be, and I hate sitting around the pool or on the beach thinking about nothing other than what my next meal may be. I like to keep active. We were staying in a great hotel, though we had the strangely unsettling feeling you get when you're the only English people there. Rachel went to the beach to top up on her tan, so I decided to check in for a massage before joining her. I have massages regularly, and after a relaxing, hour-long massage, with my tensions and tweaks gone, I strolled down to the beach to meet Rachel. I spent an hour with her, sitting on the sand, reading the newspaper . . . the usual beach routine. The only difference was I completely forgot about the massage oil I still had on! I hadn't showered after my massage, and it was only when we got back to our room that I realised the serious effect the sun can have.

Red-haired, fair-skinned people are never the best tanners, but this was unreal—you would never have seen a more sunburned man. It hurt to stand, so I sat down; it hurt to sit, so I lay down. Still the agonising, excruciating pain wouldn't go away. My skin felt like it was on fire, each slight shift or shuffle sending a burn scorching through my body. My face and torso were bright red and blistering, Rachel poured on after-sun but it did little to cool my skin. It was severe, so we went to the chemist—you can imagine the stares I got—and bought the strongest sleeping pills. I literally slept off the pain over the next four days. Using after-sun like it was going out of fashion, my skin eventually healed and I began to feel better. I found my mobile, noticed the dead battery, rummaged through my case for the charger and plugged it in. 'Ping'. I had a message. Then another. Then another. I made a drink and picked up my phone—eight texts and six missed calls.

Wigan were bottom of the table and had only won one Super League game out of seven or eight—before I had read the texts, I knew that they would be messages to tell me that Millward had been sacked and, sure enough, they all were. All, except for one. Among them was a text message from the Bradford coach, Brian Noble, who had coached me with Great Britain. The message simply read, 'How is the knee—Nobby'. I replied, telling him it wasn't too bad, but that I hadn't been doing any physical activity so it hadn't really been tested. He asked if he could meet me for a chat. I was intrigued and of course agreed, but I told him that I was away for a few more days. The phone calls kept coming telling me more about Ian's dismissal. One of the calls was from my mate, and former Wigan team-mate, Andy Johnson. Now AJ is the kind of bloke who knows everything about what is happening in the game before it happens—nothing escapes him. He told me about the situation, and that he knew who the next man in charge would be. He wouldn't tell me who it was, he was sworn to secrecy, and I respected his loyalty to his source. Besides, as soon as he said that, I knew who the next coach was going to be. The texts from Nobby, the secrecy over the new coach—it all clicked into place. For the rest of my break, all sorts of thoughts went round my head. I even dragged Rachel out of bed one morning for a run along the sea front, just to see what state I was in. I got a bit of satisfaction when she told me she was going to collapse; she's quite fit, so I knew my engine was still in half-decent shape.

A few days after returning home, and returning to my original colour, I answered a call from Nobby asking if he could come and see me. He was, by then, the Wigan coach. He drove up to my house, we had a brew and then he laid it on the line. He wanted to know if I would come back and play the rest of the season, if a physio gave me the nod.

Though I'd only retired earlier that year, I'd not touched a rugby ball for eight or nine months. I'd hardly watched any games—I'm a frustrating fan, especially when I'm injured—and I honestly didn't know what to think. I didn't say yes or no, but I told him I'd get checked out and do a bit of training. I had a couple of commitments—I'd booked a holiday to Australia—and I promised him an answer when I got back. He understood, and said there was no pressure. When he left, I knew he had offered me the chance of leaving the game as I had always intended, on my terms, and not with bitterness and an impromptu press conference like I'd had the first time around. But, I reminded myself, I had retired for a reason—my knee. I went to see Rob Harris, who told me the knee would get me to the end of the season if it was managed properly during training and rehab. I welcomed his advice, though I was still unsure, because I had so much to risk. As it stood, I'd left the game earlier than I'd planned, and while I had back ache and my knee was basically rubbing bone on bone, I could still run and I was still active, and I'd got out of the game in far better shape than many players. Was it worth coming back to risk injuring the knee again?

The decision weighed on my mind, my answer see-sawing each day, but I thought I'd better get fit in case I decided to return. I joined a small gym on the edge of town, Kilhey Court, and trained every morning for three weeks. I reached a reasonable standard of fitness before my trip to Australia. I convinced myself that Wigan were too good to go down, but during that time they kept losing even though their performances were improving. They still occupied the relegation spot, cut off from safety, half way through the season. I still wasn't fit enough to play anywhere near my best, but Nobby told me that was not the reason he wanted me. He wanted my experience. I put the dilemma to the back of my mind and flew out to Australia to visit Brian Carney, who was playing for Newcastle. I'd booked the trip months earlier, and I spent a great week out there with him. One thing about rugby league players is that, even if you have not seen somebody for a while, friendships just resume exactly where they left off when you see each other again.

I had not been there long and my mind was still hazy with jetlag, when Brian had me in a wetsuit with a spear gun in the ocean, trying to catch our evening meal! As luck would have it, that weekend Newcastle were playing the Canberra Raiders, where my good mate David Furner was the fitness coach. Furnsy cleared it with the Raiders that he was going to stay up in Newcastle after the match, and we had a top night 'on the grog'. Australian legends Gordon Tallis and Brett Mullins, former opponents who were at the game working as TV summarisers, were with us and we all ended up at a party at Andrew Johns' house. I was pretty good mates with his brother, Matthew, from his days at Wigan and those two are so close that Matty's mates are Joey's mates! Andrew Johns may be one of the greatest players I ever faced, and a superstar in Australia, but he's such a down-to-earth and genuine bloke, like his brother. It was a mad night which, not surprisingly, saw Craig Smith and I having our traditional wrestle! For some reason, after a few beers, some players love to wrestle and we're the same. We phoned our former Wigan team-mate, Dave Hodgson, in England because he was usually involved in those scuffles with us. He was in stitches laughing on the other end of the phone! I have a knack of phoning people when I'm drunk, it's just one of my things. Craig, Furnsie, Brian and myself sat up all night drinking and chatting on Craig's balcony talking about days gone by and cooking the squid that we had caught earlier that day. There we were, four blokes from four different countries, sipping beers and reminiscing—I was the happiest I had been in months. I raised the topic of whether I should play again, and all three did their best to convince me to give it a shot. The opinions of those three blokes, who I thought the world of, mattered enormously to me—other players had come and gone over the years and we were still mates.

Brian, who had scored a hat-trick that night, and Smithy had to disappear for a rehab swim on the beach, leaving me and Furnsy drinking bourbon on Craig's balcony. They returned, but any hope of catching a few winks collapsed when Brian announced some good news—we were going wine-tasting in the Hunter Valley with one of his team-mates, Chris Bailey. Brian hired a driver to take us around 15 vineyards, and we bought a bottle from every one of them, loading them into the boot of our chauffeur-driven car. The Knights boys couldn't believe it when we rolled up that night ready to go again! During my stay in Newcastle, I had many laughs with Brian but also some serious chats, and it was obvious that—though he was awesome on the pitch—he was not completely happy there. He missed home. I was already pretty fragile emotionally and to hear an admission like that really sent me over the edge. It killed me to leave him there. I told him how much I valued his friendship, but I had to leave in my taxi for the 90-minute trip to Sydney as I'd arranged to meet two more good friends, Willie Peters and Tony Mestrov. I also managed to fulfil a lifetime dream when I went to the Stadium Australia to watch a State of Origin game between New South Wales and Queensland—a brutal, brutal match. I loved it . . . not least because I won money on the first try scorer!

Adrian Lam was coaching Queensland's Under 18s side, and afterwards we went out and partied in Kings Cross, an area of Sydney. When I mentioned the possibility of me coming out of retirement, it was a cue to get more beers and stay up even later talking. Lammy absolutely loved his time at Wigan, not only living in England but playing for the club. It was obvious Wigan was still in his heart—if Nobby had turned down their approach, I think he'd have been offered the job—and he was hurting as much as any fan about Wigan's struggles that season. I remember looking at my watch and it was 6.15am—I couldn't believe it, the time had flown! 'Lammy, I've got to go,' I told him, 'I fly in a few hours and I've not even packed.'

'Just one more mate,' he replied, convincing me to stay.

How they let me on the plane that day is beyond me, and I felt so sorry for the lady who had to sit next to me—I had a week's worth of VB, Toohey's and Castlemaine streaming out of my pores. I must have stunk. It was a magical week for me, a chance to renew a few friendships and also for a bit of self-discovery. Lammy said one thing before he waved me farewell. 'Rads, think about how much you love Wigan,' he said. 'They might get relegated. If they do, and you hadn't played again, imagine how you'd feel knowing that you could have helped prevent it.'

Those words were bouncing through my mind on the long-haul flight to England. I landed back at Manchester tired, but revitalised. During my time away, Wigan still hadn't picked up any wins, and time was fast running out. It had been seven weeks since Nobby first approached me, six since he took the job. I knew in my heart I was going to return, and not just to help the club, but from a selfish point of view as well—I wanted to finish my career the right way.

It was the end of May and Wigan were playing St Helens that weekend, but I had one more pre-arranged commitment before I told Nobby what I was going to do—I had to take Rachel to watch Bon Jovi in concert (she has a thing for Jon Bon Jovi, but apparently all women do). We travelled to Milton Keynes the night before and went out for dinner with Andy Farrell and Colleen—they didn't come to the gig, Faz's wife has better taste in music! We had a good night, I filled him in on how our former Aussie team-mates were getting on, but I didn't tell him that I was going to play again. I kept it secret, and I felt guilty about that because I could always trust Faz . . . it was just that I had to get my own head around it before I talked about it.

Driving to the gig, my mind drifting away from rugby league and onto the impending thoughts of singing 'Living on a Prayer', I got a call from Mandy, Maurice Lindsay's assistant. He had just had knee surgery, but she said that he wanted to speak to me from his hospital bed. Weeks earlier, Maurice had sent me a long text message to apologise for not taking my advice when I told him things weren't right with Millward. He didn't need to, really, because in a way I understood that he was in a tricky position because he had to back his coach. Mandy connected Maurice's call, and he came on the loud speaker and said, 'I'm asking you as a friend, will you come back and play and help get us out of trouble?' He then began going into detail about the state of the club—mentioning things he perhaps shouldn't have told me—and all the while, Rachel and I were looking at each other with puzzled expressions, wondering why he was being so frank. The following day, he called again to ask if I'd help get Wigan out of trouble—but he said it with the tone of voice as if he was asking for the first time.

'Maurice, are you okay?' I asked him.

'Fine. Why?' he replied.

'You phoned me yesterday and we had this same conversation.'

He was stunned when I told him that, but then he realised that the anaesthetic had played tricks with his mind and he didn't remember a thing. He then moved the conversation onto money. I knew Wigan were having problems with their salary cap, and Maurice told me there was little he could do.

'I'm not coming back for the money,' I told him. 'I'll be at training on Monday.'

Maurice later announced my return in the press, and said I was coming back to play for free. That was not true—I was paid expenses, though it wasn't a lot, and in truth I am still owed a few quid by the club. But the money didn't matter, it wasn't an issue. I was made to feel needed, and I had the chance to end my career properly. That was enough for me.

The following day, on the first Sunday of June, I went under my bed and dug some old gear out. I also sent a text message to Chris Ashton, a teenager who was playing out of his skin at full-back, to tell him not to worry. 'I'm not coming back to reclaim my spot, I want to help the team out,' I wrote. He responded by saying it would be great to have me back. That meant a lot to me.

One thing that always surprised fans when I told them was

that, as players, we knew as much as them about what was going on. Players would only find out about signings by reading about them on teletext or in newspapers. Apart from Ashy, I'd only told Brett Dallas and Sean O'Loughlin about my comeback, so the rest of the players were quite surprised when I turned up to train on the Monday morning! They all seemed pleased to see me, which was the important thing.

That morning, we had a contact session, and it was tough. I was fit, that is to say I was treadmill fit, but it's hard to replicate in a gym the fitness you need to make tackles, get up, run, make another tackle . . . it was a punishing session. It wasn't helped by the fact Nobby went back on his promise to pull me out half way through!

The week passed quickly, and I enjoyed being back. I hadn't been involved in the earlier games, and had I not seen the league table I would have thought we had the making of a decent side. I looked at the players in training and there was quality there—Bryan Fletcher, Ashton, Brett, Lockers, Gareth Hock. Lockers and Hock are players who came through the ranks when I was in the side, and they're both players I regard highly. It was always tough for Lockers, having Faz as his brother-in-law, and it really bugged me when people criticised him as a captain because they were basing their judgement on seeing him speak to the players during breaks in play. Lockers is exemplary with everything he does. He does the little things that fans don't see, but players realise how important they are. For example, he may run a great line for an inside ball, but it will be a decoy run that bends the defensive line out of shape and—two passes later—the winger will score. And guess who gets the plaudits? Not the rangy guy with the curly hair. That year, he'd taken a lot of the stick because he was captain; fans wanted to see him rant at the players behind the sticks, the way Faz and Shaun Edwards did. Faz and Shaun used to lash out at the players, sure, but that's not what made them such great captains. They were great captains because of the way they played, the way they led by example, the way they put their heart and soul into every match and didn't give up. They also spoke a lot of sense.

Lockers is such a nice guy, and that also worked against him in one respect because fans probably thought he was too polite to be the captain. But the fans didn't see what he's like in the changing room—trust me, if someone wasn't pulling their weight he'd tell them. He never hesitated to confront a player and then, after the game, say, 'Look, I hope you realise why I did that'. Gaz is a completely different player, a bit of a freak in the nicest term. He's one of those unique talents, and my hope is that he isn't over-coached or it may stop him enjoying the career his talents deserve.

The Friday night of my comeback game, we had a home fixture against Catalans, who were struggling for form themselves. I was amazed at how relaxed I was going into the game. I walked into our changing room and saw my name back above my peg with my shirt hanging from it. I was so pleased to be back. But it didn't take me long to realise why I'd been asked back. It was so quiet, the players looked so nervy, I could see that their confidence was low. Even guys like Bryan Fletcher, a chirpy Australian who lightened the mood with his jokes, was not his usual self. The whole situation had got to the players. It was eating them up inside, and you could see why.

Wigan were bottom of the table after 16 matches, six points from safety and with only 12 games to go. In the last four months, they'd had just two wins. Huddersfield were the only team they'd beaten in 10 months! And on top of that, they knew what was being said about them. Players like to say that they don't read newspapers, but that's rubbish—they do. Most of them lived in Wigan, and even if they tried to avoid the papers and the internet message boards, you could guarantee some of their family and friends had read them, and they would relay the messages. Though the fans were awesome that year, they were understandably concerned—players told me they couldn't put petrol in their car or go to the shops without being stopped and asked about rugby. And while most of the fans were polite and meant no harm, the players couldn't escape the crisis they were in. They felt trapped, they were, in effect, imprisoned by the fear that Wigan were going to be relegated and it would be their fault.

The pressure they were under was immense. In all the Wigan teams I had played in we always had the mentality that nobody would come to our house and win, but that fear factor had gone, and teams were actually looking forward to visiting Wigan. I'm not criticising those players, had I been in the team during that time, winning just two Super League games in the whole of February, March, April and May, I'm sure I'd have been just as depressed. But because I'd come in from outside, I was buoyant and I could see things clearly while the players were in a very deep hole.

My job was to build confidence, and I tried my best to help them out. I pulled a couple of the young lads to one side and told them how good they were. I told the experienced players how much I was looking forward to playing with them. I was trying to create an atmosphere. My return generated a lot of press, which I was happy about—and not from a selfish point of view. I wanted the media's eyes and spotlight trained on me, because it took the pressure off the other players—it gave them some breathing space. About five minutes before kick-off, we gathered in a huddle in the changing room where, usually, the captain would deliver his final thoughts. Lockers asked me to do this instead. The players were already thinking about the result, and its consequences. I said, 'Go and enjoy yourselves, go and play.'

I was buzzing, I was charged. We did the traditional jog on the spot for 10 seconds and then went out.

I was playing at centre, and with Stacey Jones in the Catalans side, I was quite relieved not to be at full-back! Stacey was a great tactician, and had a wonderful kicking game. The match was certainly not a classic, but it was all about points for us. I didn't make much of an impact on the game, and I never felt the burden to, I just defended strongly down the right side, and I managed to see out the 80 minutes. It was pouring down with rain and, though Catalans never gave in, we clung on to a 24–18 win.

To say I was sore the morning after was an understatement. Not only was the knee twice its size but my whole body ached, and even breathing was difficult. It was as though I'd bruised all my insides—it hadn't been a more physical game than usual; I had just forgotten how tough playing rugby league is. It was a five-day turnaround until my next game and, with my knee slow to recover, Nobby gave me the game off against Warrington though I still went into the dressing room before the match.

The lads played awesome rugby that night, and did not look like a side in trouble of relegation. Stuart Fielden's arrival gave us another real boost—a few weeks earlier, Nobby had told me he was trying to get him in—and from that moment I knew that we'd escape from the clutches of relegation.

In two weeks, we'd got two wins. The turnaround was unbelievable. Momentum and self-belief are such important parts of the game, yet they're so hard to obtain. I once heard a saying that a losing run is like a comfy bed—easy to fall into but hard to get out of, and that's so true. Players were starting games well but, as soon as the opposition scored, their confidence melted away. After just two wins, players began turning up to training with smiles on their faces. I was so pleased for the players, because they worked so hard, spilling sweat and blood on the training pitch.

Those two wins reinvigorated the team. It was as if the shackles had been taken off. We travelled to London the following week, which was always tough to prepare for because of the travel and overnight stop. The Broncos were scrapping at the lower end of the table, too, and in scorching heat we knew it was going to be tough. Danny Orr was awesome that day, and Mark Calderwood and Ashy came up with some big plays and scored three tries between them. Calders is a player I always regarded highly, he is one of the fittest players I ever came across and is the best cover-defender I've ever known. It's like having two full-backs in the side. A lot of the headlines were about whether I could save Wigan, or Nobby, or Michael Dobson, or Stu Fielden—but in a great effort from everyone, blokes like Lockers and Calders never got the credit they so richly deserved.

In the London heat, I popped my shoulder early on in the game, and at half-time my knee was iced up as the doctor injected pain killers into my shoulder; all the while, I was still delivering messages to players, not even flinching when Dr Zaman had a four-inch needle stuck in me. It was hurting, sure, but I wanted to make a statement before the second half. We clung on for an edgy 26–24 win, it was a huge result for us, and the Wigan fans that day knew it. They were incredible, and I remember Nobby coming to me at the end and saying he couldn't believe how vocal and supportive they were.

We were still bottom, but we'd won three on the spin, and the mood of confidence had been galvanised by the gutsy win in London. Our next match was against Wakefield, and it was crucial, because they were the team we were chasing. A win would draw us level on points with them, while a loss would strike a four-point wedge between us. We were always in control, winning 42–24, and for the first time in a long time, our future was back in our hands. That in itself relieved some of the pressure, because until then we were looking out for the other results, hoping they would swing in our favour. Survival was now in sight, and after beating Salford in our next game, we took on our own aura of invincibility.

The following week we played at Warrington which was always a hard local derby, and though we played well in a high-quality match, they beat us 22–20. Wigan had managed only two wins in four months when I arrived; amazingly, in six weeks, that was our first defeat. The result was a reality check that we needed. It grounded us and made us realise that we were not out of the water. About 20 minutes into that match I hurt my knee badly for the first time since I'd been back. I probably should have gone off but I couldn't, I hobbled until the final whistle. That night, I knew that I didn't have much left to give. I was doing everything I could as far as my rehab went, spending hours in the pool, but I was limping pretty heavily. I didn't train at all in the week leading up to the next game, a home match against Catalans which we won easily 40–4. Yet no sooner had we moved two points clear of Wakefield, we started hearing rumours that we'd been docked points for breaching the salary cap, and days later it was confirmed—a two point deduction for breaking the £1.6m wage ceiling the previous year.

It was a bitter pill to swallow, because we'd been punished for something that had happened a year earlier, and it couldn't have come at a worse time, just days after we'd gone two points clear of the relegation spot. Yet the way the team responded astonished me. No one cursed Maurice Lindsay. No one moaned. We spoke about it for a minute and Lockers said, 'Look, we can't do anything about it, all we can control is what we do on the pitch'.

That was it, and while the fans were furious with Maurice, we never mentioned it again. The penalty meant that we'd dropped to be level on points with Wakefield with just five games to go.

It should have been a nervous time but, in truth, it wasn't. Wigan had been six points from safety on my return a few weeks previously, but we'd won six of our seven games since—and our only loss was by a two-point margin, at Warrington. We had a daunting trip to Leeds coming up and, though our safety was not going to be decided by that match, we all had a feeling that if we won, we'd stay up. We were playing well, momentum was in our favour and, on top of that, three of our final four matches were at home, which was great because our fans had again turned the JJB Stadium into a fortress.

The game against Leeds was vital for us. Nobby asked me the day before the match how I was. 'I'm struggling,' I told him frankly. 'But I've come this far.' He still wanted me involved. I think he felt more confident with me there, so he named me on the bench. We were definitely the underdogs and we battled for everything. I came off the bench midway through the second half—Ashton and Calders both scored great tries—and we won, 20–18. It was an epic match. It was by far our biggest test since our revival and not many people expected us to win, because Leeds were practically bullet-proof at home. We moved two points clear of Wakey, and one point behind Castleford, and with those sides playing each other on the final day of the season we knew we had the upper hand. It felt like we'd stayed up, and we sang our team song on a great journey home.

In my mind, I knew I couldn't give any more, and after a few sleepless nights, and without telling my mates, Rachel or my family, I went to the club, walked into the coaches' office and told Nobby I couldn't give him any more. My knee was constantly sore, and I was taking so many strong pain killers to cope that I was worried about becoming addicted. They numbed the pain but also calmed me down, sending my mind funny. Nobby stood up, shook my hand, and said he would never forget what I had done for him and for the town.

I thanked him, quietly left without seeing my team-mates and made my way home. I cried all the way. Part of me was sad, part of me was proud, but either way it was over. When I had retired the first time, there had been quite a fuss, but I didn't want any of that again. I always got on with the press, I always understood my role to promote the club and the game, but on that occasion I ignored their calls and messages. I was content that I'd helped the club. I'd finished my Wigan career as I had started it 13 years earlier—as a substitute.

My mind was a mess, because it had been a bit of an emotional roller-coaster for me. I kept such a low profile that I practically went into hibernation, and it was only after about four weeks that I left my house and began to live again. In the final match of the season, a home game against Hull FC, I was introduced to the fans before the match and they all stood up and applauded me. It was only then I realised the impact that I had made on both the club and the fans. Their vocal cheers that evening hit home; I can't describe the emotion I felt. Appreciated, grateful, joyous . . . all of the above, and more. I stayed and watched about 50 minutes of the game, and then, without announcing my exit, I sneaked out. No fanfare, no fuss, no farewells. Five minutes later, I sat on my garden bench drinking a beer, alone—a sad but contented man. My neighbours, Keith and Carol, returned from the game about an hour later and came over to tell me how proud they were. Keith said I could look back on a career that many sportsmen could only dream of. He knew it was an emotional time, so he told me to keep my head up high because I was a gentleman of rugby league, which was nice to hear.

In the after-season parties that followed, the messages I got from the other players were phenomenal. Brett Dallas was not exactly renowned for his sentiment, but he thanked me and told me he loved me. He was leaving the club to go back to

Australia—he had been amazing. He was a machine in training and awesome on the pitch, a pure athlete and such a brave player. And on top of that, he was a great mate. I received numerous text messages from players and friends, which I wrote down in a book. My good mate Danny Orr wrote, 'Really gutted for you mate, but at least you have left as one of the best No.1s ever, and people will always remember that'.

St Helens' full-back Paul Wellens wrote, 'Good luck champion, it's been an honour playing with and against you'. Paul Sculthorpe, Sean O'Loughlin, Wayne Godwin and many more all sent similar texts, saying how honoured they felt to have played alongside me. Harrison Hansen thanked me and told me that Wigan wouldn't have stayed up without me. Granted, he was blind drunk at the time, but it meant the world to me! And when he said that I'd helped keep the club in Super League, my mind wandered back to what Lammy had said months earlier, about having a chance to help the club I loved and to end my playing career on my terms. I was glad I'd done both of those things, but the messages I got were really satisfying. They made me incredibly proud. They made me glad I came back.

18

INSIDE WIGAN

'Talent is never enough, with few exceptions, the best players are the hardest workers.'

Magic Johnson

IN MY FIRST full season, Wigan won the Grand Slam. In my last full season, they had to fight against the real threat of relegation. In more than a decade at the club, I've experienced the great highs of sporting glory, and also faced the unthinkable lows; I'd like to think I am well qualified to talk about the changes that have taken place at Wigan Rugby League Football Club in that time.

The teams around them have undeniably grown stronger over the years, but was the Wigan RLFC club I left different to the one I joined? The answer is a resounding yes. What changed? And more importantly, why did Wigan's fortunes tumble? I think Wigan's fans deserve an insight into what I think has happened at the club they love.

Since the turn of the millennium, there's been a definite shift of power in rugby league. Bradford and Leeds have both had their successes, and St Helens too. Saints' entertaining brand of rugby league has set them apart from many of the other clubs. I've studied their success story intensely, and I believe that's because the backbone of their side has been the same for many seasons. The club retained players in key positions and they improved and grew together. The St Helens board deserve credit for that. They showed patience and a lot of faith in a group of guys, and built their team around the likes of Keiron Cunningham, Paul Wellens, Sean Long and Paul Sculthorpe, all of whom play, or played, in key positions, and supplemented that core group with quality additions. Tommy Martyn and Leon Pryce have really been their two only stand-offs in the last decade. How many stand-offs have Wigan had in that time? Since Henry Paul left in 1998, Greg Florimo, Tony Smith, Matt Johns, Julian O'Neill and Danny Orr were all signed to fill that role, in addition to guys like Phil Jones, Kev Brown, Sean O'Loughlin and even Andy Farrell playing in that position. There are some very good players in that list, but it takes time for them to settle in a key ball playing position, often a season. At Wigan, they didn't last that long. That happened with the coaches, too.

Coaches arrived, each with a two or three-year plan but they didn't get the full time to exercise their plan. I had 11 coaches in 13 years—Dorahy, West, Hughes, Monie, Goodway, Endacott, Raper, Gregory, Betts, Millward and Noble—which is a crazy number. None of them were stupid; they all knew that Wigan had 'previous' for firing coaches who didn't deliver success, so nobody could blame them for putting short-term goals before the long-term development of the club. That then moves the spotlight onto those who fired the coaches—namely Dave Whelan, Maurice Lindsay and the other directors over the years. They faced tremendous pressure from the fans to deliver a trophy, but I think that, in some instances, they should have resisted those outside influences and been strong, and given some of those coaches a decent run in charge.

As well as the high—at times alarming—turnover, of key pivotal players and coaches during my years at Wigan, I noticed the culture of the club eroded—and it was not one coach's fault. It was a gradual and inexplicable shift, from the Wigan I joined to the Wigan I left. When I went into the first team in the early 1990s, there was a very strong culture in place. A culture we all abided by. It's hard to quantify culture, harder still to explain how it changed, but there seemed to be more passion, a clearer direction, a hungrier work ethic and mutual respect in comparison to the culture present at the club when I left. I was promoted to the first team squad alongside the talented Simon Haughton. Only two of us were new, and we were shouted at for any minor detail that we got wrong. The senior players were concerned about the team, not our feelings, and they wouldn't worry about upsetting us. Shaun Edwards would sulk if he thought the training was not up to the standard he wanted.

While we didn't appreciate it at the time, it taught us lessons and made us stronger. After they'd bollocked us, we'd have to sit with them—we couldn't hang around a posse of friends our own age. That attitude, that culture, showed us the way we needed to act when, over the following years, the next crop of players came through. It underlined the standards to maintain. Yet by the end of my career, it got to the point where, if a senior player bollocked a young lad, he'd just go away and laugh about it with his mates. I'll give you an example: when I was struggling with my knee in 2005, the coaching staff gave me some stationary skill work to do, and the young lads would run past and take the piss out of me. I thought back to when I was 17, and wondered what would have happened to me if I had taken the piss out of Dean Bell or Kelvin Skerrett or Andy Platt. It just wouldn't have happened, because I had so much respect for them. I know I risk sounding like an old man moaning about young lads these days not having any respect, but the change in Wigan's culture was evident elsewhere as well. I've always believed that being a great professional is not about what you do in training, but how you live your life. I once roomed with Stuart Fielden, who had a knee injury at the time, and I remember him sitting with his laptop on his bed, looking at diagrams of the knee on medical websites, and ringing a doctor for advice. That's brilliant—he was showing an interest in his body and his recovery, which is the way all players should be. Some young players may train a lot, but then they leave training and they think that's it until the next day. They're wrong. 'Extras' are now compulsory; they're not the same as extras used to be. Shaun Edwards used to go on a pitch, alone, and imagine different scenarios in his mind. There'd be a burst of speed, a step, a glance to the left and a dummy to the right—no one told him to do it, he wanted to do it to get better. Matty Johns did the same when he came over. Every player is very aware of their weaknesses and they should want to improve them, not be forced into working on them. I have long legs so I never had the fast, quick feet of other guys. I felt I needed to improve so I had extra agility sessions. I wanted to get better and score those magical weaving tries that other players had the ability to do.

The point is, when guys like Quentin Pongia and Craig Smith came in, some of the young lads were blown away by their work ethic. It was never a case of Quentin and Craig being blown away by their work ethic. Smithy even had a rule; if you had a beer, the day after you had to kill it in the gym. I know there are plenty of stories in this book about drinking, but those blow-outs took place once every couple of months— for the rest of the time, I really worked hard to look after myself.

Team spirit is important, but not to the extent that team-mates are too afraid to tell someone to pull their finger out, for fear of ruining a friendship. Young players were spending so much time with each other that the distinctions between work and pleasure faded; they were so used to having a laugh with one another, they treated Wigan like a social club, rather than the world's most famous rugby league club. Sean O'Loughlin and Gareth Hock weren't like that. They kept most of their best friends away from Wigan, and their careers really benefited, because while they would get on with young players, they wouldn't think twice about calling one out if he wasn't putting in the effort.

So why has this cultural shift happened? I think the move to a salary cap system forced Wigan to bring young players into the first team squad en masse, and prevented them from keeping hold of experienced 'squad players'. When I came into the team, before a salary cap system, there was one other player my age so inevitably we mixed with older players. When I left, the squad was loaded with young lads who all came through together, and fell into the trap of hanging out with their peers. But by doing that, they didn't learn habits from the older players who had been there, done it and bought the proverbial t-shirt. A few years ago, they tried to introduce a 'buddy' system to tackle the problem and it was a shame it faded; senior players got tired of keeping track of the younger players when, instead, it should have been the young players watching and learning from the experienced players. Don't mistake this as a criticism of the young players; it's not their fault. This is the culture they came into, and it's been brought about through no fault of any one individual. Wigan not only need a strong core of experienced performers who the younger lads can learn from, but also young players to realise the importance of picking up good tips and habits from those who have gone before them. I'm a strong advocate of using home-grown players, and by tackling the issue of passing on professional habits—by maintaining a strong culture—more could come into the side and flourish.

Wigan has an abundance of amateur rugby league clubs, all of which have young lads who would give their right arm to play for the club, and when Andrew Farrell left, I liked the fact they invested their future in a local young lad in Sean O'Loughlin—with guys like Joel Tomkins pushing for the spot, too—because they could quite easily have gone for a quick-fix signing. I would like to see a representative from the club working hand-in-hand with these amateur clubs, offering advice and support. They could also pass on tips and thoughts but the main thing was that it would create a buzz amongst these young local lads that maybe they could get snapped up. Also age doesn't matter, Wigan could easily sign a 24-year-old if he could do a job, rather than looking down under. Like many fans, I didn't like seeing Wigan offloading local lads . . . in a lot of circumstances, but not all.

Terry Newton was heartbroken when he left the club and it should not have been allowed to happen. He wore his heart on his sleeve and drove fear into opponents, he really led by example. Sometimes the suits in the boardroom don't see the work players put in—and the impact guys like him have—in training. Teams need strong characters, and letting Tez go was a huge mistake. The same applies about Shaun Briscoe, who was a perfect student who would always ask for advice. Mark Smith, Paul Johnson and Stephen Wild are others who should not have been allowed to leave.

I don't know if the fans realise just how influential their jeers or cheers can be. Their expectations can crush a player's confidence. Kevin Brown was one of the most gifted young players I watched come through at Wigan, he could do things on the field that I could never do. He'd glide through defences, he could fire out passes both sides and his attitude was great. I remember him approaching me once after training to ask if I could run at him a few times, because his left shoulder defence needed improving. But Browny was a confidence player, and when he had a poor game, and then another one, his head would drop and—instead of fans rallying behind him—they would get on his back, which only made him worse. I know their criticism stemmed from their love of the club, but in that case it would have been better for everyone if it had been channelled differently.

I have mentioned that there are limits to keeping all our young players. That's because, despite what some fans believe, the club shouldn't keep hold of every single Wigan lad who comes into the first team. One thing I hated seeing over the years, and unfortunately I saw it far too often, was a talented teenager come into the side and make an impression, but then rest on his laurels. Just because they were rubbing shoulders with the likes of Faz, Gary Connolly, Brett Dallas, they thought they'd made it. I don't want to appear an apologist for Maurice, but there have been times when he and the club have been criticised for letting young players go—especially when their careers took off at rival Super League clubs. What fans need to understand is that often there's a reason for letting them go, and the reason is normally that they've had a couple of good games, signed a few autographs and got plenty of attention from young girls on King Street, and thought they were superstars. Sometimes I'd notice the change in a matter of days. One minute they'd be at training, desperate for a chance; the next, I'd see them roll into training in stylish clothes and acting like they had it all. What they seemed to forget was that the reason they were getting so much attention was because of the way they played, and when the club got rid of them, it often served as their wake-up call. They moved on, realised they were not at the world's most famous club anymore, and had to start again. It is then, at second-rate clubs, that these lads re-evaluate their lives and realise that they have messed up—they then mature and fulfil their potential, becoming the players we all thought they would. Many players left and went on to have successful careers at other clubs but deep down, I suspect they would rather be wearing the cherry and white.

Of course, the subject of home-grown players cannot be mentioned without discussing overseas players. It's often regarded as a power struggle, between players born in Wigan and those born in Wagga Wagga (or other ridiculous sounding towns down under). The logic is simple: when an overseas player joins, he takes a place in the team that could otherwise go to a home-grown player.

At Wigan it used to be a case of signing two or three players from overseas, but that number grew until more than half the starting line-up had an Australian or Kiwi twang. In my debut season, Wigan had no Australians and three New Zealanders—Dean Bell, Sam Panapa and Frano Botica. By the time we went into Super League in 1996, that statistic was the same though the names had changed (Henry Paul, Inga Tuigamala and Shem Tatupu, who only played three games).

Five years later there were five players from overseas (Brett Dallas, Matty Johns, Adrian Lam, Steve Renouf and Dave Furner) and in my final season, there were eight (Brett, Michael Dobson, Bryan Fletcher, Scott Logan, Iafeta Palea'aesina, Pat Richards, Jerry Seuseu and Dave Vaealiki—I've not counted Harrison Hansen, as he was an academy product). I liked overseas signings—when they were quality additions to the squad. I didn't like it when the club would sign an average utility who offered little more than a Wigan-born player would. I wish, when Wigan signed players—and this goes for English players from other clubs, too—they were made aware of the club's history. I don't just mean they should have been sat down in front of a DVD about the team's glory days, but rather, made to understand the importance of their role in the team. They need to be told the responsibilities that wearing the cherry and white jersey brings. Rugby league in Wigan is a religion, but too many jerseys have been given out to players over the years that don't fully realise the obligations that go hand-in-hand with playing for Wigan. I remember when Paul Koloi came in during the 1997 season, he was a nice guy but he was so relaxed that Neil Cowie joked, 'He thinks he's come to Center Parcs, not Central Park'. I know it's not possible to have a team loaded with superstars anymore, the salary cap prevents that, but surely it's still possible to have 17 blokes giving their all for the badge. I'm convinced that is what the fans want to see—guys who would go to war for the club.

I've known many fans organise their lives around Warriors' fixtures. They wouldn't think twice about cancelling a holiday if it clashed with a game. This is why the fans are so outspoken over defeats and issues concerning the club, it's their life. I have been stopped many times by fans while out shopping; I don't agree with everything they say—and if I've only nipped out for a pint of milk, it can be frustrating—but there is no way I'd offend them as they speak with such passion about something I also care deeply about. Every player who arrives at Wigan should be asked, 'How do you want to be remembered?'

This isn't a sweeping judgement of the overseas players Wigan have had over the years, because some of my best friends—and greatest team-mates—have come from Australia or New Zealand. Many of them have achieved good things with Wigan, and I would challenge anyone to say the likes of Dean Bell—who was captain of the side on my debut—Inga Tuigamala and Henry Paul through to Brett Dallas, Adrian Lam, Craig Smith, Dave Furner and, lately, Trent Barrett didn't give their all for the club. They were all class players, sure, but what made those players great was their hunger; their competitive spirit. There have been other, lesser-profile players, such as Robbie McCormack, who also left with dignity, and the knowledge that any time they return to Wigan in the future, they could walk into a bar and a fan will say, 'He was a good 'un'. But without getting personal, during my career at the club, there were too many overseas players who came for a big pay-day at the end of their careers. I know I would have rather played with a guy who had dreams of winning trophies, than someone who played for the coin. Sure, they wanted to get to a final, but that wasn't what motivated them.

How many overseas players would actually come and sign for Wigan if they could get paid the same money back in Australia? I think a few ambitious guys would, but many others would stay in Australia. Is that the players' fault, or the club's fault for signing them? Sometimes it is the former, but often it is the latter. For example, at the end of 2004, Wigan lost a lot of key players such as Lammy, Craig Smith, Mick Cassidy, Gary Connolly and Terry O'Connor. Andrew Farrell left a few months later. In their place, they signed—all for big money— Dennis Moran, Luke Davico, David Vaealiki and Jerry Seuseu. Luke, unfortunately, only played two minutes of a pre-season friendly before a recurrence of an injury ended his Wigan career. The other three were widely condemned by the fans because they failed to make an impact at the club. Dennis was a brilliant player at London; a roaming free-spirit on the field, he scored tries with seeming ease. He played his best rugby playing at full-back for the Broncos. It wasn't his fault that Wigan signed him and asked him to be the chief organiser, just like David couldn't have been blamed for taking the lucrative contract that was offered to him while he was coming back from major Achilles surgery. As for Jerry, he really trained the house down, and you won't find a player who didn't have the highest regard for him. Unfortunately, it was a case of two seasons too far for him, because he was playing with a knee injury that prevented him recapturing his former glory. Again, I don't blame him—on the edge of retirement—for taking the money on offer at Wigan; really, it was Wigan's fault for not doing their homework. We have heard so many times about players being homesick and whatever and I appreciate that it's a big step into the unknown for these guys but more research needs to be done. When recruiting players from overseas, do we actually know the guys we are signing or are we just listening to Australian agents who are trying to sell their star to make a quid or two for themselves? Can these players influence the team? What are their habits? Will they be distracted by the bars, given that they are no longer subjected to the same scrutiny that they had down under? I may sound harsh but I just want the best for our club.

Our fans haven't changed, and our fan-base hasn't dropped off, but the sporting landscape of Wigan has changed dramatically in the last few years. When I grew up, it seemed every kid wanted to play rugby league for Wigan. Sports day would see most of the lads wearing Wigan replica tops, with maybe the odd Man United or Liverpool shirt sprinkled among the starting line-up. How times have changed. Football, on the whole, is bigger than it once was, and a lot more fashionable; kids collect trading cards and obsess over PlayStation football games . . . even if they're not addicts of the actual game itself.

Although the Warriors still get big crowds, you can't deny—
and it's hard not to respect—Wigan Athletic's tremendous rise
from the old Division Two into the top-flight. When I walk
around town now, I see far more replica Latics tops than
Warriors tops. I know a lot of Wigan rugby fans don't like their
stablemates, perhaps they feel threatened by Latics' success;
they certainly don't support them, and vice versa. I'm told
some Latics fans cheer more if the Warriors lose than if their
own side win, which is petty and sad. This bitter split between
the two really frustrates me. This isn't like Everton-Liverpool
or City-United, we're talking about two different sports. Sure,
fans will probably have a first love—rugby or football—but I
can't see why more don't take at least a passing interest in the
town's other team. I can't understand why they don't celebrate
both teams' success. We're both playing as Wigan, and there's
no logical reason why both sports can't co-exist, and succeed,
alongside each other.

You will never turn a true rugby league fan into a football
fan and you will never turn a true football fan into a rugby
league fan. But wanting both to do well should not be frowned
upon. I've watched Latics a few times and enjoyed it; that
doesn't question or weaken my ties to the rugby league club.
The discussion about the town turning blue—it's ridiculous.
Sure, Latics' gate has rocketed from a few thousand to an
average of more than 18,000 in their first season in the
Premier League. But consider this: in 1997, the Warriors'
average gate dipped below the five-figure mark to 8,866. In
my final season as a player, the Warriors' average gate was
14,464—so obviously the Warriors' ability to attract fans has
nothing to do with whether Latics are playing in Division
Three or the Premier League. Both those crowd rises should
be celebrated, but instead, there's more chance of finding fans
bickering about the figures, with Latics fans bragging that their

crowd was higher than the rugby club's and the rugby fans questioning how many of the football gate were travelling fans. Who cares? If we are to measure each club's success by their own history, then both are doing well. Sport is parochial, so fans needs their teams to hate—but they shouldn't hate a team playing a different sport in the same town!

While some rugby league and football fans hate each other's sport, I found that the players of each team had nothing but respect for each other. We used to train at Latics' Christopher Park facility, and they always kicked a soccer ball over for us to warm-up with. I'd often have a chat to them, and they were genuinely nice guys—I shared the occasional beer with guys like Matt Jackson and Jimmy Bullard. When they got promoted to the Premiership, I was the Warriors captain and I sent a telegram to Matt, who was their captain, which he appreciated. If I'm home on a Saturday afternoon, the first result I'll check is Latics', and I always hope they've won.

With Wigan, it goes without saying that I want them to do well and I truly believe they can. It would be nothing more than the people down there deserve, and I don't just mean the players and coaches, but also those who work tirelessly for very little reward or acknowledgement. Wigan is a massive club, but it is also a family club built on strong values and ethics. Every time I go back, I know everybody's name and greet them all with a firm handshake, a kiss or a hug. There are so many unsung heroes. The club would not have operated over the last 20 years if it wasn't for Mary and Mandy in the office— two absolute diamond girls. I don't know what the club would have done without Keith Mills—who has filled many roles— and his wife, Anne, who washed the team's kits for many years. Kit man George Unsworth does an incredible job seeing to players' needs, and we have had the same two stats men for well over a decade—Gordon and Malcolm—who do it all for only a team jacket each. I love the fact they don't want anything in return except a pat on the back. I used the words 'we' and 'our' because I still feel part of Wigan Rugby League Football Club. The guy in charge now, Ian Lenagan, has a burning ambition to succeed and to bring trophies back to the club. I have been in his company and I know his vision for the team, but he's also smart enough to realise it won't happen overnight. It's easy to have the right intentions, but I think Ian also has the know-how as well. His track record in the business world suggests that.

I don't think Wigan are far off achieving their goals, but there are areas that still concern me. In addition to the issue of the changing culture, or perhaps because of it, Wigan need to grind out more wins. They don't have a problem raising themselves to play the big games, but trophies are won on the back of ugly, gutsy wins. When the pressure is on, they need to perform, and I'd love to see the JJB Stadium become a fortress so visiting teams are more afraid than excited about playing there. I'd like visiting teams to enter the ground and realise that they have just entered the most famous club in the world, and that they are about to face the cherry and whites of Wigan.

Nostalgia plays a big part in supporting Wigan, because of the club's glittering history. A lot has changed over the years. If the club could harness the same culture that we had in the early 1990s, sign the right overseas players and crank up the production line of home-grown players so that two or three great players are being drip-fed into the first team each year, they can have an exciting and successful future.

19

DISCOVERING
MY ROOTS

'Time is a companion that goes with us on a journey. It reminds us to cherish each moment, because it will never come again. What we leave behind is not as important as how we have lived.'

Captain Jean Luc Picard, Star Trek

I WAS BORN in Wigan, I fell in love with rugby league and, like thousands of youngsters, I dreamed of playing for Wigan. I was, in every sense of the word, an archetypal Wiganer. But unlike my peers, I had one distinguishing feature they never had. And I used to get asked about all the time: my name.

I wish I had a pound for every time someone asked me about the origins of my name. It's Polish. My granddad, Jan, served in the military with the Special Forces, and moved from Poland to England shortly after the Second World War ended. Until December 2006, that was pretty much all I knew about my family's origins, until I went on a remarkable pilgrimage with my dad to discover our roots.

I never knew my granddad. He had to go back to Poland a few years after the war ended, leaving my nan here with my dad, his brother Carl and sister Jean, who were all very young. My granddad was still serving with the Polish Special Forces when he was ordered to return home and, as communications were difficult in the early 1950s, he lost contact with his family.

Throughout my childhood, particularly after my nan died, I was intrigued about what happened to my granddad. My dad searched for years to try to track him down. We assumed he had died, but my dad couldn't find any record of him. Then, in early 2006, my dad's persistence and patience finally paid off. He was contacted by the pensions department in Poland. They informed my dad that Jan Radlinski had died in 1976, the year I was born, and was buried in a church in Warsaw. It was a strange emotion for my dad. He was naturally upset—perhaps he'd had that glimmer of hope that his father was still alive—but he was also relieved to have located him after years of painstaking searching. I promised my dad that we'd go over to visit my granddad's grave. I was also keen to visit Poland; it's my heritage, it's in my blood and it's in my name.

My dad and I flew out to Warsaw for a four-day visit. I actually felt guilty that I hadn't made the trip before, as it is only a two-hour flight away. On the flight, my emotions were stifling, and as we touched down at Warsaw airport the poignancy of our trip hit me like a thunderbolt. My eyes welled up . . . I couldn't believe we were in my granddad's hometown.

We caught a cab to the hotel I'd booked over the internet and leisurely strolled through the streets to find some dinner. It was late, and we agreed to visit the grave the following day. When we returned to our hotel, we asked the concierge if he knew the location of the church where my granddad was buried. He looked puzzled, and shrugged his shoulders apologetically. In his defence, Poland is very Catholic, and there are literally hundreds of churches scattered throughout the country. We bought a map and spent a couple of hours scouring each street meticulously, name by name, grid by grid, for our church. We found it . . . on the same street as our hotel, a mile down the road! Luck? Fate? I'm not sure. But satisfied that we would easily find the church we were searching for the following morning, we sank a couple of Polish beers in the lobby bar and retired to bed for an early start.

The church was three bus stops from the hotel. It was a short trip, but one I'll never forget. I had a strange blend of emotions I'd never experienced before. I was excited, sure, but I was more conscious of what my dad must be feeling and thinking. Throughout my childhood he'd wondered what had happened to his dad and, here we were, in Poland, a few hundred yards away from being with him again for the first time in more than 50 years.

We got off the bus and walked to the church. It was quaint and beautiful, but there were unmistakable reminders of Warsaw's traumatic past—bullet holes peppered the perimeter wall. A little old lady directed us up to the cemetery, and my dad reached into his pocket to produce a piece of paper he'd been sent. The paper showed the exact location of his father's grave. We walked up the correct aisle and down the row to the number on his sheet, but we couldn't find a grave with his name on. Our instinctive reaction was that there had been a mistake; that it was too good to be true.

'We can't have gone wrong,' I said. 'We did exactly what the paper said.'

Dad and I drifted, slowly walking through the maze of tombstones, checking every name. A minute or two later I heard my dad's voice calling my name, and I looked up to see him signalling me over. An old nun had pointed dad in the right direction; there were two parts to the cemetery, the aisle, row and number we'd searched for were correct, but we'd been in the wrong part.

I walked to my dad, and together we eased down the row,

counting the numbers until we reached the grave we wanted. We turned and looked down and there, emblazoned across the marble, was the name: Jan Radlinski. We paused for a beat.

'Dad, this is my son . . . your grandson,' my dad said and, in an instant, I felt a surge of pride so unbelievably powerful. We stood, looking at the grave as we allowed the emotions to sink in. Then, without prompting, we both knelt, pulled out all the weeds and cleaned up the grave. I wanted to leave my dad there alone for a moment, so I headed back up to the church, where there was a little stall selling candles and flowers. I bought a little plant, a candle in a glass cylinder and some matches, and walked back to my dad. My mum phoned me to ask if we had located the grave. When I told her we had found it, she was so relieved as she knew how important it was for my dad. We arranged the flowers in front of the grave, lit the eternal candle and said our goodbyes. Slowly, reluctantly, we backed away, before turning and walking towards the exit. My dad put his arm around me, thanked me and told me he loved me. That second, that very moment, I understood the true value of life.

Family relationships are so powerful, they should be embraced and enjoyed, because they will not exist forever. When I have children, and when they're old enough—probably about the time kids start asking why they have a different sounding name—I will tell them about that day in Warsaw, and how it made me understand the true importance of life.

We hadn't quite left the graveyard when the heavens opened, and the heaviest thunderstorm I have ever witnessed rumbled across the sky. We hid under trees, but then we looked at each other and realised that neither of us cared about getting soaked, so we ran through puddles to catch our bus with not a care in the world.

That journey to my granddad's grave changed me. It gave me a sense of closure, of understanding, but more importantly it changed my outlook on life and what was important. Being loved, I discovered in Warsaw, was the best feeling in the world. The value of all of my material possessions plummeted; they didn't matter, not really.

Throughout my career, I kept a book in which I wrote down memorable phrases I was told or heard. One was a poem called 'The Guy in the Glass' by Dale Wimbrow. The last passage reads:

> *You can fool the whole world down the pathway of years,*
> *And get pats on the back as you pass,*
> *But your final reward will be heartaches and tears,*
> *If you've cheated the guy in the glass.*

I found that passage particularly appropriate, and it's one I've been conscious of obeying since—being truthful to myself.

In the two days that followed visiting my granddad's grave, my dad and I spent time exploring his wonderful homeland and I learned so much about the history of Poland. Warsaw has a history like no place I'd ever visited. It was completely demolished, apart from one church, during the war yet was built up again through the spirit and hard work of its proud people. To look at the Warsaw natives, their pain is still etched on their faces, but it's impossible not to respect them for rising from the horrors of their past to stand proudly in their own right as citizens of one of Europe's most wonderful cities. During our trip, I also visited the Auschwitz concentration camp, the death factory where two million Polish Jews were executed. As I walked through the wrought iron entrance gates, I couldn't help feel sadness and remorse. Painted on the side, in what would have been clear view for the captives, were the words, 'Arbeit Macht Frei' which translates as 'Work shall set you free'. Maybe it was written to try to discipline the Jews, or maybe it was a cruel joke by the Nazis, as no matter how hard they worked they would never walk free. We toured the camp in a small group and many cried as soon as we entered the gas chambers, where hundreds of prisoners were marched supposedly for a shower, only for the doors to be slammed and cyanide-based Zyklon B pellets dropped through a small hole in the ceiling. They died in minutes, their corpses burned in a furnace next door. The inhumanity, and the scale of murder, was too great to comprehend. I couldn't help wonder how many thousands more may have lost their lives had two prisoners not escaped and made an 85-mile, 15-day trip to make the world aware of the atrocities that were taking place.

Many took photos of the sites, but I couldn't. I found it distasteful and, in any regard, I didn't need to—those images are etched in my mind, and will be until I die. The only picture I took was of where Rudolph Höss, the commander of Auschwitz, was executed. I didn't feel the slightest tinge of guilt in taking that photo.

Behind one of the glass walls in the museum was a display of human hair that the Nazis had shaved off the captives, accompanied by the words, 'Those who fail to remember the past are bound to live it again'. I'll always remember that phrase along with the fact that millions died in order to give us the life that we lead. And I'm grateful that my own personal pilgrimage to visit my granddad's grave also put some perspective on my own life.

I'm very proud of my Polish heritage. I love Wigan and I love England but, equally, I'll never forget that in a churchyard in Warsaw stands a grave with the name 'Radlinski' on it. My granddad's grave.

20

ROYAL WEDDING

'God only knows what I'd be without you.'
> **Beach Boys** (my wedding first dance song)

SOME RECKON sleep is the perfect cure for a hangover. In Dublin, where I was in the May of 2007, the locals swear by hair of the dog. But as I nursed a sore head one particular morning, and made an empty promise to myself not to match Gary Connolly drink-for-drink ever again, I was presented with the perfect tonic. And one I'd never even dreamed about.

Gary and I had flown to Ireland to watch Brian Carney play for Munster. It was the morning after his game, though in truth it may have been approaching lunchtime, and we were in a pub waiting for our late breakfast to arrive when my phone rang. It was my mum. I answered, expecting her to ask if we were having a good time, but she was flustered. She said that a letter for me had been delivered to their house. That wasn't unusual—I still got junk mail despite leaving home years earlier—but she then said, 'Kris, on the envelope, there is a stamp from the Prime Minister and another one from The Queen'. I froze. What the hell could that be? I urged her to open it, and she read the letter to me down the phone. Very politely worded, it was informing me that I had been put forward as a potential recipient of an MBE, an award given to people who have excelled in their chosen field and represented it in a special way.

The letter did not say that I had got it, but that I had to reply to say if I would accept it. There was no way I was going to emulate The Beatles and turn it down! I was with three friends, Gary, Wilf Roden and my neighbour Dave Heaton, and when I returned to my table they could tell something had happened. The letter, though, made it clear that it had to remain a secret and that I would not hear another thing until it was announced to the press in June on the Queen's birthday.

'Nothing's up, honest,' I assured them, but they didn't believe me. They thought I'd received some bad news, and that I was putting on a brave face, but in actual fact I was just shocked. They were worrying unnecessarily, and so I reluctantly told them why my mum had called. They couldn't believe it. They were made up, and visibly emotional, in ways men don't normally express, especially not in a group or in public. Of course, as soon as their concern for me had melted away, I realised that I'd not done such a good job at keeping it secret! I told them that they couldn't tell a soul.

'Agreed,' Gary smiled. 'But does that mean we can't celebrate it?'

Before I'd even replied, he'd ordered four pints of Guinness from the bar. Maybe the locals were right about the hair of the dog, after all. My dad called to congratulate me a few minutes later, and told me to practise my bow, but it was a little surreal because it was still a guarded secret, and would remain that way for another five weeks. I knew in my heart that the letter—asking whether I would accept the award if I was offered it—was deliberately worded that way to ensure they don't give them out to people who would refuse. But even so, I did not receive any contact after returning the letter to tell them I'd accept. There was no call, no further letters, and so I had that paranoid itch in the back of my mind that wouldn't go away: what if I didn't get it?

It was a huge relief when 15th June arrived and I got a call from a journalist to tell me the MBE had been announced. Finally I could, officially, speak about it. It just so happened I was eating my breakfast at the time. I told the café owner, Dave, and he became very emotional at being the first person to find out. I didn't tell him about the few people who already knew; I may not have received a free breakfast that day if I had done! I wanted to show people, because the award was a tribute to those close to me, too: I wanted them to share my happiness.

Within minutes, my phone began ringing constantly, with family and friends, team-mates and opponents old and new calling to congratulate me. Their interest made me realise I'd joined a select few. For years I idolised Ellery for having an MBE, and now I had joined him. It was the pinnacle of my career. I was being honoured by the monarchy and becoming a Member of the British Empire . . . it was a surreal and amazing feeling. I was told on more than one occasion that I'd be able to walk a flock of sheep across Tower Bridge, and eventually my children could get married in the great Westminster Abbey. This was big time.

Official confirmation soon arrived, informing me to be at the gates of Buckingham Palace at 10am on Tuesday, 11th December, dressed in a morning suit. I could bring three guests, and so the obvious choices were mum, dad and Rachel. My dad, though, insisted I took my sister Nicola, and said the fact I'd been handed the award was pleasing enough. We'd just spent an emotional few days together in Poland, but still, it was a great gesture on his part.

For several weeks Rachel, Nicola and my mum discussed what to wear and I grew tired of hearing, 'Does this look alright?' Women are bad for this sort of thing at the best of times, but going to one of the most important buildings in the world, their decisions see-sawed frequently as they tried to look their best.

We went down to London a day earlier on the train to make the most of the trip. I was calmer than I thought I would be. The only sadness was that I wished my dad could have come with us as well. After checking into our hotel, I headed to my favourite shop in the world, Abercrombie and Fitch, which sells casual, American-style college clothing. I'd shopped there for years, stocking up every time I visited Florida, but the first store in England had recently opened in London, so I went to visit it.

That night I had a little surprise planned for my three women. I'd booked a table at The Ivy restaurant in London, a celebrity haunt that was notoriously difficult to get into: my friend Shamu—Colin Welland's son—arranged it. His contacts book was as big as he was! When I told them where we were eating, they were more excited about going there than they were about going to the Palace the following day! It was a nice place, surprisingly not ridiculously priced, but it was an experience none of us will forget as we all became—how did I put it at the time—'food perverts'. In between courses, we tried to look the part, and we would have succeeded, too, had my mum not craned her neck and fixed her stare on Len Goodman, from *Strictly Come Dancing!* I was more impressed that Baldrick from *Blackadder* was facing me from the next table, though I dragged my attentions back to the food when my meal arrived—corned beef hash with a fried egg on top. You can take the boy out of Wigan, but you can't take Wigan out the boy! The food was sensational, as good as I'd tasted, and the experience was capped off perfectly when we walked out to be greeted by a mob of paparazzi photographers. Sadly, no bulbs flashed as we passed.

We woke early on the Tuesday morning; I was still calm and composed, but the women wanted plenty of time to look their best. They were panicking a bit, but they didn't let me down—they all looked stunning, and their outfits complemented each other. My mum was visibly nervous—it must have been a very proud day for her, to be in Buckingham Palace with her two children and her daughter-in-law, who she loves dearly. We walked outside and hailed a black cab. 'Where you off to, guv'nor?' he asked in a chirpy, Cockney accent.

'Buckingham Palace, please,' I replied. That threw him, let me tell you! As we pulled up, flocks of tourists were outside, some looking at the guards, others having their photos taken in front of the gates.

We still had no clue where we should be heading—it's not as if you can go to the front door and knock! Luckily, there was a policeman outside, and as I approached him to ask where I should go, he recognised me—Wigan fans get everywhere, eh?—and, after checking our passes, he led us through a gate.

Then, we walked across the most famous courtyard in the world, in front of Buckingham Palace, with hundreds of tourists peering through the iron bars wondering who we were. A few even took our pictures. For the first time, I was excited. The archway in front of the Palace leads to another open courtyard, which was roped off, directing people around the side and into the facing building. I watched other people, dressed in their best outfits, walking around with their mouths open at the sheer splendour of the place. We walked through a big grand door, where we were welcomed, and shown to a cloakroom where we had to put our cameras—they're forbidden during the ceremony. There were two massive Christmas trees in front of us, and instead of the customary multi-coloured decorations, they were covered with miniature gold crowns.

My family—and the other guests there—were invited into the ballroom to take their seats, while I was welcomed into the Long Room where I had a drink with the other investitures. Television screens showed the guests in the ballroom, all waiting patiently. I spotted my mum, Nicola and Rachel on the second row—my mum later told me that, if Rachel hadn't needed a toilet stop on their way in, they would have been on the front row!

I think Rachel just wanted to tell people that she has been to the loo in Buckingham Palace. A member of staff addressed us, telling us the correct protocol when meeting the Queen, which was a huge relief because I was beginning to worry about saying the wrong thing. When my name was called, I was to walk straight forward from the left, stop about four feet in front of Her Majesty, turn to face her, bow, then walk forward to meet her. The Queen would then pin on my medal and begin a conversation, which she would signal an end to by offering her hand to shake. Then, and I forced myself to remember this, I was to back away from the Queen, bow again, turn and walk away to my right.

I repeated in my mind the correct order: walk straight, turn, bow, walk, chat, shake, walk backwards, bow again . . . with my nerves already frayed, I hoped I wouldn't mess it up. We were called forward in groups of 10, so those of us left behind waited in the Long Room watching the recipients before them and rehearsing the correct protocol.

I spent an hour in there. By chance, the great Manchester United footballer Ryan Giggs was being honoured that day. I'd met Ryan a few years earlier and we had been mates ever since, though not the type of mates to be on the phone to each other all the time. Ryan is a big rugby league fan and I'd read in an interview a few years earlier that I was his favourite player of the time, which I really buzzed off, because he is such a well-respected and brilliant footballer. He's a genuine and down-to-earth guy, too.

When it was time for my group to be called through, it suddenly dawned on me how big the occasion was. I ran through the routine in my head again, because I was anxious not to mess it up. 'Walk straight, turn, bow, walk, chat, shake, walk backwards, bow again . . .' My train of thought was interrupted by a loud call of my name. Walking in a straight line had never been such a difficult task! I walked out slowly, affording a little glance to my right to look at my mum, Nicola and Rachel, and then turned left and stood directly in front of the Queen of England.

The obvious question is 'What did she say?' Well . . . I can't really remember! Between my nerves and making sure I didn't speak after she offered a handshake, I can't remember her exact words, or the order of her questions. I know she told me that she loved watching rugby league on television, and she said that she had recently watched the Great Britain v New Zealand Test series. She asked if I had ever played against the Kiwis. 'Yes, a few times,' I offered.

'They are very big men,' she replied. I couldn't help smile at that remark. She then asked about the differences between rugby league and rugby union, and resisting the temptation to milk my date with royalty and list all the differences, I told her that there was too many to mention.

She finally said that I was a very brave and tough man, and thanked me for offering so much on and off the field to the world of rugby league. She then extended her hand, signalling the end of our conversation, which I shook warmly but gently and I backed off, bowed and walked away. I hadn't made a single mistake! It seemed as though I'd been talking to her for a long time, in reflection, it was probably about four minutes.

I handed my medal over to be placed in a decorative case, and then walked to the back of the ballroom to watch the remaining guests receive their awards. Finally, she stood and walked through the middle of the room, serenaded to a rousing rendition of our national anthem.

I met my family for some official pictures, as well as some candid shots taken with Nicola's Kodak, and then we made our way out of Buckingham Palace. As we did, I phoned my dad to tell him about the experience. He told me he was outside the Palace gates. That was a complete shock . . . he'd come to London for a business meeting and arranged it so he could be there when I came out. It was a proud moment for him, and I was glad that all my family could share my special day in some way. Who'd have thought the proudest day of my rugby league career would be not on a pitch, but at Buckingham Palace? My sister had arranged afternoon tea at a hotel facing the Palace, so we spent the rest of the day eating cream cakes and drinking champagne. I could not imagine a better way to end one of the most memorable days of my life.

The experience was soured a little—only a little—by the under-whelming reaction from some people I'd known for years. Although getting the award was hugely satisfying and rewarding, I couldn't help but think whether others thought I deserved it. Many were genuinely happy for me, but others were silent—and that spoke volumes. I had friends who I thought would show their joy for me, but they didn't, and they never mentioned it afterwards either. I don't know whether they were jealous, or if they just didn't think my career warranted royal recognition.

Ultimately, though, I can hold my head up high and walk into any rugby club in the country, knowing I gave my all to the game. I played rugby league for the right reasons and in the right spirit, and I think I got the award not just for my performances, but for championing the game. When I hear people talk about my career, they often mention the Challenge Cup Final in 2002 and my decision to turn down offers from rugby union. Probe a little deeper, and they may volunteer the fact I came out of retirement to play for Wigan when they were in relegation danger.

They're all significant parts of my career, and I'm proud of them, but I don't think my MBE was for any one or any combination of those. During my career, I tried to be a good ambassador for the game, and I was always happy to help out amateur clubs or visit schools. And when other players cancelled a scheduled appearance, I'd be the first person to be called to help them out of a mess—I don't think I once turned them down. I tried to help out charities, too, donating memorabilia whenever I could. I never wanted any acknowledgement for that, though I think I got it in the end, and it came from the most impressive woman in the world. The Queen.

In December of 2007, I'd already been to Poland to discover my routes and been honoured by the Queen with an MBE. It was certainly an eventful month, and it wasn't over yet. Forget Christmas and New Year—I was getting married. On Sunday 30th December Rachel and I tied the knot, one of the happiest days of my life.

A few weeks earlier, 19 mates, assorted family members and I flew to Las Vegas for my stag party. It was a trip to remember. The party included people from all walks of life— players, businessmen, teachers—of varying ages, but we all got on famously. Many of the lads had never been to Vegas; in that respect, I felt a tinge of guilt that they didn't get to see any of the sights. From the moment the coach picked us up outside my favourite sandwich shop on Wigan Lane at five in the morning, the beer started flowing, and it only stopped when we slept. We followed the same punishing schedule for five solid days, with occasional rest breaks allowed for the odd gamble or bite to eat.

We had to travel on two separate flights due to availability, 16 members of the party on one flight that had a two-hour stop in Atlanta, and the four remaining party members—including me—on the direct flight to Vegas. When we arrived at the airport, our banter faded away as we glanced at the check-in monitors and discovered the flight with 16 on was delayed by four hours. Because the flight was only going to Atlanta, the group would then miss their connection to Vegas. No one had any idea how long it would take them to arrive. It was a terrible start to my stag party; I looked at everyone's faces and they looked miserable. I felt terrible because I had planned the trip and also because my direct flight was on schedule. Luckily Rachel's dad, Frank Twigg, was with us. He asked the help desk, very politely, if there were 16 spare seats on the direct flight to Vegas.

The checkout girl tapped at her keyboard, looked up and said, 'Yes we can do that for you sir, and there will be no extra charge'. If it had been a play on a rugby pitch, fans would still be eulogising about it now, because I'd never seen so many men's moods change so swiftly. Within a few minutes, we'd shuffled through passport control, found the bar and the pints began to flow. I thought the guys would ease themselves into the trip, it was a five-day marathon, not a sprint, but the setback of the delay—and the surprise recovery—had swelled their excitement. We were separated on the plane in little groups, Frank, my cousin Gareth, my good mate, Lee-thal, though that nickname is deceptively flattering, and I shared a bottle of brandy. I pitied Kevin Brown, my former Wigan team-mate. He was sat with Gary Connolly and the Duffy brothers Kevin and Conal, two musician friends of mine, and was being plied with Southern Comfort . . . this was after at least 10 pints. We were fooling no one: three hours into the flight, we were all asleep!

When we arrived in Vegas, we split up to find our rooms and get changed. I was sharing a room with Gary, my best man, and as we checked in, Gaz told the check-in girl that he was the worst best man ever, and would she help him out by putting us in a suite. Surprisingly his charm worked, and we made our way to a spacious, stunning room on the 27th floor of the Luxor, complete with bar living room and panoramic views of the strip.

It was a shame we couldn't stay to appreciate its splendour, but we'd promised to meet the lads downstairs a few minutes later, so I threw my case on my bed, opened it and pulled on a clean pair of jeans. 'Take them off,' ordered Gaz, as he walked in my room. Before I could ask what he was talking about, he threw a costume my way that I snatched out of the air, and held up with my outstretched arm. It was a pirate's costume. I put it on and looked an absolute idiot, but at least he didn't make me wear it alone as he had one for himself. The following night, he pulled the same trick, and again the night after—he said he was wearing the costume every night. I love Gary—but he's so weird!

We had an absolute ball, drinking by the pool all day and then getting changed and hitting the Irish bar in the New York New York hotel by night. And that was it, for five days solid. No shows, no trip to the Grand Canyon. In the gambling capital of the world, we hardly played cards—the reason we went there was to party ourselves crazy. Many friendships were forged on that trip, because not many came from the rugby league fraternity.

Everyone warmed to Kevin Brown. He is misunderstood—

he has a natural swagger and some fans mistake that for arrogance, but he's such a polite and humble guy. I remember standing outside the Bellagio hotel, watching the fountain display, which runs in sync with the music. They are performed every 15 minutes, each time with a different musical score, and we watched the arrangement to Lucianno Pavarotti singing Nessun Dorma in awe. It is one of the most celebrated pieces, sung by one of the most famous singers, but amazingly, Browny had never heard the classical piece. He nudged me, and said, 'It's a good record this Rads, who sings it? I'll have to get it for my iPod'.

Whilst walking through a casino one night, we all decided to have a go at a darts game at which you could win a guitar. Franco, a restaurant owner and good friend, actually won one. This guitar kept us in great company as we sang and played it most nights. We were just a group of guys singing and having fun, I never realised Italians were good at darts until then.

As a thank you to all the guys for finding the money for the trip, I bought tickets to see Elton John in the Coliseum in Caesar's Palace. We took our seats, and the place next to me was vacant. 'Where's Gary?' I asked. Everyone just shrugged. Five minutes later, he strolled along carrying an ice bucket packed with bottles of Budweiser. 'Six bottles for five dollars,' he said. 'How good's that?' Instead of sharing them, he downed one and started on his second. Elton was about to come on, but we all went for a bucket as well!

We returned before Elton came on, and it was a great night. He was on top form and we were as drunk as monkeys. Towards the end of the gig, Gary went missing again and returned with Elton's drummer's drumstick! I asked him how he'd got it the next day, and he genuinely didn't remember. Classic Connolly, those things only ever happened to him. That drumstick is on display in my house—the lads all chucked in to have it framed for me. The lads took good care of me, there were no pranks and I was devastated! I'd been to a few stag parties, and at every one the groom-to-be ended up being stripped off. Expecting that, I'd spent weeks leading up to the trip hitting the gym every day, working hard. My torso was cut, but not once did I get pinned down and have my shirt ripped off whilst taped to a lamppost. I must be the only bloke to be upset that he wasn't stripped on his own stag do! Apart from that, it was a stag do to savour—and the perfect 'send-off' before marriage.

Rachel and I tied the knot in a civil ceremony in the Park Hall hotel in Chorley, on the outskirts of Wigan, with the traditional wedding breakfast and function at the same venue. It was a magical day that went exactly to plan. We put a lot of thought into it, and spent months going over every single detail. Rachel also did a good job sticking to the budget!

I was relaxed on the day, and why shouldn't I have been? All the hard work had been done, I was positive she was going to show up, plus that month I'd already practised being dressed up for a big occasion in front of hundreds of people when I'd met the Queen. The only thing that pulled on my heart-strings was when my mum returned from taking a basket to Rachel I'd prepared—filled with an assortment of white gifts, such as a Christian Dior diamond watch and matching purse, sunglasses and luggage tags saying 'Mrs Radlinski'—and told me she had cried her eyes out.

Gary was calm, which was unlike him. He's got a showman streak that only flares up on rare occasions—I'd once been at a plush black-tie dinner when he had, uninvited, climbed on stage to sing a number with The Drifters—but usually, he avoided crowds and kept himself to himself. He was the obvious choice to be my best man. He has been a friend for more than 15 years and I'd always been able to count on him.

If I ever write another book, it will be called *Stories About Gary Connolly!* Gary and I shouldn't really get on as well as we do. We're completely different individuals. He is so laid back and relaxed, while I'm quite intense and serious and when I do let my hair down, there's always that paranoia about who might be watching.

I'm comfortable in his company, we can be the life and soul of the party when we're out together, though he suffers from short-term memory loss when he's had a few drinks and I have the pleasure of reminding him, sometimes convincing him, of what he did the night before! When Andrew Johnson and his partner Alex got married in Dubai, Gary and I were invited along with our partners and Andy and Alex's families.

For a reason I've yet to understand, Gary turned up to the ceremony dressed as if he owned a boat, complete with linen trousers, hat and cravat. It was incredible. At the party that night, Gary and I dimmed the lights and told all the guests to lie on the floor and look at the ceiling as we played Snow Patrol's 'Chasing Cars' over the sound system. I know it sounds weird, but believe me when I tell you it was a surreal, magical moment—even if the waiters were puzzled. Yep, that story would certainly make it into my *Stories About Gary Connolly* book; I dare say that if I asked many players and coaches, they'd all have their own unique tale to tell.

To thank him, I had a special piece of art commissioned called 'Gary's memory lane', which was a picture filled with reflections from his life and career. He told me it was the best gift he'd ever received. Brian Carney was one of my ushers. He again had provided unconditional friendship over the years. My two other ushers were Rachel's brother, Ian, and my little mate, Lee. We asked Lee to do a reading at the ceremony and he provided a moment that everybody present would never forget. He wrote a piece himself called 'The

Essence Of Love', and he delivered it with real passion. It was breathtaking and I'll never forget it. My sister Nicola, and Ian's partner Tracey, were Rachel's bridesmaids. Both looked stunning and had helped us greatly in planning our day. I got emotional in my speech, especially when I spoke about Nicola, because she's been an incredible influence on my life. She has a beautiful heart. Gary's little boy Adam was our ring bearer, and it was such a cute sight as he walked down the aisle, his gaze fixed on the cushion he was carrying, concentrating hard on not dropping the ring! Rachel's two little nieces, Jasmine and Phoebe, completed the wedding party as our flower girls.

My mum and dad looked great, and they were quite calm considering. Brandy probably helped my dad, while mum was drunk on pride and love—the many weeks visiting bridal boutiques had certainly paid off: she looked wonderful. Everything went to plan. My dad checked the room before Rachel and the rest of the guests arrived, making sure that every table was correct and the lighting was just right. My dad is a real attention-to-detail guy. I thought I'd ticked every box and prepared myself for every event, but I was caught out when I looked down the aisle and saw my bride walking towards me. I know I'm slightly biased, but she was the most beautiful bride you could ever wish to see. She was simply stunning, and guests later commented that she was the most stunning bride they'd ever seen . . . they got no arguments from me on that one. It was such an emotionally charged day, and people were on edge momentarily, until Rachel's dad Frank sat down and knocked over the candles—that broke the ice and calmed everyone's nerves.

The rest of the day was a blur, and that wasn't just the emotion—I got drunk! I wasn't 'stumbling about drunk', but one of the few vivid memories I have was of looking down and seeing a glass of red wine, a glass of white wine, a glass of champagne, a pint of Guinness and a Jack Daniels and Coke. And I hate wasting good drinks. Rachel was completely different. She only had two drinks all day, and after my Duffy mates and their band had finished their set (they rocked the place) and the guests had scattered, I can only imagine what she thought when we made it into our hotel suite. Without going into too fine a detail, there weren't any fireworks—I collapsed on the bed and passed out!

For our honeymoon, we spent eight days in Miami and then a week in Jamaica, but first we flew to London and spent a night there. As a little surprise for Rachel I'd bought tickets to watch the Spice Girls at the O2 Arena. She's a huge fan, and we travelled by boat up the River Thames to the venue. Marriage, we were told more than once, is all about give and take, and we practised that on our honeymoon. There was no way I could have spent all our time on a sun-kissed beach, so we compromised and got the best of both worlds by going to Miami first, allowing me to shop and hit the bars, and then Rachel had her way and got the beautiful beaches of Jamaica. We had a magical time.

21

THE FUTURE

'I don't know what I will do when my career is over. I'll probably have to go back to crime.'

Terry Newton

WHAT HAPPENS when the cheering stops? What happens when everything you dreamed of, and worked hard for, ends? I'd asked myself those questions at various stages in my career but, before I paused to consider the answers, my mind drifted elsewhere. I didn't want to think about it. I dreaded the end of my career; it's the day every sportsman dreads. Sure, the prospect of 'retiring' 30 years before most people may sound great but, believe me, for most athletes it's scarier than any opponent. Thousands have hung up their boots before me, thousands more will follow, but I hope my experiences will provide an insight into what an athlete faces when his (or her) career ends. I hope it will make current players aware of the day they can't put off forever . . .

I'm not sure what I miss the most. The crowd, the banter, the tries, the wins. Even the little things that I never noticed when I was playing: the smell of the changing room, the bus journey home, even that overall soreness that woke me up the morning after a game. I loved the hug from my mum and the approving look from my dad.

But I think maybe it was that feeling I got seconds after I made a great play. The 20,000 people in the crowd might have missed it, but not my team-mates; they would slap my back, or yell words of encouragement, and recall it afterwards in the showers. I was one of 17 proud men . . . I still desperately miss the feeling of being a good team-mate.

I'm still struggling to come to terms with the loneliness of retirement. It hurts to think that my life will never be the same again. One minute, I was worshipped and wearing the Wigan and Great Britain number 1 shirt, with a purpose in life; the next, I was a has-been. The months after I retired were the most difficult. I don't like to admit that I was depressed, but I was. I was engulfed in a feeling of complete despair, it was almost like a time of mourning. I felt lost. People call it a transition period in a player's life, but that suggests a gradual change; not an overnight lightning bolt. Shane Webcke, the former Brisbane prop, compared the feeling of retirement—of losing the routine of the past few years as an athlete—to prisoners being institutionalised and then struggling to adapt to society, and he's right.

I'd fought back from bad times before. Any player who has been sidelined by injury for a considerable spell will tell you that it's a painstaking and lonely time. You feel helpless, unable to contribute to the team. But every time I'd been injured, there had been light at the end of the tunnel—a recovery time-line, or a possible date for a return to playing. Adjusting to retirement was different. I was down and depressed, but I couldn't see any light. Unlike being injured, I had nothing to aim for, and without that motivation there didn't seem to be an end to the misery. I've always been a people person, but I pushed everyone away, and found my solace walking alone along the canal. Some nights, I couldn't sleep so I'd jump out of bed and just drive. In hindsight, being alone with my thoughts was dangerous. The sense of confusion accompanying both the decision to retire and deciding what to do next is a depressing mix.

I had many arguments with my dad about it. He couldn't understand the emotional turmoil I was going through, it was black and white to him, but that wasn't the reason I didn't really confide my darkest secrets to anyone. I was using up so much of my energy by putting on a brave face, I didn't want to risk letting my guard down. I wish I'd spoken to my family more, because I'm so lucky to have a loving family. My dad has always been the realist, he's loving but also keen to emphasise the challenges that life throws up. My mum is incredible. She could be having a terrible day but would drop everything if somebody needs help. Everybody loves her, and never once in my life has she let me down. She looked after my thoughts and feelings all my life. My sister is an angel, and not once did she ever see me as Kris Radlinski the rugby player—the Superman outfit didn't work in our home; she just saw me as her brother, and loved me with affection.

Like all traumas and losses, time has been the greatest healer. Gradually, I started going out more, socialising more and, all in all, returning to my old self. But 2008 was definitely the hardest year of my life. I think what made it tougher was the fact I didn't know what to do with myself. Those who have made a seamless transition from sports star into a new career often know what they want to do next, before they've finished playing. They're ready for the end of their careers, and excited by the future—whether that's moving into coaching, broadcasting, business or a complete career shift. They had new goals to aim for. But all I ever wanted to do was play rugby league, I had no ambitions to do anything else, and after having dedicated so much of my life to one sport only for it all to end in an instant . . . well, it left a pretty big void in my life. I tried to fill the extra time productively, training every morning in the gym, writing this autobiography, reading books and playing one of my guitars, but the long days can be hard when my friends are at work. It may sound like fun, but it can be very boring. Some friends I thought would be there for me forever disappeared, which was tough, because I needed them more than ever. For a guy who was always the first to call them up for no other reason than a chat, I found that hard to take. Neil Cowie said to me years ago that when you retire you will be able to count on one hand the number of true friends that you have in life; once again he was right, and they're my priority.

It was hard to bring closure to my career when, in my soul, I couldn't help think that I still could have been playing. That question about whether I retired too soon will haunt me until I die. No matter how proud I am of all of my achievements, I can't shake that niggling question, 'What if?'

After months of struggling with injuries and battles with depression, I saw retirement as the obvious—and my only—feasible option. My dreams were slipping away from me, and there didn't seem I could do anything about it. But once I retired for good—after my brief comeback—and underwent further knee surgery, and gave the joint a good rest, I honestly felt like a million dollars. With my knees holding up and my back pain under control, I felt as though I could play another few years. I played my final game at 30, which was a premature end to my career. And when I see guys who started out before me still playing—Jason Croker, Stacey Jones, Steve Menzies—I can't help wonder whether I should be playing too. I won't make another comeback, but my body feels great; maybe if I'd had a little luck, time and support towards the end of my career, I'd still be playing now.

Maybe that's the reason I find it so hard to watch rugby league. When I went to see Wigan play in 2007 and 2008, and I saw Trent Barrett play for them, I regretted my decision to retire. I would have loved to have played in the same Wigan side as him, especially being a full-back. He was constantly thinking, playing the game two plays ahead of everyone else. As I watched him play, I would think to myself, 'Where would I run here', 'What would I say to the lads now' . . . I was so fidgety, I found it impossible to relax. When I first retired in 2005, I had become disheartened with criticisms of my dropping performance levels. I should have been mentally stronger, but I was mentally drained at the time in dealing with my injury problems. If I had my time again, I would have contacted Ellery and asked him how I could get through it. I'm content with what I achieved in my career, but I would have loved to have gone on longer. It wasn't to be.

Rachel was incredibly supportive and tolerant of my moods. I have been out with a few girls in my life who have all helped to make me into the person I am, and I've tried to remain on good terms with them all—I wish them all the happiness in the world. I know I've made the right choice in settling down with Rachel. She makes me feel good about myself, and can read me so well—she'll know when I want cheering up, and when I want to be left alone. She's a few years younger than me, but she amazes me when she shows wisdom well beyond her years. She's very mature and I can put her in any situation and she adapts very comfortably. My friends adore her and they're glad when I invite her on lads' nights out, because she'll join in and have a beer herself.

Even before I returned to Wigan in a junior coaching role, the Wigan club were very hospitable to my wife and me. We've been frequently invited into the chairman's box and had meals with old friends. Rachel recently met Maurice Lindsay for the first time, and she couldn't believe how charming he was. I always got on well with Maurice. I know he can polarise opinions, but I only judge people on how they have been with me and we never crossed words in a decade of working together. We met him recently at a fans' awards night and we had a great evening, reminiscing with Maurice, Gary Connolly and Mick Cassidy and their respective partners. Maurice was on top form, and had the whole table in the palm of his hand.

I may have not planned properly for this transition in my life, but fortunately my financial advisor did. Neil Harrison was a terrific guy, and I was very sad when he died of cancer early in his forties in 2007. While I don't have a bottomless pit, I've got investments and properties to see me over while I try to discover what I'm going to do for the rest of my life.

The rest of my life, that an issue I find impossible to ignore. I seem to get asked about it every time I leave the house! I'm not afraid to roll up my sleeves, but it's tough to adapt back into 'normal' life when I live in the same town where I played my whole career. And what is normal life? The only life I ever knew was rugby league; training, playing, recovering. I've never written a job application in my life. I've never had a job interview. People may say I've got so many Test caps and trophies on my CV, but what good will that do in a normal life?

I have become a shareholder in a hotel and bar in Wigan called the Bel Air, with Brian Carney and a couple of business associates. It came at a good time for me, and it helped me adapt to life as an ex-player because the launch phase took up a lot of my time. For such a small bar on the outskirts of Wigan, the problems we have encountered take some believing. We had a manager who was addicted to adult chat lines, we had hotel bandits who scammed us into thinking their house was flooded, money has gone missing and, on top of that, there has been grief from neighbours. But it's been a good, if harsh, induction into the realities of running a business. On New Year's Eve, Wilf Rhoden, one of the business partners, hadn't organised enough staff so me, Brian and Gary served behind the bar while my mum and Kath, Gary's wife, waited the restaurant. Rachel, who had only been my wife a day, was glass collecting—not the ideal way to treat a new bride!

The hotel also gave me a ready-made answer for when I hear, 'What are you up to with yourself?' Even Dave Whelan enquired about it the last time we met after a Wigan game. Before walking off, he asked how much I paid for the building. I told him it was leased, not bought, because the building cost well over a million and we couldn't afford to buy it. He then quipped, 'You should have scored more tries then'. Classic Dave. He then just walked off, leaving me to pick my knee-caps off the floor! He always had to have the last say just to prove that he was still the man.

The hotel doesn't take up all my time. I recently returned to the Wigan Club to work alongside some of my old mentors, John Pendlebury, Ray Unsworth and Brian Foley in the youth development side of the club. After numerous meetings with Ian Lenagan, who succeeded Maurice as chairman, he decided that I had something to offer. It is a great start for me, and it's a responsibility I've not taken lightly.

Wigan's young players all harbour the same ambitions I had. Sadly, it's inevitable that they won't all make it at Wigan, but I want to give them all the ingredients for successful career. I see it as a real challenge to reinforce the culture that I was exposed to when I was their age. I want to help instil good habits in them that will serve them well, wherever their career takes them. And I know the importance of qualities such as honesty, integrity and confidence—the good players we produce can be fine young men, too. I have always felt that the minute you stop learning is the minute you stop living and, to an extent, that's why I was so depressed in the months after my retirement. Now, I'm not only content with where I've been but I'm excited about where I am, and where I'm going. It's a nice feeling going to bed knowing I've had a productive day; knowing I've helped someone.

On my first day in the job, I went for a coffee with Shaun Wane, Wigan's reserve team coach who was a no-nonsense prop for Wigan in the 1980s. His enthusiasm and passion for his hometown club is incredible, and it's great working with people like him and John in setting Wigan down the right path towards a successful future. I am so glad to be a part of it and who knows? Maybe a kid I am coaching now will one day pull on the most famous jersey of all. I look at the kids and feel almost jealous of the journey they are about to embark on. If they work hard, the next decade or so will be the best days of their lives. I strive to get this message across to them.

Having a goal to aim for makes retirement easier, which is why I didn't hesitate to volunteer for a fund-raising cycling challenge from the South of France to London—with the channel crossing made by dragon boat. The money raised is for the Trust set up by Steve Prescott, the former St Helens player who is battling cancer.

Now I've grown used to life as a retired rugby league player, I've been able to enjoy my free time more. Rachel and I spend lots of time together and we love to travel and eat out. We have visited some wonderful cities around the world and it's such a great feeling doing it with someone you feel so strongly about. We want children one day, so that's another reason to travel so much now while we have free time. I treated her, my mum and my sister to a holiday in Las Vegas and we had a great time. One afternoon, the girls went out shopping, leaving me to play a few hands of three-card poker in the lobby casino.

Maybe because it was at the time when the disappointment of retirement had been replaced by satisfaction in my career, maybe it was an early mid-life crisis, I went wild. I gambled on the cards, won a few dollars, and decided to celebrate in the most decadent way possible—I drunk Jack Daniels, bought a guitar and got a tattoo. It was the most rock 'n' roll thing I'd ever done! As Richard Ashcroft is one of my heroes, I had one of his most popular The Verve song titles branded on my foot—'Lucky Man'.

I've still got faint ambitions of returning to the spotlight, though not as a rugby league player. I've seen my good mate Martin Offiah take part in *Strictly Come Dancing* and I'd love to do something like that. I've always loved West End musicals, and when I've taken my acoustic along to an 'open-mic' night at my local pub, I've found performing comes naturally to me. The challenge of doing something like that would excite me, though I wouldn't do it to try to make the most of any lingering fame I may have. It's the greatest feeling in the world having thousands of fans applaud you, but being famous has never interested me. In fact, I've only once felt famous in the last two years since retiring, and it was one of the most embarrassing moments of my life. Singer Don McLean, of 'American Pie' fame, was doing a CD signing in Manchester. I waited in the queue for ages, desperate to meet a performer I'd always admired. Before he came out, an official addressed all the waiting music-lovers and said that, in order to sign everyone's CDs, Don would have to rush through them. That was fine by me. I approached the front of the queue, said, 'Hi', shook his hand and handed him my copy of his CD to autograph. He handed it back to me and thanked me for coming. Conscious of the stewards hurrying the queue along, I turned to leave, when the guy next in line to see Don, a guy in his 70s or 80s, stopped in his tracks.

'Oh my God, it's Kris Radlinski', he exclaimed, excited, grabbing my hand to shake, 'You're the best full-back I've ever seen . . . I can't believe it's Kris Radlinski.'

Normally, I'd appreciate such a compliment, but I was completely embarrassed. Don McLean looked at me puzzled, probably wondering who the hell the impostor was stealing his thunder. Fortunately, I don't get that often! The people of Wigan are far less imposing. Often, if I'm in the coffee shop next to the gym, there could be 20 people walk past before I've finished my drink and nearly all of them will say, 'Morning Kris'. I don't know these people, but it feels great when they acknowledge me with a little hello. It makes me feel respected. Does it make me feel famous? No, but it does make me feel a bit like Norm from the American sitcom *Cheers*. He would walk into the bar and everyone shouted, 'Hey Norm!'

Rugby league has made me feel like Norm in my own hometown. I'm proud of that . . . and I don't think that would change, even if I went on *Strictly Come Dancing!* That, of course, is more than likely a pipedream. As is performing the lead role in *Joseph and his Amazing Technicolor Dreamcoat* at Wigan Little Theatre (I'm serious). It took me a while to get over the loneliness and shock of finishing rugby league, and occasionally I'll relapse and think, 'What if?' But, for the most part, I'm happy and confident, and looking forward to whatever life throws up. That's why I wanted to write this book—it gave me a chance to reflect on my career and share some of my memories and insights.

I suggested in an earlier chapter that Wigan's new signings should be asked the question, 'How do you want to be remembered?' when they sign for the club. It seems only fair that I answer that question, too. I've not glorified my career in this book; I know I wasn't the quickest, fittest or most skilful player in the game. But I hope people remember me for wearing my heart on my sleeve and for fulfilling my dream through sheer determination. I always put my team-mates first. When I was Super League's top try scorer in 2001, I was given £1,000 prize money that I put straight into the players' fund for our end-of-season party. I didn't have to do it, but I wouldn't have scored those tries without my team-mates, so why should I be the only one who benefited? I never set out to be the best player in the world, but I'd like to think I worked as hard as anyone else. Wigan's crest features the words 'Ancient and Loyal' . . . well, I'm not that old, but I think I did justice to that emblem. Fans may have specific highlights of my career, but I don't—there's not one, stand-out memory. If the players I played alongside remember me as a good team-mate, I'd be happy with that. If, in 10 years time, I walk into a bar and I hear blokes mumbling among themselves, 'Not many got past him,' that would be satisfying.

At the start of this book, I mentioned that I sent Ellery Hanley one of the three original copies of the book I had. When Mike Gregory died, it really hit me hard how fragile and precious life is, and I made a promise to myself that I would never be afraid to show my emotions because no one knows what's around the corner. I wanted Ellery to know what an impact he had on my life and career, so I posted him a copy with a brief explanatory note.

A few days later, at about 5.30pm on a Monday evening, I got a call on my mobile phone. I didn't recognise the number and, though I don't normally pick up in those instances, for some reason I did. 'Hi Kris, it's Ellery,' said the voice. My whole world stood still. Not many people have received calls from their all-time hero. He was really emotional on the phone, and told me that he was overwhelmed by my gesture. He went on to say how highly he regarded me as a player, and how he wished he'd had the chance to play alongside me. That blew me away. Ellery said he would treasure the book as a reminder of what an inspiration he had been to others; he said the book meant more to him than any trophy he had ever won.

Long before £100,000-a-week footballers, a generation of kids in Wigan had grown up dreaming of being Ellery Hanley. Every kid needs a hero, and Ellery was mine. The phone call from him was, in a sense, the final approval that I needed to lay some insecurities to rest—it brought a sense of closure to my playing career, and I was completely at one with myself and what I had achieved. I'm ready for the next chapter in my life.

Before I sign off, I just want to say to my friends, family, former team-mates and opponents, and rugby league fans everywhere, thank you. Thank you for a career that surpassed even my wildest dreams. Fairytales don't often intrude in a brutal sport like rugby league; I'm glad my career was an exception to this. My life and career have been filled with so much joy, so many laughs and so many highlights—memories that, I'm sure, the future years won't erode. My body makes it impossible for me to forget my career with Wigan—I wake up every day with a stiff back, a sore wrist and a knee that just doesn't feel right! And if I want any further reminder of how blessed I have been, I only need bow my head and look at the two-word tattoo etched on my foot: 'Lucky Man.'